# Rice: A Cookbook

# RICE

## A Cookbook

*Maria Luisa Scott
and Jack Denton Scott*

Consumers Union
Mount Vernon, New York

Copyright © 1985, 1989 by Maria Luisa Scott and Jack Denton Scott
Published by Consumers Union of U.S., Inc., Mount Vernon, New York 10553

Library of Congress Cataloging-in-Publication Data
Scott, Maria Luisa.
Rice : a cookbook / Maria Luisa Scott and Jack Denton Scott.
p.  cm.
Includes index.
ISBN 0-89043-267-8
1. Cookery (Rice)   I. Scott, Jack Denton.   II. Title.
TX809.R5S34   1989
641.6'318—dc 19                          89-30399
                                            CIP

Design by Susan Hood
First printing, June 1989
Manufactured in the United States of America
Originally published in 1985 by Times Books

*Rice: A Cookbook* is a Consumer Reports Book published by Consumers Union, the nonprofit organization that publishes *Consumer Reports*, the monthly magazine of test reports, product Ratings, and buying guidance. Established in 1936, Consumers Union is chartered under the Not-For-Profit Corporation Law of the State of New York.

The purposes of Consumers Union, as stated in its charter, are to provide consumers with information and counsel on consumer goods and services, to give information on all matters relating to the expenditure of the family income, and to initiate and to cooperate with individual and group efforts seeking to create and maintain decent living standards.

Consumers Union derives its income solely from the sale of *Consumer Reports* and other publications. In addition, expenses of occasional public service efforts may be met, in part, by nonrestrictive, noncommercial contributions, grants, and fees. Consumers Union accepts no advertising or product samples and is not beholden in any way to any commercial interest. Its Ratings and reports are solely for the use of the readers of its publications. Neither the Ratings, nor the reports, nor any Consumers Union publications, including this book, may be used in advertising or for any commercial purpose. Consumers Union will take all steps open to it to prevent such uses of its materials, its name, or the name of *Consumer Reports*.

# Contents

# The World's Most Important Food

"A meal without rice," the Chinese say, "is like a beautiful woman with only one eye." They should know; they've been cooking rice for 7,000 years. In fact, their word for culture is the same as their word for rice.

Do the Chinese know something we don't? Probably. They've long been aware of the remarkable energy it provides, which enables a Chinese coolie, who eats mainly rice, to work at dockside all day unloading ships and handling three times his weight with every load he carries. In their heyday, the rice-eating rickshaw coolie could pull two passengers for hours, running at the speed of a trotting horse.

For those of us with less-strenuous pursuits, it'll probably come as a surprise to know that rice can actually supply 80 percent of our daily food requirements, 1 pound delivering four times the food energy of an equal weight of potatoes.

We hasten to add that rice is also delicious, a recipe rage, a menu classic in most countries, and the main ingredient in countless extraordinary dishes.

Yet a serving of rice costs just pennies, less than five cents, even in the United States. With all of its other assets, rice also is considered by professional chefs to be the most versatile of all foods.

Exactly what is this remarkable, prolific grain that is responsible for the survival of over 2 billion people and has such a magical way with world menus?

*Oryza sativa* is a cereal said to have 40,000 varieties in all. It is a member of the grass family, which grows on a slender stalk 2 to 4 feet high. It originally came from wild plants found in Asia, India, and Indo-China. Some archeologists believe that it was cultivated in Southeast Asia and Southern China 5,000 years before Christ; then it spread to India, Indonesia, the Philippines, the remainder of China, Japan, and Korea. Other historians say that rice originated in India in 3000 B.C. They relate it to a wild plant, "newaree," which grew at that time.

Wherever it originated, credit for its first cultivation came out of China in 2800 B.C., when Emperor Shen Nung wrote of yearly rice-planting ceremonies he created, during which he himself planted the first choice seeds.

Archeological excavations in China, in 1974, unearthed rice more than 6,960 years old; in India, rice was uncovered which dated back to 4530 B.C.; and in northern Thailand, rice was found that was grown in 4000 B.C.

It isn't surprising that in Asia rice is considered much more than food. In Indonesia, it is the gift of the goddess Dewie Srie; there, no girl can be considered ready for marriage until she can skillfully prepare rice. The Javanese believe that rice has a soul and must never be stolen. In Madagascar, throwing rice or playing a flute while rice is growing is certain to bring a harmful hailstorm. An old Chinese cure for aching bones, stomach upsets, and colds involved combining toasted brown rice and minced gingerroot in a cloth and then simmering it in whiskey. The compress was then rubbed on the joints or stomach. Alternately, it could also be inhaled.

Rice fields in Japan are given names as if they were people. Throughout Japan there are thousands of miniature shrines of Inari, the rice god. For centuries, Japan's standard of wealth was rice; feudal lands were valued according to their rice yield, and the famous *samurai*, or warriors, were paid in rice.

In China, an entire day of the New Year is set aside in memory of the first planting of rice, 7,000 years ago. Quitting or losing a job in China is called "breaking the rice bowl." It is considered very bad luck to upset a bowl of rice, and the deadliest insult of all is to pick up a bowl of someone else's rice and spill it on the ground. Chinese parents admonish their children to eat all of a serving of rice. For every grain of rice not eaten, they point out, there will be a pockmark on the face of their future husband or wife.

The custom of pelting newlyweds with rice originated in China and India as a fertility rite. The thrown grains are supposed to grant young couples many children and prosperity.

The story of how this greatest of grains came to America began in 1685, with a storm off the coast of South Carolina. Blown off course, a British brigantine en route from Madagascar put in to port at Charleston. As one token of his gratitude for the hospitality of the colonists, the ship's captain, James Thurber, presented a leading South Carolina citizen, Henry Woodward, with a bag of rough rice ready for planting.

Some historians disagree with this romantic version, claiming that the introduction of rice to America was neither an accident nor a single historical event, but that it was gradually developed by English colonists whose African slaves knew how to grow rice. It is a fact that many of the slaves in the Carolinas came from the West African coast south of the Sahara, where rice had been grown for centuries.

The rice-from-the-ship supporters claim that the single gift bag of rice soon supplied not only both Carolinas but Georgia as well. That could be within the realm of probability, as 100 pounds of seed planted per acre yield 5,000 pounds.

For a long time in the United States we probably threw more rice at weddings than we ate. Disgruntled rice farmers claimed that Northerners only made pudding out of it and Southerners just put gravy on it. Today, however, 84 percent of U.S. households use rice often, and it is important as a health food, in cereal, and in a rapidly growing number of unique recipes. Finally, we are discovering rice!

Ninety-nine percent of the rice we eat in the United States is grown in the Southern "rice belt" and in California, where the farming relocated when it petered out in the Carolinas after the Civil War. Established in Louisiana in 1888, it soon spread to Arkansas, California, Mississippi, Missouri, and Texas, where 18.5 billion pounds are raised each year on 3.3 million acres.

Our gourmet president, Thomas Jefferson, risked his life to smuggle a pocketful of seed out of Italy. Impressed with the quality of the rice grown in the Po Valley, and knowing that smuggling it out of the country was a crime punishable by death, Jefferson took the chance and brought Italian rice back to Monticello.

Less distinguished mortals all over the world are also taken with rice, not because it supplies more food for the money, but more taste for the food. It has such a remarkable way with other foods that it not only imparts its own flavor but seems to accentuate the flavors of the foods with which it is combined.

The Italians have made their *risotti* minor masterpieces, and in some areas they replace pasta. Spain's *paella* with seafood, sausage, and chicken, baked with saffron rice, is so outstanding that it is regarded as the national dish. The French *riz pilafs* and India's *pulaus* are classics, served with all kinds of seafoods and meats. The Creoles in Louisiana create poetry with rice, their gumbos and jambalayas making seafood sing. South Americans and other Latins consider it ridiculous to serve chicken without rice. The Indonesians, old hands with rice, set an entire table with rice and assorted savory dishes to serve with it. Called *rijsttafel*, it is such a spectacular offering that it has been adopted by the Dutch as one of Holland's major culinary attractions. The Chinese and the Japanese are the rice-eating champs of the world: The Chinese polish off at least a pound a day, and the Japanese eat half a pound daily. In both countries, the word for meal is the same as the word for rice.

But some United States rice eaters rank right up there with the people of the Orient. In Louisiana, rice is often eaten three times a day, and it is included in most Creole dishes. It is said that the Cajuns of that state can look at a field of growing rice and rattle off the number of gallons of gravy needed to serve with that amount of cooked rice.

We could have saved reading time and summed up the foregoing by simply saying that rice is the world's most popular food—but we're too enthusiastic for that. We had to prove it by writing a book in which we recount some of the experiences we had in discovering rice recipes in a dozen trips around the world.

We were fortunate in signing a contract to write a travel book in which we would record our adventures in as many off-the-beaten-track places of the world that we could find. We were given plenty of time and could wander anywhere that we thought might be rewarding.

Not only did we collect sights, sounds, and experiences (for example, searching for tigers on the backs of trained elephants in the foothills of the Himalayas), but we filled pages of notebooks with recipes of the various dishes we had. Most important, we made friends everywhere: Africa, India, the Philippines, Spitzbergen (above the Arctic circle), all of Europe, Sri Lanka (then Ceylon), Hong Kong, Cambodia, Thailand, and other places in the Near and Far East. Everywhere we went we found color and adventure, and rice—the world's common food denominator, served in many uncommon ways.

Along with some of these unique rice recipes, we also offer a few of the adventures associated with rice.

# 1

# The Rewards of Rice

The food world today is full of fads that flare and then fizzle out like fireworks on the Fourth of July. For a while the favorite was the exotic but bland fruit, kiwi, which appeared in all manner of recipes. Then came the palate-dominating peppers, large and small, sweet and hot, overwhelming recipes in silly combinations. But this fad, like all fads, disappeared.

Rice is no fad. The Orientals first discovered its rewards many years ago: Each pound triples in volume when cooked, so that you can get 18 servings from a pound of raw rice. The same amount of potatoes yields only 3 servings. Uncooked, rice needs no refrigeration, stores on a shelf indefinitely, doesn't spoil, sprout, shrivel, or lose nutritional value. Cooked, rice holds its personality well for up to four hours, which, compared to pasta or potatoes, is a unique convenience.

In the United States, rice has been hailed as the new American staple that can be used in all courses. We're also discovering that it adds appeal to most dishes, especially curries, stews, vegetables, and even salads. Rice dramatically gets the host or hostess out of the meat-and-potato rut and also is superb for meatless meals: Many of us have discovered the old Chinese favorite, fried rice with eggs and vegetables, and we're adopting the Middle Eastern technique of stuffing vegetables (eggplants, peppers, tomatoes, and zucchini) with rice. Rice also is excellent as a stuffing for pork chops, poultry, or game birds.

Rice rejuvenates all kinds of leftovers, and is unbeatable as a flavorful extender, making a little chicken, meat, or seafood look and taste like a lot. It is so compatible with seafood that crab, scallops, and shrimp with rice have become international favorites.

Although it is not native to America, and most of the classic dishes using rice did not originate here, American rice is, to our minds (and taste buds), the world's best. Research and scientific farming here (seeding by airplane, harvesting with the assistance of laser beams, and the creation of hardy, prolific new types) have produced rice that is superior to any other in flavor, in cooking and storing qualities, and in cleanliness. Most other rices have to be washed, drained, and then washed again, but not ours. In fact, we are advised not to do this with American rice, as vitamins, its abundant food value, can be washed away.

# Nutritional Value

We are trying to become an "eat light" society. Rice not only ranks at the top of the light foods, but it is the dream food for dieters and health fans: Low in calories (just 84 in ½ cup, supplying enough energy to dance for 18 minutes, or walk for 35), rice is free of cholesterol, has all of the body-building essential amino acids, and is very low in sodium. It also is the most digestible of the important complex carbohydrates. Most food requires 2 to 4 hours to digest; rice requires just one. It is also gluten-free and nonallergenic.

Like bread, most of the rice we buy in supermarkets is enriched, which means it also contains calcium, iron, and B complex vitamins in addition to its other assets. It also is the answer for natural food devotees—if they eat brown rice, it has all of the nutrients naturally, without enrichment. The bran layer in brown rice (removed in white rice) also has beneficial fiber and oil and another bonus, vitamin E.

# Varieties of Rice

Although other types of rice are available here, the United States mainly produces twenty types, which are classified by length into just three categories: long grain, medium grain, and short grain.

Long-grain rice is about five times as long as it is wide. The cooked grains are usually separate and fluffy. It is the most popular rice in the United States. Although it is excellent for general use, long-grain rice is especially good in curries, pilafs, risotti, and salads.

Medium- and short-grain rice are much shorter and plumper and cook much the same: moist and tender, clinging together more than long-grain rice does. They are used best in desserts, molds, meat loaves and croquettes, where their "cling" is advantageous. Short grain is raised only in California and sometimes is difficult to find, so you can substitute medium grain for recipes that call for short grain.

The three types of rice are also found in different forms, or different degrees of processing.

*Regular milled white rice* is sometimes called *white* or *polished* rice. This is probably the most widely used form of rice. The outer husk of the grain is removed, and the bran layers are then milled until the grain is white.

*Brown rice* is the whole, unpolished grain that still retains most of its bran layer. That bran gives a "nutty" flavor and slightly chewy texture to the rice.

*Parboiled rice* (or "Converted rice") has extra-fluffy, separate grains, which hold after cooking for a longer period of time without "clumping." The fluffy characteristic results from the steam-pressure process the rice goes through before it is milled.

*Precooked rice* (so-called minute rice) is the fastest, and, for us, the least satisfying of all rices to prepare or eat. Already fully cooked and dehydrated, this type simply needs to be rehydrated and it is ready to be eaten.

There are also a growing number of premixed *specialty rices* on the market, designed for those who'd rather eat fast than eat well. Just follow package directions. These dehydrated mixtures do not compare in flavor, aroma, and presentation with freshly cooked rice combined with fresh ingredients.

In doing research for this book, we collected all of the American and foreign rices we could find and tested them.

We tried Boil-in-Bag precooked long-grain rice; the Texas long-grain basmati; and a regular milled medium grain, much like a Japanese rice that was "coated with an edible cereal." Even though this was American-grown rice, the cooking directions advised us to wash it in water (Japanese style) until the water ran clear; then soak in water for 30 minutes before draining and cooking. A California medium-grain brown rice had similar complicated directions.

Four regular milled long grains were excellent, but a California pearl short grain needed washing first. We didn't care for the results of three long-grain precooked rices that cooked in 5 minutes. We liked the ten brown rices we tried, long grain, medium grain, and short grain, and were very taken with a Wild Pecan Rice from Louisiana, a long-grain rice with a lovely nutty, slight pecan-like flavor and aroma. That rice isn't wild rice, and there are no pecans in it, but it is an exceptional aromatic rice, grown only in the Evangeline farmland of south Louisiana.

We also tried a glutinous, "sweet" or "sticky," rice, which costs more than twice the amount of other American rices. It sure was sticky! Despite recommendations from friends who had eaten it in numerous ways in China, we didn't find it worth the effort. It required washing four times, or until the water ran clear; then it had to be soaked for at least 1 hour and then strained for 2 hours. After all this, it had to be steamed.

We also sampled imported "bagged" Chinese long grain, Japanese medium grain, Italian Arborio, and Indian basmati. Rices we tried from Latin America were usually broken, and all needed washing. The Italian rice (which was difficult to find and expensive) required special attention, constant stirring (for about 18 minutes), and frequent additions of hot water or broth until it was absorbed and al dente, slightly moist, risotto style. It was good, but it was not superior to our long-grain rice. No foreign variety had the fluffy, firm separation of grains of American rice.

Besides finding the foreign rices at least twice as expensive (sometimes more) as ours, slow retail movement of those rices produced some that we found rancid. And some were contaminated with insects.

Our recommendation is to stay with American rice in the American styles, regular milled long grain, medium grain, or short grain, or the parboiled or converted rice in the same grains. Or use long-grain or medium-grain brown rice. These rices will do for any recipe in this book, and they will be easy to cook, reasonable in price, and excellent in taste.


# Ingredients

Rice keeps coming up with rewards: Unlike many foods, it absorbs and magnifies flavors while it is cooking and usually is not drained.

Although it may also be dressed with various sauces and cheeses, the cook should begin adding taste-making ingredients right in the pot.

Onions add flavor to about anything except ice cream and chocolate cake. They work taste wonders with rice. The Italians, when preparing a risotto, generally sauté onions in butter and then stir in the rice. We learned our technique from them. But briefly sautéing rice in butter or margarine before adding the liquid does more than add flavor to the rice-flour coating. It also helps prevent the rice from getting sticky.

Broths and stocks: It is always preferable to make your own. For example, we make a basic stock in our Old-fashioned Chicken and Rice Soup (page 30). But today many of us are pressed for time, so cans and cubes are helpful.

Using these liquids (beef or chicken stocks) instead of water adds new taste textures. It's also interesting to experiment with tomato, lemon, and orange juices diluted with water (1 cup of juice to 1 cup of water). With pork, we've had rice simmered in apple or pineapple juice mixed with water. We've found it rewarding and very different.

Rice cookery also encourages the use of imagination. Try tossing hot rice with chopped scallions and fresh mushrooms sautéed in butter or margarine, a medley of cooked fresh vegetables, chopped pimento, or chopped broadleaf (Italian) parsley leaves, even chopped mixed nuts. We like plain white rice tossed with chutney when we serve a curry.


# Cheeses

We like to use almost as much cheese in cooking rice as we do in preparing pasta. Readers will note that in the recipes (although several other kinds of cheese are used) we mainly recommend two cheeses: Asiago and Parmesan. Parmesan is widely known, but Asiago we discovered only a few years ago. Like Parmesan, it is a Grana type, a grating cheese that originated in the Italian province of Vicenza. Properly aged (it should be golden, hard, nutty, and 2 or 3 years old), it has, in our opinion, more flavor than Parmesan—at about half the price.

# Equipment

Not much equipment is involved in rice cookery. For such an exotic food, its requirements are simple. We, however, like the cast-iron, enameled heavy pots with tight-fitting covers made in France, Belgium, or The Netherlands. These pots are perfect conductors of heat, cooking evenly (rice will not burn or stick on the heavy bottoms, and the tops fit snugly for the perfect simmering of rice), and are easy to clean, good for storing in the refrigerator or for serving from stove to table.

Our pots (we are collectors; we have ten) range in size from 1¼ quarts to 11 quarts; they are what the French call round *cocottes*, casseroles with tight-fitting covers.

We also like the oval au gratin dishes. We have five, ranging in size from 7¾ to 14 inches. These go from oven to table with rice dishes that have cream and cheese, so-called casserole dinners.

We hasten to add that all this equipment isn't necessary for rice cookery. For us, having these handsome pots and dishes enhances the whole idea of cooking and brightens the kitchen, but you can use whatever you have. Just make sure the pot or dish is large enough to handle the amount of rice you are cooking or serving.

We use a wooden fork for stirring the rice in its pot, and a metal fork for tossing up to mix and for fluffing the rice with butter for serving.


# Molds

Depending upon what you're serving with the rice, you can be creative and dramatic if you present the dish in a mold. We have found that short- and medium-grain rice molds best. It clings, and that is important if you are trying to achieve various shapes. But all rice—long grain, brown, wild—can be molded if you're careful. The rice should not be cooked al dente; longer cooking is advised. Molded rice also may need butter or margarine stirred in before it is molded to help it stay in the desired shape. Also, the mold itself should be well coated with butter or margarine.

The molds can be in any form (there are many sizes and shapes on the market, mainly for various pastries, hearts, flowers, balls, loaves, etc.); dainty espresso cups make neat little molds. For example, unmold a quartet beside an offering of curried shrimp. The presentation opportunities are limitless. But that's another rice reward: eye appeal.

## Ring Molds

For example, consider the piece of equipment that we think is the most important and use most often when we are entertaining: ring molds. We have several recipes that illustrate how they dramatize and decorate a dinner table. The rice is usually cooked, placed in a mold coated with butter or margarine, and then briefly baked in the oven. Unmolded on a hot platter, the rice ring can be filled with any number of creamed dishes—chicken, fish, shrimp, chipped beef, or chicken livers in a sauce. The possibilities are plentiful. Or if you're having a roast or a broiled chicken, the ring can be filled with creamed (or plain) vegetables. Even serving from a ring mold is interesting: A large spoonful of rice is placed on each diner's warm plate; then the creamed offering is spooned on top of the rice. Or it can be placed beside the rice, with diners handling it the way they prefer. We have ring molds in several sizes, ranging from 7¼ to 9½ inches in diameter.

# Storage

White rice will keep indefinitely on the shelf, virtually unchanged for 1 to 2 years. Once opened, however, it should be placed in containers that keep it clean and free from moisture. Brown rice, however, because of the oil in the bran, has a shelf life of just 6 months. Refrigeration will retard spoilage. Wild rice may be stored in a tightly covered container in a cool, dry place. It will keep indefinitely, like white rice, virtually unchanged for 1 to 2 years.

All cooked rice can be refrigerated for up to a week, or frozen for 4 months. It should go immediately into the refrigerator and, if not used within 2 or 3 days, into the freezer. A dish of leftover rice should be covered tightly with plastic wrap so that it won't pick up any refrigerator flavors or odors. It is a hypersensitive food that latches onto other flavors quickly.

Leftover rice reheats perfectly, coming back to a flavor that is as good as when it was first prepared. Simply add 2 tablespoons of hot liquid for each cup of cooked rice and heat on top of the stove for 5 minutes, stirring and fluffing the rice with a metal fork.

# 2

# How to Cook Rice

As we do in all matters pertaining to cooking, we sought advice while writing this book from our mentor, Antoine Gilly, one of the greatest of French chefs. We spent nearly two decades working with and learning from this talented man, probably the longest cooking course on record. Antoine has been the chef for a king of England, a prince of Wales, and a prime minister; he created the cuisine for France's famous Blue Train, and he was master chef for several of France's most distinguished restaurants.

Antoine Gilly's recommendations and suggestions are important to us, so we put the question to him: What American rice should we use for most dishes? What does he use?

Antoine went right to the point. "American Converted rice is fail-proof," he said, "cooking just right every time. It is parboiled by a special process, but not precooked. It is not an 'instant rice.' Some people are put off or confused by the word 'converted.' This rice has been prepared by the processors to cook easily and perfectly and retain its natural vitamins and flavor. Most chefs I know use it because it holds on a steam table, on top of the range, or in an oven without becoming sticky."

We do use other types of rice, and we give explicit cooking directions in every recipe in this book, but cooking parboiled rice, which has also become our favorite, is as simple as reading the directions on the box. Here are our directions (which differ from those on the box only slightly) for cooking 1 cup of raw parboiled rice, which yields about 3 cups or five ⅗-cup servings.

1. In a pot with a heavy lid and heavy bottom (large enough to handle 2½ cups of liquid and the eventual expanded 3 cups of cooked rice), over medium heat, melt 1 tablespoon of butter or margarine. Add 1 small onion, chopped, and cook for 2 minutes

stirring. (We don't always add the onion. It depends on how the rice will be used.) Stir in 1 teaspoon of salt (if using broth, taste before adding the salt) and 1 cup of rice, blending well.

2. Pour 2½ cups of liquid (broth, water, etc.) into the rice pot, stirring the rice with a wooden fork. Raise the heat and bring to a boil.

3. Cover tightly, lower the heat, and simmer for 20 minutes, or until the liquid has been absorbed and the rice is tender.

*Note:* For firmer rice, use less liquid (2 cups) and simmer 5 minutes less, 15 rather than 20 minutes. For softer rice, use more liquid (¼ cup more) and simmer 5 minutes longer, 25 minutes, rather than 20.

- Directions on some boxes of rice suggest bringing the liquid to a boil first, then adding it to the rice that has been briefly sautéed with butter or margarine, salt, and onion. Bringing the liquid to a boil first is a step that we discovered isn't necessary. We found that adding the liquid to the sautéed rice, then bringing it to a boil worked just as well. Either way, the choice is yours. Rice cooperates.
- Some directions suggest that the pot be removed from the heat after 20 minutes and allowed to sit, covered, for 5 minutes, while the absorption is taking place. We have not found this necessary, but it does result in a somewhat drier rice.
- For regular milled rice, use 2 cups of liquid for 1 cup of rice.
- If using water, always add butter or margarine.
- Stir the rice with a wooden fork only *after* the liquid comes to a boil. Then lower the heat and simmer the rice with the pot covered.
- *Keep* the lid *on* the pot. After the rice is simmering do *not* peek to see how it is doing.
- The heat must be low, but constant, so the simmer is even.

## Some Questions and Answers

*Why Does Rice Become Gritty?* The cover has been frequently removed during the cooking period. It's like lifting your head to watch where the golf ball will go after the swing. Bad technique.

Keep your head down, and keep the lid on the rice pot down on top of the pot, not lifted so you can watch the progress of the cooking rice.

**Why Does Long-Grain Rice Sometimes Become "Chalky" and Hard When Refrigerated?** A chemical change takes place with some rices when they become cold. It's a starch change called *retrogradation*. It can be corrected by adding small amounts of boiling water or broth to the hard refrigerated rice, stirring gently with a metal fork, and reheating slowly. Also, if rice is going to be refrigerated, cooking it in more liquid than usual will soften it and retard that hardening process. For 1 cup of Converted rice, use 3 cups of liquid rather than 2½ cups; for 1 cup of regular milled rice, use 2½ cups of liquid rather than 2 cups.

**Why Is Rice Sometimes Sticky?** Rice gets sticky if you stir it while it's cooking or if you cook it for too long a time.

**What Do I Do If the Rice Isn't Dry Enough?** Simply remove the cover and place over low heat for about 3 or 4 minutes, or until the rice is as dry as desired.

**Most American Rices Seem to Take About 20 Minutes, Covered, to Cook. Is There an American Rice That Takes Longer?** Yes, brown rice. There are many brand names on the market, but all brown rices are natural and have had less milling than white rice. All need about 45 minutes of cooking, covered, and some directions also state, "After simmering in 2½ cups of water for 45 minutes, turn off the heat and let the rice pot sit on the hot burner for 10 minutes. Do not remove the cover until ready to serve." We found that this was good advice. It is also wise to check the directions carefully on the boxes of brown rice. Different processors vary procedure, some increasing the liquid and cooking time.

After cooking all rices (except dessert rice), we add room-temperature butter or margarine to the hot rice just before serving. We then fluff the rice with a metal fork, lifting the cooked grains with the fork rather than stirring. This not only increases the fluffiness of the rice but also helps separate the grains. We use "sweet" butter or margarine; added at the last minute, it also gives additional flavor.

You'll note that we use the Italian term *al dente* in some recipes.

By that we mean that the rice should be slightly chewy, slightly underdone. We suggest that the rice be al dente when it will be cooked further, such as baking in a casserole with other ingredients. We also recommend it for risotti.

# Other Cooking Methods

## Oven

In order to save energy we often use this method (it's also the method of many French chefs) when we have a roast or other dishes in the oven.

Place 1 cup of rice in a baking dish, add 1 tablespoon of butter or margarine and 1 teaspoon of salt. Pour in 2½ cups of boiling liquid. Stir with a fork. Cover tightly and bake in a preheated 350-degree oven for 25 to 30 minutes, or until the rice is tender and the liquid has been absorbed. (Brown rice needs 1 hour.)

## Microwave

For regular milled, parboiled, or brown rice: In a 2-quart microwave baking dish place 1 cup of rice, 1 tablespoon of butter or margarine, and 1 teaspoon of salt. Add 2 cups of liquid (not boiling) and stir well with a fork. Cover tightly and cook on high (maximum power) for 5 minutes, or until boiling. Reduce setting to medium, or 50 percent power, and cook for 15 minutes, or until the rice is tender and the liquid has been absorbed. For brown rice, reduce the setting to 30 percent power and cook for 30 minutes, or until the rice is tender.

## Rice Cookers and Steamers

There are a number of automatic and nonautomatic rice cookers available. We don't use one (or a steamer either), as we are partial to the simple never-fail, top-of-the-stove method. If you choose to use one, it is important to follow the manufacturer's directions carefully. Generally, about ½ cup less liquid is required with the rice cookers. We offer the same advice for steamers, which are becoming popular: Follow the manufacturer's directions.

## Double Boiler

Sometimes when rice is cooked in milk for dessert recipes, it is simmered over boiling water. Place 1 cup uncooked regular milled medium- or short-grain rice in the top of a double boiler with 3½ cups of milk and 1 teaspoon of salt. Heat the mixture to boiling. Place over boiling water in the bottom of the double boiler and cook, covered, for 40 minutes, or until the rice is tender and the milk has been absorbed.

Before you read the recipes, we again remind you that in all recipes where we use long-grain rice, rice that is Converted or parboiled, we do so for the reasons that we have already detailed. If another type of rice is called for, we state that in the recipe.

For example, another type of rice may be the Rolls-Royce of rices, wild rice, which is not a rice at all. It is *Zinzania aquatica,* the seed of a grass plant that grows in shallow fresh water, primarily in lakes in Minnesota, which produces 80 percent of the world's crop. But we all call this luxury (more than $10 a pound) "rice," so we include it here.

# Preparation of Wild Rice

## Stove Top

Wash by running cold water over the wild rice in a wire strainer until the water runs clear.

Use 3 to 1 as the rule of thumb for the amount of liquid to use, i.e., for 1 cup of uncooked wild rice, boil 3 cups of water salted to taste. When the water boils add the rice. Return to the boil, stir, and lower the heat until the water slowly simmers. Cover and cook until the rice puffs open and reveals a white interior. The degree of doneness is a matter of personal taste. Some prefer a nutty, chewy texture; others prefer soft wild rice.

If the wild rice is to be cooked again, such as in a casserole or stuffing, it should be cooked only to the point where it puffs but does not open.

*Yield:* One cup of wild rice yields 3 to 4 cups when cooked.

## Oven

Wash 1 cup of wild rice thoroughly in cold running water until the water runs clear. Combine with 3 cups of water in a 2-quart casserole. Stir, cover, and bake in a preheated 350-degree oven for 1 hour. Check the wild rice. Add more water, if needed, and fluff with a fork. Continue cooking for 30 minutes. Wild rice should be moist, not dry.

## Microwave

Wash 1 cup of wild rice thoroughly in cold running water until the water runs clear. Combine with 3 cups of water in a 2-quart microwave baking dish. Stir well. Cover and microwave on high for 5 minutes. Microwave on medium (50 percent power) for 30 minutes. Let stand for 15 minutes; then drain.

# 3

# Rice with Soups

Among other adventurous ambitions, we had always wanted to travel to the North Pole. Finally, a few years ago we decided that if we were ever going to do it we had better get the plan into motion. So we chartered a special ice-breaking 57-foot diesel ketch, *Havella*, with a five-man Norwegian crew. It broke ice all right, some of which we used in our predinner cocktails.

The steward (read "cook"), Aage Rutwold, proved to be somewhat of a genius, producing excellent meals on seas sometimes so rough that we often could not stand upright. Often all we could get down was a delicious soup, always rice in a rich broth, sometimes floating bright green specks (parsley, chives?).

We had, of course, brought along provisions—beef, pork, poultry—and several times we had bagged eider ducks to give the menu variety. But that rice soup was on the table almost every other day, and we always looked forward to it. We asked Aage for the recipe—several times. He always bobbed his head and said that he wouldn't forget to give it to us. But he never did. We wondered what meat or poultry (wild duck?) made the broth so rich, so consistently delicious.

As we were about to leave *Havella* for the last time, Maria Luisa said to Aage, "You haven't forgotten that you were going to give us the recipe for the rice soup?"

He shook his head, went to his galley, and came back with three items. Abashed, he held out one package of chicken bouillon cubes and one of beef.

The last item he gave us was a box of American long-grain rice.

"This is the secret," he said. "I couldn't make a pot of decent soup without it."

# Savoia Rice and Cabbage Soup

One 1½-inch cube of fatback, blanched in boiling water for 5
   minutes, drained, and cut into ¼-inch cubes
2 tablespoons butter or margarine
3 large ripe tomatoes, peeled, seeded, and finely chopped
One 1-pound firm head Savoy cabbage, cored and shredded
1 medium onion, minced
1 garlic clove, minced
Salt and freshly ground black pepper to taste
6 cups beef broth
½ cup long-grain rice
½ cup grated Asiago or Parmesan cheese

1. In a large pot, over medium heat, cook the fatback in the butter or margarine until it is golden and crisp but not brown. Add the
tomatoes, cabbage, onion, and garlic and simmer for 10 minutes.
Lightly season with salt and pepper.

2. Add the broth and bring to a simmer. Stir in the rice, cover,
and simmer for 15 minutes, or until the rice and cabbage are tender. Taste for seasoning, adding salt and pepper if needed. Serve
with the cheese sprinkled on top.

*Serves 4 to 6*


# Cream of Carrot-Rice Soup

2 tablespoons butter or margarine
3 large leeks (white part only), trimmed, well washed, and
   thinly sliced
3 carrots, scraped and thinly sliced
¼ teaspoon ground mace
Salt and freshly ground black pepper to taste
6 cups chicken broth
¾ cup cooked long-grain rice
About ¾ cup half-and-half
½ carrot, scraped and finely grated

1. In a large pot, over medium heat, melt the butter or margarine. Add the leeks and cook for 1 minute, stirring. Do not brown. Add the sliced carrots and cook, stirring, for 1 minute. Stir in the mace, salt, and pepper. Add the broth and half of the rice. Cover and simmer for 30 minutes, or until the carrots and rice can be mashed against the side of the pot.

2. Cool slightly and pour into the container of a blender or food processor, and blend into a smooth liquid.

3. Before serving, stir in 2 tablespoons of half-and-half for each cup of soup. Heat just to a simmer. Taste for seasoning, adding salt and pepper if needed. With a metal fork, mix the remaining rice with the grated carrot and sprinkle over the top of each serving.

*Serves 4 to 6*

## Bolognese Chicken Liver Soup

*We enjoyed this in Bologna, where Thomas Jefferson risked his life to smuggle out that short-grain, nutty Italian rice. He needn't have bothered; U.S. rice is superb. But it took time and Jefferson was in a hurry.*

2 tablespoons butter or margarine
½ pound chicken livers, trimmed
2½ cups water
1 teaspoon salt (optional)
1 cup long-grain rice
7 cups chicken broth
½ teaspoon dried leaf sage, crumbled
Salt and freshly ground black pepper to taste
½ cup grated Asiago or Parmesan cheese
2 tablespoons chopped broadleaf (Italian) parsley leaves

1. In a frying pan, over medium heat, melt the butter or margarine and cook the livers for 4 minutes, or until they are brown outside and slightly pink inside. Remove from the heat and cut into ¼-inch pieces.

2. In a saucepan, bring the water to a boil. Stir in the salt and

rice. Lower the heat, cover, and simmer for 20 minutes, or until the rice is tender and the liquid has been absorbed.

3. In a large pot, bring the chicken broth to a boil. Stir in the chicken livers, rice, and sage. Heat for 1 minute. Taste before seasoning with salt and pepper (the broth may have supplied enough). Serve piping hot, sprinkled with the cheese and parsley.

*Serves 4 to 6*

# Old-fashioned Chicken and Rice Soup

*This is a classic that many processors try to reproduce in cans but can't quite master. Rice doesn't like cans.*

1¼ cups water
2½ teaspoons salt (optional)
½ cup long-grain rice
6 meaty chicken backs
2 large onions, halved and each half nailed with a
    whole clove
2 celery stalks, coarsely chopped
2 medium carrots, scraped and coarsely
    chopped
½ teaspoon freshly ground black pepper
1 bay leaf
½ teaspoon dried thyme
3 quarts water
4 chicken thighs

1. In a saucepan, bring the 1¼ cups of water to a boil. Stir in 1 teaspoon of salt and the rice. Lower the heat, cover, and simmer for 15 minutes, or until the rice is tender and the liquid has been absorbed. Reserve.

2. Put the chicken backs, onions, celery, carrots, 1½ teaspoons of salt, pepper, bay leaf, and thyme into a large pot. Pour on the 3 quarts of water. Bring to a boil, cover, lower the heat, and simmer for 45 minutes, or until the chicken is tender, skimming the scum from the top as necessary. Remove the cover and reduce the stock

by one-third over high heat. Strain the stock, discarding the vegetables and bay leaf.

3. Discard the skin and bones from the chicken backs, reserving the good pieces of meat.

4. Pour the strained stock back into the pot and add the chicken thighs. Bring to a boil. Lower the heat and simmer, partially covered, for 25 minutes, or until the thighs are tender. Remove the thighs to cool. Discard the skin and bones and cut the meat from the backs and thighs into bite-size pieces.

5. Add all of the chicken meat to the stock. Stir in the rice and taste for seasoning, adding salt and pepper if needed. Bring to a boil and serve piping hot.

*Note:* If the stock is not as rich as you would like after it has reduced, add 2 or 3 chicken bouillon cubes.

*Serves 6*


## Greek Rice and Lemon Soup

*The Greeks sometimes vary this soup by adding small pieces of cooked meat or poultry during the last, simmering stage.*

7 cups rich chicken broth
6 tablespoons long-grain rice
3 eggs
¼ cup fresh lemon juice
Salt to taste

1. In a pot large enough to hold all the ingredients, bring the broth to a boil. Add the rice, cover, lower the heat, and simmer for 15 minutes, or until the rice is tender. Remove the pot from the heat and let stand for 5 minutes.

2. Beat the eggs and lemon juice together. Then stir the egg-lemon mixture into the soup. Taste and add salt if needed. The broth may have supplied enough seasoning. Heat just to a simmer and serve immediately in hot soup bowls.

*Serves 6*

# Chicken Gumbo Soup

One 3- to 3½-pound chicken
1 celery stalk, including leaves, coarsely chopped
2 carrots, scraped and coarsely chopped
1 large onion, nailed with 2 whole cloves
1 bay leaf
½ teaspoon dried oregano
1½ teaspoons salt (optional)
½ teaspoon freshly ground black pepper
3 quarts water
½ cup long-grain rice
One 1-pound can plum tomatoes with liquid (Pour into a bowl
    and break up the tomatoes with your hands.)
1 small green bell pepper, cored, seeded, and chopped
1 medium onion, chopped
½ cup corn kernels, preferably fresh (or frozen, defrosted)
1 cup thinly sliced fresh okra

1. Put the chicken, celery, carrots, onion with the cloves, bay leaf, oregano, salt, and pepper into a large pot. Pour in the water. Bring to a boil, lower the heat, and simmer, partially covered, for 1 hour, or until the chicken is tender and the liquid is reduced by one-third. (If the chicken is tender before the liquid has reduced, remove the chicken, raise the heat, and reduce the liquid.) Remove the chicken and strain the stock.

2. Return the stock to the pot and stir in the rice, tomatoes, green pepper, and chopped onion. Simmer, covered, for 20 minutes; then stir in the corn and okra and simmer, uncovered, for 10 minutes, or until the rice and vegetables are tender.

3. Remove and discard the skin and bones from the chicken and cut the meat into small cubes. Stir the chicken into the soup pot. Taste for seasoning, adding salt and pepper if needed. Bring to a boil and serve.

*Note:* If the stock is not as rich as you would like after it has reduced, add 2 or 3 chicken bouillon cubes.

*Serves 6 to 8*

# Consommé with Rice

*Rice is classic with simple soups, because it adds character and flavor.*

1 cup water
½ cup long-grain rice
9 cups beef broth
Salt and pepper to taste
1 bunch watercress, washed and stems removed

1. In a small saucepan, bring the water to a boil. Stir in the rice, cover, lower the heat, and simmer for 5 minutes. Drain if any liquid remains in the pan.

2. Pour the broth into a pot and bring to a boil. Stir in the rice, cover, lower the heat, and simmer for about 15 minutes, or until the rice is tender. Taste for seasoning, adding salt and pepper if needed. The broth may supply enough seasoning. Serve in hot bowls with watercress leaves floating on top.

*Serves 6*


# Cock-a-leekie with Rice

## *Brown Rice with Chicken and Leeks*

8 leeks, including all of the white part and 1 inch of the light
    green part
One 3½- to 4-pound chicken with its giblets
2 teaspoons salt (optional)
½ teaspoon freshly ground black pepper
Water to cover (about 3½ quarts)
6 pitted prunes (optional)
½ cup long-grain brown rice
2 tablespoons chopped broadleaf (Italian) parsley leaves

1. Remove and discard the root end of the leeks. Cut the leeks into halves lengthwise. Wash well under cool running water and cut into ½-inch-long pieces. Set aside.

2. Put the chicken, its giblets, salt, and pepper into a large pot. Pour in the water and bring to a boil. Lower the heat, cover, and simmer for 40 minutes, skimming the scum from the top as necessary.

3. Add the leeks and prunes and simmer, uncovered, for 20 minutes, or until the chicken is tender.

4. Remove the chicken from the pot. When cool enough to handle, separate the breast and thighs and reserve them for another meal. Remove the skin and bones from the rest of the bird and cut the meat, along with the giblets, into small, bite-size pieces. Reserve this cut-up chicken.

5. With a slotted spoon, remove the leeks and prunes and reserve them.

6. Raise the heat under the pot and reduce the liquid by half. Stir in the rice. Bring to a boil, lower the heat, cover, and simmer for 30 minutes, or until the rice is tender but not too soft.

7. Return the cut-up chicken, leeks, and prunes to the pot with the rice. Bring to a boil. Taste for seasoning, adding salt and pepper if needed. Sprinkle with the parsley.

*Note:* If the stock is not as rich as you would like after it has reduced, add 2 or 3 chicken bouillon cubes.

*Serves 6*

## Genovese Rice and Egg Soup

8 cups rich chicken broth
¾ cup long-grain rice
1 tablespoon chopped fresh thyme, or ½ teaspoon dried
3 eggs
¼ cup chopped broadleaf (Italian) parsley leaves
1½ cups grated Asiago or Parmesan cheese
Salt and freshly ground black pepper to taste

1. In a pot, bring the broth to a boil. Stir in the rice and thyme. Cover the pot, lower the heat, and simmer for 15 minutes, or until the rice is almost tender (al dente).

2. In a bowl, beat the eggs with the parsley and half of the cheese, blending well. Stir 1 cup of the broth into the egg-cheese mixture. Quickly stir this mixture into the pot with the rice. Simmer for 5 minutes, stirring constantly. Taste and season with salt and pepper. Serve immediately. Pass the remaining cheese at the table to be sprinkled on each bowl of soup.

*Serves 6*

## Porro Brodo

### *Leek, Prosciutto, Rice, and Spinach Soup*

8 cups chicken broth
6 medium leeks (white part only), trimmed, well washed, and cut into ¼-inch-long pieces
½ cup long-grain rice
One 10-ounce package fresh spinach, trimmed, washed, and coarsely chopped, or one 10-ounce package frozen leaf spinach, defrosted and coarsely chopped
2 tablespoons butter or margarine
½ cup small prosciutto slivers
Salt and freshly ground black pepper to taste
1 cup grated Asiago or Parmesan cheese

1. Pour the broth into a large saucepan. Add the leeks and bring to a simmer over medium heat. Cover and cook for 10 minutes.

2. Stir in the rice and cook, covered, for 12 minutes, or until the rice is tender but still a little al dente.

3. Add the spinach (if using fresh) and cook for 5 minutes. Add the butter or margarine and prosciutto and the spinach (if using frozen) and cook for 3 minutes. Taste for seasoning, adding salt and pepper if needed. The broth may have supplied enough. If the soup is too thick for your taste, add more hot broth. Serve the cheese on the side.

*Serves 6*

# Athenian Fish Soup

2 pounds firm white fish fillets (haddock, cod, etc.)
Cheesecloth, sufficient to completely wrap the fish
1 quart water
1 cup clam juice or Fish Stock (page 48)
1 cup dry white wine
1½ teaspoons salt (optional)
½ teaspoon freshly ground black pepper
6 whole scallions, trimmed and diced
2 celery stalks, scraped and chopped
1 small turnip, peeled and diced
One 1-pound can plum tomatoes, chopped and liquid reserved
¾ cup long-grain rice

1. Wrap the fish in the cheesecloth, then place in a large pot. Add the water, clam juice or fish stock, wine, salt if desired, and pepper. Bring to a boil, cover, lower the heat, and simmer for 15 minutes, or until the fish begins to separate. Remove and flake the fish, discarding any skin and bones. Reserve. Strain the stock.

2. Return the stock to the pot. Add the scallions, celery, turnip, tomatoes and their liquid, and the rice. Bring to a boil, cover, lower the heat, and simmer for 20 minutes, or until the rice is tender.

3. Stir in the flaked fish and simmer until the soup is very hot. Taste for seasoning, adding salt and pepper if needed. Serve in warm deep soup bowls, with hot, crisp French or Italian bread.

*Serves 6*

# Zuppa alla Abruzzese

## *Rice, Anchovy, Lentil, and Tomato Soup*

1 cup dry lentils, picked over, rinsed, and soaked in water to
    cover for 3 hours, and then drained
Salt to taste
½ cup long-grain rice
1¼ cups water
1 tablespoon butter or margarine
2 tablespoons olive oil
2 large celery stalks, scraped and chopped
2 garlic cloves, minced
4 large ripe tomatoes, peeled, seeded, and diced
8 cups chicken broth
8 anchovy fillets, drained of oil and mashed
3 tablespoons chopped broadleaf (Italian) parsley leaves
Freshly ground black pepper to taste
1 cup grated Asiago or Parmesan cheese

1. Put the lentils and 1 teaspoon salt into a saucepan. Pour in
enough water to cover and bring to a boil. Cover the pan, lower the
heat, and simmer for 45 minutes, or until the lentils are tender. Do
not overcook. Reserve the lentils and the liquid in which they
cooked.

2. In another saucepan, combine the rice and 1¼ cups of water.
Bring to a boil, cover, lower the heat, and simmer for 20 minutes,
or until the rice is tender and the liquid has been absorbed. Reserve
the rice.

3. In a large pot, over medium heat, heat the butter or margarine
and oil. Stir in the celery and garlic. Cook for 5 minutes. Do not
brown. Add the tomatoes and cook for 5 minutes. Pour in the
chicken broth. Stir in the anchovies and bring to a boil. Lower the
heat and simmer, uncovered, for 20 minutes.

4. Add the lentils with their liquid, the rice, parsley, and black
pepper. Taste before adding more salt, as the broth and anchovies
may have supplied enough. Heat through. Sprinkle cheese on each
serving.

*Serves 6 to 8*

# Cream of Rice Soup

6 cups beef broth
1 cup long-grain rice
2 cups hot milk
3 egg yolks, beaten
2 tablespoons butter or margarine, cut into small pieces
Salt and freshly ground black pepper to taste
2 tablespoons finely chopped fresh chives
1 cup unseasoned croutons

1. In a pot, bring the broth to a boil. Stir in the rice, cover, lower the heat, and simmer for 20 minutes, or until the rice is tender. Drain the rice, returning the broth to the pot. Rub the rice through a fine sieve and return it to the pot with the broth.

2. Gradually beat the milk into the egg yolks. Stir into the pot with the broth and rice, along with the butter or margarine, blending well. Heat thoroughly, but do not boil.

3. Taste before adding salt and pepper; the broth may have supplied enough. Sprinkle with the chives and float the croutons on top of each serving.

*Serves 4 to 6*

# Mulligatawny Soup

1¼ cups water
1 teaspoon salt (optional)
½ cup long-grain rice
1 large whole chicken breast
6 cups chicken broth
1 onion, quartered
1 carrot, scraped and quartered
4 tablespoons (½ stick) butter or margarine
6 whole scallions, trimmed and minced
2 celery stalks, scraped and minced
1 green apple, peeled, cored, and finely chopped
1 tablespoon curry powder, or to taste (page 79)
1½ tablespoons all-purpose flour
½ teaspoon dried thyme
2 medium ripe tomatoes, peeled, seeded, and finely chopped
Salt and freshly ground black pepper to taste
½ cup half-and-half

1. In a saucepan, bring the water to a boil. Stir in the salt and rice. Lower the heat, cover, and simmer for 20 minutes, or until the rice is tender and the liquid has been absorbed. Reserve the rice.

2. Put the chicken in a pot with the broth, onion, and carrot. Bring to a boil, lower the heat, cover, and cook for 30 minutes, or until the chicken is tender, skimming the scum from the top as necessary. Remove and cool the chicken. Discard the skin and bones and cut the meat into slivers. Strain and reserve the broth.

3. In a large deep pot, over medium heat, melt 2 tablespoons of the butter or margarine. Add the scallions, celery, and apple and cook for 5 minutes. Do not brown. Stir in the curry powder, flour, and thyme. Add the tomatoes and cook off most of the liquid, about 7 minutes. Gradually add the broth, stirring. Simmer for 10 minutes. Taste for seasoning, adding salt and pepper if needed. Stir in the chicken, rice, half-and-half, and the remaining butter or margarine, and bring just to a boil. Serve immediately.

*Serves 4 to 6*

# Turkey-Yogurt-Rice Soup

9 cups chicken broth
⅔ cup long-grain rice
2 cups diced cooked turkey
2 tablespoons butter or margarine
1½ tablespoons all-purpose flour
1 cup plain yogurt
½ teaspoon ground cumin
Salt and freshly ground black pepper to taste
2 tablespoons chopped fresh dill

1. In a large pot, bring the broth to a boil. Stir in the rice, cover, lower the heat, and simmer for 20 minutes, or until the rice is tender. Stir in the turkey and remove from the heat.

2. In a saucepan, over medium heat, melt the butter or margarine. Stir in the flour, blending it into a smooth paste. Add the yogurt and cumin and simmer, stirring, for 1 minute.

3. Stir the yogurt mixture into the pot with the rice and turkey and simmer, uncovered, for 5 minutes, or until the soup thickens. Taste for seasoning before adding salt and pepper, as the broth may have supplied enough. Sprinkle dill on each serving.

*Serves 6 to 8*

# Pork Balls and Rice Soup

*Serve this soup in deep bowls, accompanied by warm, crusty, French or Italian bread.*

*Vegetable Soup Base*
3 large leeks, including all of the white part and half of the green
9 cups chicken broth
2 garlic cloves, minced
2 large celery stalks, scraped and chopped

2 medium carrots, scraped and chopped
One 1-pound can tomatoes with their liquid (Pour into a bowl and
    finely break up the tomatoes with your hands.)
1 teaspoon salt (optional)
½ teaspoon freshly ground black pepper

*Pork Balls and Rice*
¾ pound ground lean pork
1 medium onion, finely chopped
1 garlic clove, minced
½ teaspoon salt (optional)
⅛ teaspoon hot red pepper flakes
1 teaspoon ground allspice
3 tablespoons finely chopped broadleaf (Italian) parsley leaves
1 egg, beaten
⅔ cup long-grain rice

1. To make the soup base, cut off and discard the root end of the
leeks. Cut the leeks in half lengthwise and wash them well under
cool running water; then chop them.
2. In a large pot, bring the broth to a boil. Lower the heat and
simmer, stirring in the leeks, garlic, celery, carrots, tomatoes with
their liquid, salt, and pepper. Stir, cover, and simmer for 30 minutes. Taste for seasoning, adding more salt and pepper if needed.
3. To make the pork balls, combine all the ingredients but the
rice in a large bowl. Blend well.
4. Moisten your hands with cold water and form the pork mixture into compact balls ½ to ¾ inch in diameter. With a slotted
spoon, lower the balls into the simmering vegetable-chicken broth.
Stir in the rice, cover, and simmer for 25 minutes. Taste for seasoning, adding salt and pepper if needed.

*Serves 6*

# Rice and Potato Soup

One 1-inch cube salt pork, blanched in boiling water for 5
   minutes, drained, and finely chopped
2 tablespoons butter or margarine
1 medium onion, finely chopped
2 medium potatoes, peeled and cut into ½-inch or smaller cubes
½ cup chopped celery leaves from the center of the bunch
6 cups beef broth
1 large ripe tomato, peeled, seeded, and finely chopped
¾ cup long-grain rice
Salt and freshly ground black pepper to taste
1 tablespoon chopped fresh chives

1. In a large pot, over medium heat, cook the salt pork with the
butter or margarine for 4 minutes, or until the salt pork is golden.
Add the onion and cook for 3 minutes, or until the onion is soft. Do
not brown. Add the potatoes and celery leaves and cook, stirring,
for 2 minutes.

2. Pour in the broth. Add the tomato and bring to a boil. Lower
the heat, add the rice, and simmer, covered, for 15 minutes, or until
the potatoes and rice are tender. Taste for seasoning, adding salt
and pepper if needed. The broth may have supplied enough seasoning. Serve sprinkled with the chives.

*Serves 6*

# Caribbean Pumpkin and Rice Soup

3 tablespoons butter or margarine
1 medium onion, chopped
1 garlic clove, minced
½ teaspoon salt (optional)
½ teaspoon ground coriander
½ teaspoon ground allspice
1 bay leaf
½ cup long-grain rice
4 cups chicken broth (or more, see below)

2 cups fresh pumpkin, cut into ½-inch cubes
Pinch of hot red pepper flakes, crumbled
2 cups cooked chicken, cut into ½-inch cubes
2 tablespoons chopped fresh coriander leaves, or 1 tablespoon
   chopped fresh parsley leaves mixed with 1 tablespoon chopped
   fresh chives

1. In a large pot, over medium heat, melt the butter or margarine. Add the onion and garlic and cook for 3 minutes, or until they
are soft. Do not brown. Add the salt, coriander, allspice, and bay
leaf. Add the rice and cook, stirring, for 1 minute. Pour in the 4
cups of broth and bring to a boil. Stir with a wooden fork, lower
the heat, cover, and simmer for 10 minutes. Add the pumpkin and
hot red pepper flakes and simmer for 10 minutes, or until the rice
and pumpkin are tender but still slightly firm. Remove and discard
the bay leaf. Taste for seasoning, adding salt and pepper if needed.
2. Stir in the chicken and cook until it is just heated through. If
the soup seems too thick for your taste, add more hot broth. Sprinkle each serving with the fresh coriander or parsley-chive mixture.

*Serves 6 to 8*

## Rice with Yogurt Soup

3 tablespoons butter or margarine
1 medium onion, finely chopped
¾ cup long-grain rice
8 cups chicken broth
1½ cups plain yogurt
1 egg
2 tablespoons chopped fresh mint leaves, or 2 teaspoons dried
Salt and freshly ground black pepper to taste

1. In a pot large enough to hold all the ingredients, over medium
heat, melt the butter or margarine and cook the onion until it is
soft and slightly golden. Stir in the rice and chicken broth. Bring
to a boil, cover, lower the heat, and simmer for 15 minutes, or until
the rice is almost tender.

2. In a bowl, beat the yogurt with the egg until smooth. Stir 1 cup of the broth into the yogurt-egg mixture. Stir the mixture and the mint into the pot with the rice. Heat, stirring, for 3 minutes, but do not allow to boil. Taste and add salt and pepper if needed. (The broth may have supplied enough seasoning.)

*Note:* This can also be served cold, but if allowed to stand the rice will absorb much of the liquid. If the soup seems too thick, stir in additional broth.

*Serves 6 to 8*

# 4

# Rice with Fish
# and Shellfish

All over Asia, the birthplace of rice, no matter what variety of seafood is served, or how it is prepared, it is always presented with rice. Often rice is an integral part of the dish or used as a border or a garnish—but it's always there.

We asked about this several times. Some, who knew America, compared it with our habit of serving potatoes with meat. Others merely smiled and said, "Rice first; everything else second. For Asians, rice always leads the way and sets our tables."

But perhaps we found the basic reason in the Typhoon Shelter in Hong Kong, the floating city of the Tam Ka people. One night we dined on one of the boats with a family of eight, friends of a friend of ours assigned to Hong Kong. It was an experience we'll remember for a long time.

One fish, a big red one that looked like our red snapper, called a *garoupa*, fed eleven hungry people. The fish was cooked in stock in a wok over a brazier on deck. We all had small portions of the fish in its stock, which was sparked with ginger, ladled over large servings of slightly gummy but very white and delicious rice. We didn't ask, but we were certain that the rice had been cooked in seawater, dipped from that dark, overpopulated harbor.

Rice not only made that fish go a long way, but it magnified and extended its flavor. That, we believe, is the real magic of rice.

# Fish Stock

*There are several ways to obtain fish stock. The simplest way is to use fish bouillon cubes. The second simplest way is to use equal parts of bottled clam juice, dry white wine, and water. The third is this classic way.*

2 pounds fish heads, tails, and bones (or buy less-expensive
   fish, using the whole fish cut up), washed
2 quarts water
2 cups dry white wine
1 large onion, cut in half and each half nailed with a
   whole clove
2 sprigs fresh parsley
2 carrots, scraped and cut up
Leaves from 2 celery stalks
1 bay leaf
1 teaspoon dried thyme
10 whole black peppercorns, cracked
2 teaspoons salt (optional)

Combine all the ingredients in a large pot. Bring to a boil, lower the heat, and simmer, uncovered, for 45 minutes, skimming the scum off the top as it appears. Strain the stock through a fine sieve or cheesecloth, discarding all the solids. Store in glass jars in the freezer.

*Makes about 2 quarts*


# Lisbon Cod and Rice

*We've had this dish several ways in Portugal and Spain, with tomatoes and potatoes, but also just creamed. We found that the rice version always came off best. Cooked properly, salt cod is surprisingly delicious.*
   *The Portuguese serve a green wine, Vinho Verde, with this. We like an Italian Pinot Grigio.*

2 pounds dried salt cod (soaked for 24 hours in cold water,
  the water changed 3 times)
1 bay leaf
½ teaspoon dried thyme
2 sprigs fresh parsley
2½ cups water
3 tablespoons butter or margarine
1 cup long-grain rice
3 tablespoons olive oil
3 large onions, chopped
2 garlic cloves, minced
½ teaspoon freshly ground black pepper
8 pimiento-stuffed olives, sliced
3 tablespoons chopped broadleaf (Italian) parsley leaves

1. Drain the cod and put it in a deep saucepan with the bay leaf, thyme, parsley sprigs, and water. Turn the heat to high and bring the water to a boil. Cover, lower the heat, and simmer for 20 minutes, or until the fish flakes with a fork. Remove the fish. Strain and reserve the liquid. Remove and discard the skin and bones from the fish and cut it into small bite-size pieces. Reserve.

2. Melt 2 tablespoons of the butter or margarine in the saucepan. Stir in the rice and cook, stirring, for 2 minutes. Pour in the reserved fish cooking liquid. Bring to a boil, cover, lower the heat, and simmer for 20 minutes, or until the rice is tender and the liquid has been absorbed. If the liquid is absorbed before the rice is tender, add small amounts of hot water and continue cooking.

3. In a large heavy-bottomed pot, over medium heat, heat the remaining butter or margarine and olive oil, and cook the onions and garlic for 5 minutes, or until they are soft, seasoning with the pepper. Do not brown. Carefully stir in the olives, fish, and rice, and simmer for 5 minutes, or until heated through. Serve garnished with the parsley.

*Serves 6*

# Scalloped Fish and Rice

*A little leftover fish plus rice, served in scallop shells or small ramekins, topped with a cream sauce and sprinkled with cheese, produces an elegant offering. Leftover rice can also be used. We often use leftover haddock or cod, but any white-fleshed fish will do.*

4 tablespoons (½ stick) butter or margarine
2 cups seasoned cooked rice
1 cup grated Gruyère cheese
2 cups flaked cooked fish
2 tablespoons all-purpose flour
1½ cups warm milk
¼ cup clam juice
2 tablespoons fresh lemon juice
1 egg, beaten
Salt and freshly ground black pepper to taste

1. In a saucepan, over medium heat, melt 2 tablespoons of the butter or margarine. Using a wooden fork, stir in the rice and 4 tablespoons of the cheese, blending well. Remove from the heat. Preheat the oven to 350 degrees.

2. Lightly butter 4 scallop shells or small ramekins with a capacity of at least one cup each. Divide the rice and fish among the shells, arranging a smooth layer of rice and topping it with one of fish. Transfer the scallop shells to a baking sheet.

3. In a saucepan (you can use the one in which you heated the rice), over medium heat, melt the remaining butter or margarine. Add the flour and cook, stirring, into a smooth paste. Lower the heat and gradually add the milk; then add the clam juice and lemon juice, stirring into a smooth sauce. Remove from the heat and quickly blend in the egg. Taste and season with salt and pepper if needed.

4. Spoon the sauce over the fish and rice, sprinkle with the remaining cheese, and bake until golden and bubbling.

*Serves 4*

# Fish and Rice Casserole

2 pounds ½-inch-thick firm fish fillets, from any white fish (cod,
    haddock, scrod, etc.), cut into 6 serving pieces
Salt and freshly ground black pepper to taste
Juice of ½ lemon
1 cup long-grain rice, simmered in 2½ cups of water until al
    dente, drained
2 tablespoons butter or margarine
1 tablespoon olive oil
2 medium onions, finely chopped
1 garlic clove, minced
4 medium ripe tomatoes, peeled, seeded, and chopped
½ cup dry white wine
3 tablespoons chopped broadleaf (Italian) parsley leaves

1. Coat the inside of a covered casserole or baking dish with butter or margarine, and arrange fillets so there is some space
between them. Sprinkle with salt, pepper, and lemon juice. Spoon
the rice between the fillets. Preheat the oven to 350 degrees.

2. In a frying pan, over medium heat, heat the butter or margarine and oil. Add the onions and garlic and cook for 5 minutes, or
until they are soft. Do not brown. Add the tomatoes and wine, and
cook briskly for 7 minutes. Spoon the tomato mixture over the fillets and rice.

3. Bake, covered, for 30 minutes, or until the rice is tender and
the fish flakes with a fork (but not too easily, or it will probably be
overcooked). Sprinkle with parsley before serving.

*Serves 6*

# Bluefish Fillets with Avocado and Saffron Rice

2 tablespoons butter or margarine
1 cup long-grain rice
2½ cups chicken broth
¼ teaspoon powdered saffron (or ¼ teaspoon turmeric), mixed
    with 2 tablespoons of broth or water
1 large ripe but firm avocado, peeled and cubed
1 tablespoon rinsed and drained capers
2 whole scallions, trimmed and thinly sliced
1 medium ripe tomato, peeled, seeded, and diced
2 tablespoons fresh lemon juice
2 tablespoons olive oil
A light dash of hot sauce
Salt to taste
Four 6- to 8-ounce bluefish fillets with skin on
Pepper to taste
Soft butter or margarine

1. In a saucepan, over medium heat, melt the 2 tablespoons of
butter or margarine. Stir in the rice and cook, stirring, for 2 minutes. Add the broth and bring to a boil. Stir with a wooden fork,
cover, lower the heat, and simmer for 20 minutes, or until the liquid has been absorbed and the rice is tender. Stir in the saffron and
cover again. Keep warm.

2. Combine and blend well, but carefully, the avocado, capers,
scallions, tomato, lemon juice, olive oil, hot sauce, and salt.

3. Preheat the broiler. Arrange the bluefish on a large buttered
baking sheet. Sprinkle the fillets with salt and pepper and coat
them lightly with soft butter or margarine. Broil 3 to 4 inches from
the heat for 5 minutes, or until the fish is golden and flakes easily
with a fork (but not too easily, or it will probably be overdone).

4. Arrange the fillets on a large, hot serving dish. Spoon the avocado mixture over them and surround with the saffron rice.

*Serves 4*

# Pesce e Riso in Conchiglie

*An Italian Specialty: Rice and Seafood*

8 tablespoons (1 stick) butter or margarine
2 shallots, or 1 small white onion, minced
1 cup diced uncooked lobster, shrimp, crabmeat, or scallops
3 tablespoons all-purpose flour
1½ cups milk, warmed
2 tablespoons dry vermouth
Salt to taste
⅛ teaspoon cayenne
1 cup cooked and flaked white fish (sole, cod, halibut, etc.)
1½ cups cooked long-grain rice
2 tablespoons fine fresh bread crumbs
4 tablespoons grated Asiago or Parmesan cheese

1. In a frying pan, over medium heat, melt 3 tablespoons of the butter or margarine. Add the shallots and cook until they are soft. Do not brown. Stir in the shellfish and cook for 3 to 4 minutes. (If you are using lobster, shrimp, or crab, cook until they just start to turn pink; if you are using scallops, cook until they begin to become firm.)

2. In a saucepan, melt 3 tablespoons of the butter or margarine. Add the flour and cook, stirring, into a smooth paste. Gradually add the milk and cook, stirring into a smooth, thickened sauce. Stir in the vermouth, salt, and cayenne. Mix the sauce with the shellfish and the flaked fish. Preheat the oven to 400 degrees.

3. Rub 4 scallop shells or small ramekins (capacity at least 1½ cups each) with butter or margarine. Divide the rice among them. Spoon the sauced seafood over the rice. Sprinkle with the bread crumbs, then the cheese, and dot with remaining butter or margarine.

4. Bake for 15 minutes, or until the top is golden and the sauce bubbling.

*Serves 4*

# Paella

*Paella could be the national dish of Spain, with different varieties being offered in various parts of the country. Some people prefer it mainly with seafood, others prefer it with poultry, and others like mainly sausage, and then there are many that like all three. But the "Queen of the Paellas" is* Paella Valenciana, *which contains everything. Rice remains the principle and most important ingredient—yellow rice, made so by saffron. Saffron (dried stamens of the crocus) is expensive and, we believe, contributes little to the flavor of the dish. Thus, as it is mainly cosmetic, turmeric can be substituted. But do it your own way as this is simply an economic tip.*

*We learned how to make the dish at Madrid's Botin Restaurant, working with their chef for several days, and even bringing back to the United States a couple of Botin's special metal paella pans, the* paelleras. *These pans aren't necessary to produce the dish, but as you cook and serve in them they're handy and, we think, dramatic.*

3 *chorizos* (Spanish sausages), or ½ pound Italian sweet sausage
½ cup olive oil, approximately
One 2- to 2½-pound chicken, cut into at least 8 pieces (Do not use wings or back.)
Salt and freshly ground black pepper to taste
6 to 8 small serving pieces fresh haddock
1 cup diced lean ham
1 large onion, finely minced
1 garlic clove, minced
3 cups long-grain rice
½ teaspoon powdered saffron
1 large ripe tomato, peeled, seeded, and chopped, or 1 cup canned tomatoes, drained and chopped
7 to 8 cups chicken broth
½ cup shelled peas, slightly undercooked in salted boiling water, or ½ cup frozen peas, defrosted
12 medium shrimp, shelled and deveined
12 mussels or clams, scrubbed and beards removed from the mussels
1 large pimiento, cut into 8 or more strips
1 lemon, cut into 8 wedges

1. Prick the skins of the sausages in several places and simmer them in water for 10 minutes. Drain and brown in 2 tablespoons

of the olive oil. Drain on paper towels and cut into ¼-inch-thick slices. Reserve.

2. In a large paella pan, a large deep frying pan, or a large flame-proof casserole, over medium-high heat, heat ¼ cup of the olive oil and evenly brown the chicken pieces, seasoning them with salt and pepper. Remove and reserve. Add the haddock and season lightly with salt and pepper. Cook for 45 seconds on each side, adding more oil if needed. Remove and reserve. Add the ham and more oil if needed, and cook for 2 minutes. Remove with a slotted spoon and reserve.

3. Add the onion and garlic to the pan and cook for 5 minutes, or until they are soft. Do not brown. Add the rice and cook, stirring, for 2 minutes. Stir in the saffron, tomato, and 7 cups of the broth. Simmer for 10 minutes. Preheat the oven to 350 degrees.

4. Stir in the peas. Arrange the sausage slices and chicken on the rice, partially burying them. Bring to a boil on top of the stove, cover with foil, and bake for 20 minutes. Add the haddock, shrimp, mussels or clams, partially burying them, and bake, uncovered, for 15 minutes, or until the meats, rice, and shellfish are cooked. Halfway through the cooking time, taste for seasoning, adding more salt and pepper if needed. If the liquid is absorbed before the rice is tender, add small amounts of hot broth.

5. Garnish with the pimiento strips and lemon wedges just before serving.

*Serves 6 to 8*

# Mussels Greek Style

36 large fresh mussels with tightly closed, unbroken
  shells
½ cup olive oil
2 medium onions, finely chopped
½ cup pignoli
¾ cup long-grain rice
¼ cup currants
½ teaspoon ground allspice
⅛ teaspoon ground cinnamon
1 teaspoon salt (optional)
¼ teaspoon freshly ground black pepper
1¼ cups chicken broth
½ cup dry white wine
Water
1 bay leaf
Lemon wedges

1. Scrub the mussels with a stiff brush and remove the beards.
Rinse in several changes of cool water, or under cool running
water.

2. In a saucepan, heat ¼ cup of the olive oil. Add the onions and
cook until soft and golden, for about 6 minutes. Add the pignoli and
cook for 2 minutes, or until they are golden and crisp. Stir in the
rice, currants, allspice, cinnamon, salt, pepper, and broth. Bring to
a boil, stir with a wooden fork, cover, lower the heat, and simmer
for 20 minutes, or until the liquid has been absorbed.

3. Open the mussels with a sharp knife, leaving the two parts of
the shell attached at the joint. Stuff each mussel with 1 tablespoon
of the rice filling. Close the shells and tie with kitchen string.

4. Arrange the stuffed mussels in a large heavy saucepan, in two
layers. Pour on the wine, remaining olive oil, and just enough water
to cover. Add the bay leaf. Set a heavy plate on top of the mussels
to prevent them from moving around. Bring to a boil, cover the
saucepan, lower the heat, and simmer for 20 minutes. Remove
from the heat and cool in the pan.

5. Remove the mussels with a slotted spoon. Remove the string
and serve the mussels at room temperature, garnished with lemon
wedges.

*Note:* The mussels can be cooked in advance, chilled, and then brought to room temperature before serving.

*Serves 6*

## A Note on Rice Rings

When cooking rice for a ring, cook enough (more than you need for the number of people being served because leftover rice makes very good croquettes). Also, it is annoying to end up with a skimpy ring. The rice should fill the ring.

Coat the ring mold well with butter or margarine and, after the rice is cooked, stir in two or three spoonfuls of soft butter or margarine. This makes it easier to turn the ring out intact. For insurance, before turning it out, run a knife blade around the inside of the ring. Vegetables can be served on the same dish, colorfully bordering the ring.

Fill the ring with creamed mushrooms, creamed chicken, or any sauced vegetable, fish, or meat dish.

# Curried Lobster in a Singhalese Rice Ring

*Singhalese Rice Ring*

    6 tablespoons butter or margarine
    2 medium onions, fully chopped
    2 cups short- or medium-grain rice
    3 whole cloves
    4½ cups chicken broth
    ½ cup unsalted cashews, toasted and broken into small pieces
    ½ cup golden raisins, plumped in 1 tablespoons butter or
        margarine over medium heat and then halved
    3 tablespoons finely chopped fresh coriander leaves, or 1½
        tablespoons chopped fresh parsley leaves and 1½ tablespoons
        chopped fresh chives
    Salt and freshly ground black pepper to taste

*The Curried Lobster*

    4 tablespoons (½ stick) butter or margarine
    2 medium onions, finely chopped
    1½ tablespoons curry powder, or to taste (page 79)
    3 tablespoons all-purpose flour
    1 cup chicken broth
    ½ cup clam juice
    ½ cup dry sherry
    2 tablespoons tomato purée
    ½ cup half-and-half
    ⅛ teaspoon cayenne, or to taste
    Salt to taste
    4 cups diced cooked lobster meat

    1. To make the rice ring, melt 3 tablespoons of the butter or margarine over medium heat in a saucepan. Add the onions and cook for 5 minutes, or until they are soft. Do not brown. Add the rice and stir until it is well coated. Cook for 2 minutes. Add the cloves and broth and bring to a boil. Cover, lower the heat, and simmer for 20 minutes, or until the rice is just al dente and the liquid has been absorbed. Discard the cloves.
    2. Stir in the cashews, raisins, coriander, salt and pepper, and the remaining butter or margarine (in small pieces). Preheat the oven to 350 degrees.
    3. Coat a 6- or 8-cup ring mold with butter or margarine, and

press the rice into it (the rice should fill the mold), cover with foil, and bake for 10 minutes. Unmold onto a hot serving dish and spoon the lobster and sauce into the ring. If the ring cannot accommodate all of the lobster, serve the remainder in a bowl.

4. To make the curried lobster, melt the butter or margarine in a saucepan over medium heat. Add the onions and cook for 5 minutes, or until they are soft. Do not brown. Stir in the curry powder and flour, stirring until well blended. Gradually stir in the chicken broth, clam juice, sherry, and tomato purée and cook, stirring into a smooth sauce. Stir in the half-and-half and cayenne. Taste and season with salt if needed. Add the lobster meat and heat through. Do not overcook as the lobster will toughen.

*Serves 6*


## Risotto di Frutti di Mare

*This seafood-rice offering that we found on the Italian "Riviera" could be our favorite.*

12 clams in their shells, well scrubbed
12 mussels in their shells, well scrubbed and debearded
4 tablespoons (½ stick) butter or margarine
2 tablespoons olive oil
1 medium onion, finely chopped
1 garlic clove, minced
1 celery stalk, scraped and finely chopped
12 medium shrimp, shelled and deveined
1½ cups long-grain rice
1½ cups clam juice or Fish Stock (page 48)
1½ cups water or Fish Stock (page 48)
¼ teaspoon powdered saffron
½ cup dry white wine
3 tablespoons chopped broadleaf (Italian) parsley leaves
Salt and freshly ground black pepper to taste

1. Put the clams and mussels in a large pot with 2 cups of water and steam over medium heat until the shells open. As they open, remove the clams and mussels from the shells and pour the liquid from the shells into a bowl. Discard any mussels and clams that do not open. Reserve the shellfish.

2. In a deep saucepan, over medium heat, heat 2 tablespoons of the butter or margarine with the olive oil. Add the onion, garlic, and celery and cook for 5 minutes, or until they are soft. Do not brown. Stir in the clams, mussels, and shrimp and cook for 4 minutes, or until the shrimp are pink and the clams and mussels become firm. Do not overcook or they'll toughen. Remove the clams, mussels, and shrimp with a slotted spoon. Reserve and keep them warm.

3. Stir the rice into the saucepan. Pour in the clam juice and water and the liquid saved from the shells. Dissolve the saffron in the wine and stir the mixture into the rice with a wooden fork, blending it well. Bring to a boil, lower the heat, stir with a wooden fork, cover, and simmer for 20 minutes, or until the rice is al dente and most of the liquid has been absorbed. The risotto should be slightly moist but not soupy. If it seems dry, add a small amount of hot liquid.

4. Stir in the shellfish, remaining butter or margarine (in small pieces), and parsley with a metal fork, fluffing up the rice. Taste for seasoning, add salt and pepper if necessary. Cover the pot and heat for 1 minute.

*Serves 4*

## Crabmeat Cocer

1 pound crabmeat, fresh or canned
1 bunch (about 1½ pounds) broccoli
7 tablespoons butter or margarine
4 tablespoons all-purpose flour
3 cups half-and-half, heated
Salt to taste

⅛ teaspoon cayenne
⅓ cup thinly sliced scallions (white part only)
1 canned pimiento, coarsely chopped
3 cups al dente–cooked long-grain rice
3 tablespoons fresh lemon juice
¼ cup toasted slivered almonds

1. Pick over the crabmeat to remove any bits of cartilage or shell.

2. Separate the florets from the stems of the broccoli. Scrape the stems and cook them in salted boiling water until crisp-tender. Remove from the water with a slotted spoon. Cook the florets in the same water until crisp-tender; then drain. Reserve and keep warm. Coarsely chop the broccoli stems and reserve separately.

3. In a saucepan, over medium heat, melt 4 tablespoons of the butter or margarine. Stir in the flour and cook, stirring, into a smooth paste. Gradually add the half-and-half and cook, stirring into a smooth sauce. Season with salt and cayenne. Stir in the crabmeat, scallions, and pimiento. Preheat the oven to 375 degrees.

4. In a shallow baking dish coated with butter or margarine, spread a smooth layer of the rice. Arrange a layer of the chopped broccoli stems over the rice. Spoon the crabmeat mixture over the broccoli. Bake for 20 minutes, or until heated through and the sauce is bubbling.

5. Heat the lemon juice with the remaining butter or margarine and pour the mixture over the broccoli florets.

6. Arrange the florets around the rim of the dish with the crabmeat and rice and sprinkle the almonds over the top.

*Serves 4 to 6*

# Tuna with Rice

*Canned tuna is an American favorite, and with good reason: flavor, ease of handling, and versatility. And teamed with rice it's a winner. We like the solid white, albacore; it's finer textured, less oily, and more delicate than regular tuna.*

6 tablespoons butter or margarine
2 medium white onions, chopped
1 cup long-grain rice
2½ cups chicken broth
One 10-ounce package frozen tiny peas
8 medium fresh mushrooms, thinly sliced
Salt and freshly ground black pepper to taste
One 7-ounce can solid white tuna (albacore), drained and flaked

1. In a large, deep frying pan, over medium heat, melt 3 table-spoons of the butter or margarine and cook the onions for 5 minutes, or until they are soft. Do not brown. Add the rice and cook, stirring, for 1 minute. Pour in 1 cup of the broth, bring to a boil, lower the heat, cover, and simmer for 10 minutes. Stir in the peas and the remaining broth. Bring to a boil, lower the heat, cover, and simmer for 10 minutes, or until the peas and rice are tender and the broth has been absorbed.

2. In a small frying pan, over medium-high heat, melt the remaining butter or margarine and cook the mushrooms for 3 minutes, or until any liquid has cooked off and they are slightly brown. Use a metal fork to combine the mushrooms and the butter or margarine they cooked in with the rice. Taste and season with salt and pepper if needed.

3. Blend in the tuna and heat through, fluffing the rice mixture with a metal fork. Spoon into a hot serving dish.

*Serves 4*

# Mussels Marinara

*This one we discovered in Taranto, in the south, on the heel of the boot that is Italy.*

4 tablespoons olive oil
2 garlic cloves, flattened with the broad side of a knife blade and peeled
½ cup dry red wine
36 fresh mussels, well scrubbed and debearded
One 1-pound can imported Italian plum tomatoes, finely chopped and liquid reserved
½ to 1 cup clam juice
5 tablespoons butter or margarine
1 medium onion, finely chopped
1 garlic clove, minced
1 cup long-grain rice
Salt and freshly ground black pepper to taste
3 tablespoons chopped broadleaf (Italian) parsley leaves

1. In a large pot, heat 2 tablespoons of the olive oil. Add the flattened garlic cloves and cook until they are golden. Discard the garlic. Remove the pot from the heat and quickly (to avoid spattering) pour in the wine. Add the mussels, cover tightly, and cook over high heat, shaking the pot occasionally, for 5 minutes, or until they open. Discard any mussels that do not open.

2. Drain the mussels in a strainer over a bowl to reserve the liquid. Set aside 4 mussels in their shells. Remove the remaining mussels from their shells, adding any liquid in the shells to the liquid in the bowl. Strain all the liquid through a very fine cheesecloth. Pour the strained liquid into a 4-cup measuring cup. Add the liquid from the tomatoes and enough clam juice to bring the liquid up to the 2½-cup mark.

3. In a large saucepan, over medium heat, heat 2 tablespoons of the butter or margarine with the remaining oil. Add the onion and minced garlic and cook for 5 minutes, or until they are soft. Do not brown. Stir in the rice and cook, stirring, for 2 minutes.

4. Heat the clam juice–tomato liquid to a boil. Pour 1 cup of it onto the rice. Stir with a wooden fork, cover, lower the heat, and cook for 10 minutes, or until the liquid has been absorbed. Add the

remaining hot liquid with the tomatoes and cook for 15 minutes, or until the rice is almost tender, but still quite al dente, allowing the rice to absorb the liquid.

5. Stir in the mussels (including the 4 in the shells) and cook for 5 minutes, or until the mussels are just firm. Do not overcook or they will toughen. Taste for seasoning and add salt and pepper if necessary. Stir in the parsley and the remaining butter or margarine (in small pieces) with a metal fork, fluffing the rice. Transfer to a hot serving dish, setting the 4 mussels in their shells on top. Place 1 on each individual serving.

*Serves 4*

# Sweet-and-Sour Shrimp in a Spinach-Rice Ring

*See page 57 for a note on preparing rice rings.*

*Rice Ring*
>    10 tablespoons (1¼ sticks) butter or margarine
>    1 medium onion, minced
>    2 cups short- or medium-grain rice
>    4½ cups chicken broth
>    1 cup finely chopped spinach
>    6 medium fresh mushrooms, finely chopped

*Sweet-and-Sour Shrimp*
>    ¼ cup white vinegar
>    ½ cup chicken broth
>    ¼ cup dark brown sugar
>    2 teaspoons soy sauce
>    1½ pounds medium shrimp, shelled and deveined
>    1 tablespoon peanut or vegetable oil
>    2 medium carrots, scraped and thinly sliced
>    1 garlic clove, minced
>    3 whole scallions, trimmed and cut into ½-inch lengths

1 green bell pepper, seeds and ribs removed, cut into narrow
   strips
1 tablespoon cornstarch, dissolved in 2 tablespoons cold water
Salt to taste

1. To make the rice ring, melt 2 tablespoons of the butter or margarine in a saucepan over medium heat. Add the onion and cook
for 3 minutes, or until soft. Do not brown. Add 2 more tablespoons
of butter or margarine to the pan. When it is melted, add the rice
and cook, stirring, for 2 minutes. Pour in the broth and bring to
a boil. Lower the heat, cover, and simmer for 25 minutes, or until
the rice is tender and the broth has been absorbed. Stir in the
spinach.

2. In a frying pan, melt 2 tablespoons of the butter or margarine
and cook the mushrooms over medium-high heat, cooking off all
of the liquid that the mushrooms produce. Add to the rice with the
remaining butter or margarine (in small pieces), and blend well
with a fork. Press into a 6- or 8-cup ring mold (the rice should fill
it), cover, and keep warm in a 200-degree oven until ready to
unmold.

3. To prepare the sweet-and-sour shrimp, combine and blend
well the vinegar, broth, sugar, and soy sauce. Set aside.

4. Bring a large saucepan of water to a boil. Drop in the shrimp
and the moment they start to turn pink (about 30 seconds after you
have added them to the water) remove from the heat and drain.
Set aside and keep warm.

5. Heat the oil in a wok or a large frying pan. Add the carrots,
garlic, scallions, and green pepper and stir-fry over medium-high
heat for 2 or 3 minutes, or until crisp-tender.

6. Pour in the vinegar-broth-sugar mixture and simmer for 1
minute, stirring to dissolve the sugar.

7. Add the cornstarch and water and stir for 1 or 2 minutes, or
until the sauce starts to thicken. Add the shrimp and heat through.
The shrimp should be pink but tender and the sauce thick. Taste
for seasoning, adding salt if necessary.

8. Unmold the rice ring onto a serving dish. Spoon the shrimp
into the center of the ring. If the ring won't accommodate all of the
shrimp, serve the remainder in a bowl.

*Serves 4 to 6*

# Creole Rice and Shrimp

*Rice*

2 tablespoons butter or margarine
1 medium onion, finely chopped
2 cups long-grain brown rice
1 small green bell pepper, cored, seeded, and coarsely
   chopped
2 celery stalks, scraped and coarsely chopped
4½ cups chicken broth
2 whole cloves
4 tablespoons soft butter or margarine
1 cup grated Asiago or Parmesan cheese
Salt to taste

*Shrimp*

8 tablespoons (1 stick) butter or margarine
2 tablespoons olive oil
2 pounds medium shrimp, shelled and deveined
1 large garlic clove, minced
¼ teaspoon cayenne, or to taste
Salt to taste
3 tablespoons chopped broadleaf (Italian) parsley
   leaves

1. To prepare the rice, melt the 2 tablespoons of butter or margarine in a saucepan, over medium heat. Add the onion and cook for 3 minutes, or until the onion is soft. Do not brown. Stir in the rice and cook, stirring, for 2 minutes. Add the pepper, celery, chicken broth, and cloves and bring to a boil. Lower the heat, stir with a wooden fork, cover, and simmer for 30 minutes, or until the rice is tender and the liquid has been absorbed. Discard the cloves. Just before serving, stir in the soft butter or margarine and cheese, fluffing up the rice with a metal fork. Taste for seasoning and add salt if needed.

2. To prepare the shrimp, heat the butter or margarine and oil in a large frying pan over medium-high heat. Add the shrimp and garlic and sprinkle with the cayenne and salt. Cook, turning, just until the shrimp are pink and firm. This will take about 3 minutes. Do not overcook or the shrimp will toughen.

3. Spoon the rice onto a hot serving dish. Arrange the shrimp over the rice and pour the sauce in the frying pan over it. Sprinkle with the parsley.

*Serves 6*

# Rice Savannah

3 medium ripe tomatoes, peeled, seeded, and chopped, or
    one 1-pound can imported Italian plum tomatoes, drained
    and chopped
6 tablespoons butter or margarine
1 cup long-grain rice
2½ to 3 cups chicken broth
Salt and freshly ground black pepper to taste
1 cup grated Asiago or Parmesan cheese
1 pound medium shrimp, shelled, deveined, and cut in half
    lengthwise
2 tablespoons brandy
1 cup shelled fresh peas, cooked al dente, or frozen peas,
    defrosted

1. In a saucepan, over medium heat, cook the tomatoes for 10 minutes, or until much of their liquid has evaporated. Set aside.

2. In another saucepan, over medium heat, melt 3 tablespoons of the butter or margarine, stir in the rice, and cook, stirring, for 2 minutes, or until well coated. Pour in 2½ cups of the broth, bring to a boil, stir with a wooden fork, lower the heat, cover, and simmer for 15 minutes, or until the rice is almost tender and most of the liquid has been absorbed. If necessary, add more broth. The rice should be slightly moist, but not soupy. Taste for seasoning, adding salt and pepper if needed.

3. Stir ¼ cup of the cheese into the rice with a wooden fork and cook for another 3 minutes, or until the rice is tender. Remove from the heat and keep warm.

4. While the rice is cooking, melt the remaining butter or mar-

garine in a large frying pan over medium-high heat. Add the shrimp and cook for 1 minute, stirring. Add the brandy and cook off half of it. Stir in the tomatoes and peas and simmer for 2 minutes, or until the shrimp just turn pink. Season with salt and pepper.

5. Transfer the rice to a hot serving dish. Spoon the shrimp-peas-tomato sauce over the top and serve with the remaining cheese at the table.

*Serves 4*

# Tuna Rice Quiche

3 cups cooked short- or medium-grain rice, cooled
1 egg, beaten
⅔ cup grated Gruyère or Swiss cheese
1 medium tomato, peeled, seeded, and chopped
One 7-ounce can solid white tuna (albacore), drained
    and flaked
2 tablespoons butter or margarine
1 medium onion, finely chopped
2 tablespoons all-purpose flour
1½ cups half-and-half, warmed
3 eggs, beaten
1 teaspoon salt (optional)
¼ teaspoon ground mace
⅛ teaspoon cayenne
¼ teaspoon paprika
¼ cup grated Asiago or Parmesan cheese

1. In a bowl, combine and blend well the rice, the beaten egg, and the Gruyère cheese. Coat the inside of a 10-inch pie plate with butter or margarine, and line it with the rice-cheese mixture.

2. Distribute the tomato over the "crust" and the tuna over the tomato.

3. In a saucepan, over medium heat, melt the butter or margarine. Add the onion and cook until it is soft. Do not brown. Stir in the flour and blend well. Gradually add 1 cup of the half-and-half

and cook, stirring into a thickened sauce. Remove from the heat. Preheat the oven to 350 degrees.

4. In a bowl, combine and blend well the remaining half-and-half, the 3 beaten eggs, salt, mace, cayenne, and paprika. Stir into the sauce. Carefully pour over the tuna. Sprinkle on the Asiago cheese.

5. Bake for 30 minutes, or until set and a knife blade inserted just off center emerges clean. Do not overbake.

*Serves 6*

# Scallops à la Kerala

*We discovered this, or an approximation of it, in Kerala on India's west coast. This is a South Sea–like area where we were introduced to several interesting dishes. This was prepared with very small, very sweet shrimp, but we have substituted scallops to offer variety, and we have also added what we hope are palate-pleasing touches of our own.*

*Rice*

> 3 tablespoons butter or margarine
> 2 medium onions, finely chopped
> 1 cup long-grain rice
> 5 whole black peppercorns, cracked
> ½-inch piece cinnamon stick
> 1 small bay leaf
> ¼ teaspoon ground cardamom
> 2½ cups water

*Scallops*

> 7 tablespoons butter or margarine
> 2 garlic cloves, minced
> 1 tablespoon curry powder, or to taste (page 79)
> 1 pound scallops (If you are using bay scallops, leave them whole; if you are using sea scallops, cut them in half.)
> Salt and freshly ground black pepper to taste
> 3 tablespoons all-purpose flour
> 2 cups Fish Stock (page 48)

1. To prepare the rice, melt the butter or margarine in a deep saucepan over medium heat and cook the onions for 5 minutes, or until they are soft and golden. Do not brown. Add the rice and cook, stirring, for 2 minutes. Stir in the peppercorns, cinnamon stick, bay leaf, cardamom, and water. Raise the heat and bring the liquid to a boil. Cover, lower the heat, and simmer for 20 minutes, or until the rice is tender and the liquid has been absorbed. Remove and discard the peppercorns, cinnamon stick, and bay leaf. Keep the rice warm while preparing the scallops.

2. To prepare the scallops, melt 3 tablespoons of the butter or margarine in a saucepan over medium heat and sauté the garlic until it is soft. Do not brown. Stir in the curry powder and cook for 1 minute, stirring. Add the scallops, season with salt and pepper, and cook for 5 minutes, turning. They should be just firm. Do not overcook or they will toughen. Remove the scallops and keep them warm.

3. Stir the remaining 4 tablespoons of butter or margarine into the saucepan. When it has melted, stir in the flour, blending and stirring into a smooth paste. Lower the heat and gradually add the fish stock, stirring into a smooth sauce. Return the scallops to the pan; cook for 1 minute to heat through. Taste for seasoning, adding salt and pepper if needed. Spoon the scallops with their sauce over the rice.

*Serves 4*

# Chili Rice

*Although chili peppers were developed by the Aztecs in Mexico, the Spaniards brought them to Europe, making them their own. The peppers eventually landed in Asia where they are very popular. We discovered this dish in Bangkok. If fresh chilies aren't available, most supermarkets have them canned. They'll do as a substitute.*

    3 tablespoons olive oil
    2 medium onions, chopped
    2 fresh (or canned) green chilies, seeded and thinly sliced

1 large pork chop, both fat and lean, finely chopped
½ pound fresh shrimp, shelled, deveined, and coarsely chopped
4 cups cooked long-grain rice
2 eggs, beaten
Salt and freshly ground black pepper to taste
6 whole scallions, trimmed and chopped

1. In a large frying pan, over medium heat, heat the oil and cook the onions and chilies for 5 minutes, or until they are soft. Do not brown. Stir in the pork and cook for 10 minutes. Add the shrimp and cook just until the shrimp start to turn pink, about 3 minutes.

2. Add the rice and eggs, and use a wooden fork to blend them well with the other ingredients. Season with salt and pepper. When the eggs have set, quickly stir in the chopped scallions and serve.

*Serves 4 to 6*

# Shrimp Jambalaya

*The Creoles of Louisiana (descended from French-Canadian settlers, their cooking is a mixture of French haute cuisine and provincial, also African and Indian) probably are as versatile with rice as the Orientals and eat almost as much. Here's one of their classics.*

3 tablespoons butter or margarine
2 medium onions, finely chopped
1 garlic clove, minced
1 celery stalk, scraped and finely chopped
1 small green bell pepper, cored, seeded, and finely chopped
1½ cups long-grain rice
3 cups chicken broth
3 medium ripe tomatoes, peeled, seeded, and chopped
¼ teaspoon dried thyme
¼ teaspoon hot red pepper flakes, crushed
Salt to taste
1 cup cubed cooked ham
3 scallions, trimmed and thinly sliced
1½ pounds medium shrimp, shelled and deveined

1. In a large pot, over medium heat, heat the butter or margarine. Add the onions, garlic, celery, and green pepper and cook, stirring, for 2 minutes. Stir in the rice, mixing well. Add the broth, tomatoes, thyme, hot red pepper flakes, and salt. Bring to a boil, stir with a wooden fork, cover, lower the heat, and simmer for 30 minutes, or until the rice is almost tender but still al dente.

2. Stir in the ham and scallions and cook for 5 minutes. Stir in the shrimp and cook for 5 minutes, or until they just turn pink (do not overcook the shrimp or they will toughen). Taste for seasoning, adding salt and pepper if needed, and serve.

*Serves 6 to 8*

# Scallops en Brochette on Curried Rice

*We learned to respect scallops in Spain, in Santiago de Compostela, home of the magnificent Cathedral of St. James, and at one time a holy place second only to Rome in all of Christendom. Pilgrims came from all over Europe to visit the shrine of St. James of Compostela. They ate scallops as a "penance," and wore the shells on their hats on the trip home.*

*A favorite dish of ours, Coquilles St. Jacques, is also named after St. James. Santiago is one of our favorite places, a historic, yet sparkling city that hasn't been overwhelmed by the present; it offers the best seafood in Europe in our view. In the province of Galicia, in the mountains of the northwest, with the Bay of Biscay to the north, Portugal to the south, and the Atlantic Ocean breasting the west, Santiago introduced us to this dish—and many others. The chef at the beautiful Hostal de los Reyes Católicos, beside the cathedral, was delighted to give us his recipes for the dishes we applauded. In France we would have needed a gun to get them.*

*The Scallops*

    1 medium onion, chopped
    ½ cup chopped broadleaf (Italian) parsley leaves
    1 teaspoon ground cumin
    ½ teaspoon ground coriander

4 whole cloves
⅛ cup olive oil
⅛ cup fresh lemon juice
⅛ cup dry sherry
1 teaspoon salt (optional)
½ teaspoon freshly ground black pepper
30 sea scallops, about 1 inch in diameter (If they are larger,
    use fewer and halve them.)

### The Curried Rice

3 tablespoons butter or margarine
1 medium onion, finely chopped
1 garlic clove, minced
1½ cups long-grain rice
3½ cups chicken broth
2 teaspoons curry powder, or to taste (page 79)
2 canned chili peppers, drained and cut into short strips
3 tablespoons golden raisins

### Vegetables for the Brochettes

2 large firm green bell peppers, halved, seeded, deribbed, and
    parboiled for 5 minutes
12 very small white onions, root ends scored, parboiled for 7
    minutes
12 fresh mushroom caps, sautéed in 2 tablespoons butter or
    margarine for 2 minutes
Salt and freshly ground black pepper to taste

1. To prepare the scallops, combine and blend well the onion, parsley, cumin, coriander, cloves, olive oil, lemon juice, sherry, salt, and pepper in a large stainless steel or Pyrex bowl. Add the scallops and stir to coat them evenly. Cover tightly and marinate in the refrigerator for at least 6 hours, stirring 2 or 3 times. Bring to room temperature before assembling the brochettes.

2. To prepare the rice, melt the butter or margarine in a deep saucepan over medium heat. Add the onion and garlic and cook for 5 minutes, or until they are soft. Do not brown. Stir in the rice and cook for 2 minutes, stirring. Pour in the broth and bring to a boil. Cover, lower the heat, and simmer for 20 minutes, or until the rice is slightly al dente, almost tender. With a metal fork, stir in the curry powder, chilies, and raisins, fluffing up the rice as you stir. Cover and allow to sit for 10 minutes.

3. To prepare the brochettes, thoroughly drain the peppers and onions. Cut the peppers into bite-size squares. Drain the scallops, reserving the marinade. Starting with a scallop and ending with one, arrange the scallops, green peppers, onions, and mushrooms on 6 skewers, dividing them equally. Brush with the marinade and sprinkle with salt and pepper.

4. Cook in a preheated broiler with a drip pan 3 or 4 inches from the heat for about 1 minute; then turn and brush with the marinade every minute for 5 minutes, or until the scallops are golden and somewhat firm. Do not overcook or they will toughen.

5. Serve each skewer on a bed of rice, spooning over the rice any drippings collected in the drip pan.

*Serves 6*

# 5

# Rice with Poultry and Game

Often, recipes have stories. This one takes us into the jungles of Central India where we were studying the habitat of the tiger, as research for a novel. Our camp cook, a wisp of a man with a thick gray moustache and few words of English, was from Goa, a Portuguese possession in India. Every time he prepared a meal he gave us an inferiority complex. His stove was a few stones on which he rested his pots; his fire, wood reduced to glowing ashes. On this he prepared everything from bread to a sort of pot roast called "boilybrown."

In camp were a pair of brown-and-white goats, cute as kittens, brought along in case our rations ran short. This was probably a psychological gambit, for whenever we needed fresh meat, our hunter, or *shikari*, Rao Naidu, would say, "Shall we have some nice fresh kid in a curry tonight, or do you want to shoot for the pot?"

So, of course, we shot for the pot—doves or more often peacock, for the jungles were full of exotic birds. The recipe for Curried Chicken with Rice (page 79) is an approximation of one of the dishes we had. We've substituted chicken for the peacock. The cook made his own curry powder, so we offer that recipe as well.

# Nested Rice and Chicken

4 tablespoons (½ stick) butter or margarine
1 tablespoon olive oil
6 chicken thighs
6 chicken drumsticks
Salt and freshly ground black pepper to taste
⅓ pound pork sausage meat (about ½ cup)
2 medium onions, chopped
1 celery stalk, scraped and chopped
1 cup long-grain rice
One 10-ounce package frozen corn kernels, defrosted, or 10
    ounces fresh corn kernels
2½ cups chicken broth
1 large pimiento, cut into strips

1. Preheat the oven to 350 degrees.

2. Over medium heat, in a large flameproof casserole, heat the butter or margarine and oil and evenly brown the chicken pieces, sprinkling them with salt and pepper.

3. Remove the chicken and pour off any excess fat. Over medium heat, in the same casserole, cook the sausage for 5 minutes, breaking it up with a wooden fork. Add the onions and celery and cook, stirring, for 5 minutes. Do not brown. Stir in the rice and corn. Pour in the chicken broth and bring to a boil.

4. Remove from the heat and place the chicken on top, pushing it down slightly into the rice. Cover and bake for 25 minutes, or until the liquid has been absorbed and the chicken and rice are tender. Garnish with the pimiento strips.

*Serves 6*

# Curried Chicken with Rice

*Curry Powder*

    2 teaspoons ground cumin
    ½ teaspoon ground ginger
    2 teaspoons ground coriander
    1 teaspoon ground turmeric
    ⅛ teaspoon cayenne pepper
    ¼ teaspoon freshly ground black pepper
    1 teaspoon ground cardamom

*Chicken-Rice Curry*

    3 tablespoons butter or margarine
    2 tablespoons olive oil
    2 pounds boned chicken breast, cut into 1-inch cubes
    Salt and freshly ground black pepper to taste
    3 medium white onions, chopped
    2 garlic cloves, minced
    1 medium apple, peeled, cored, and chopped
    2 tablespoons all-purpose flour
    2 cups chicken broth
    ½ cup dry white wine
    2 medium ripe tomatoes, peeled, seeded, and chopped
    1 cup long-grain rice

1. Blend all of the ingredients for the curry powder together. Makes approximately 2⅛ tablespoons. Reserve.

2. Preheat the oven to 350 degrees.

3. In a flameproof casserole, over medium heat, heat the butter or margarine with the oil. Add the chicken and season lightly with salt and pepper. Brown the chicken evenly. Stir in the onions and garlic and cook for 5 minutes, or until they are soft. Stir in the apple and blend in the flour and curry powder.

4. Gradually stir in the broth, then the wine and tomatoes. Bring to a boil; then, with a wooden fork, stir in the rice. Cover and bake for 35 minutes, or until the chicken and rice are tender and the liquid has been absorbed. Taste for seasoning, adding salt and pepper if needed. The broth may have supplied enough.

*Serves 4*

# Roman Chicken and Rice

1 cup all-purpose flour
2 teaspoons salt (optional)
1 teaspoon freshly ground black pepper
½ teaspoon dried oregano
Two 3-pound chickens, cut into serving pieces (Do not use the
    backs or wing tips; save them for making stock.)
8 tablespoons (1 stick) butter or margarine
2 tablespoons olive oil
3 tablespoons all-purpose flour
2½ cups chicken broth
½ cup half-and-half
Juice of ½ lemon
Salt and freshly ground black pepper to taste
1 medium white onion, minced
3 tablespoons chopped broadleaf (Italian) parsley leaves
⅛ teaspoon dried thyme
2 cups long-grain rice, cooked al dente

1. Combine the 1 cup flour, salt, pepper, and oregano. Dredge the chicken pieces in the seasoned flour.

2. In a deep frying pan, over medium heat, heat 4 tablespoons of the butter or margarine and the oil. Add the chicken, cooking as many pieces as you can at a time until they are evenly browned. Remove and reserve.

3. Pour off any fat remaining in the pan. Melt the remaining butter or margarine in the frying pan. Slowly blend in the 3 tablespoons of flour, stirring into a smooth paste. Gradually pour in the chicken broth, stirring into a smooth, thin sauce. Stir in the half-and-half and lemon juice and season with salt and pepper to taste. Stir in the onion, parsley, and thyme, and simmer for 1 minute, stirring. Preheat the oven to 375 degrees.

4. In a large casserole, arrange the rice in a smooth layer, but do not pack it. Spoon one-third of the sauce over the rice. Arrange the chicken pieces on top, overlapping if necessary. Spoon on the remaining sauce. Cover the casserole and bake for 30 minutes, or until the chicken is tender and the sauce has thickened. Taste for seasoning, adding salt and pepper if needed.

*Serves 6 to 8*

# Frango com Arroz

## Portuguese Chicken and Rice

3 tablespoons extra-virgin olive oil
2 thin slices boiled ham, chopped
8 medium chicken thighs
Salt and freshly ground black pepper to taste
3 medium onions, chopped
1 medium red bell pepper, cored, seeded, and chopped
1 cup long-grain rice
½ cup port wine
2½ cups chicken broth
Pimiento-stuffed olives
Peeled and seeded orange slices

1. In a large, deep, heavy saucepan over medium heat, heat ½ tablespoon of the olive oil and cook the ham until it is almost crisp. With a slotted spoon, remove and reserve the ham.

2. Add the remaining olive oil and the chicken to the saucepan, season with salt and pepper, and brown it evenly. Remove and reserve the chicken.

3. Stir the onions and pepper into the fat remaining in the pan. Cook for 5 minutes. Add the rice, port wine, and chicken broth. Return the ham and the chicken to the pan. Blend well. Bring to a boil, lower the heat, cover, and simmer for 20 minutes, or until the chicken and rice are tender. Taste for seasoning, adding salt and pepper if needed.

4. Serve the chicken on the rice. Garnish with the olives and the orange slices.

*Serves 4*

# Casablanca Chicken and Rice

*One of rice's great assets is its ability to complete a quick and easy meal. We had a dish much like this in North Africa, except that the meat was pigeon.*

*Serve this spicy dish with individual bowls of plain yogurt and a simple tomato or avocado salad or with slices of fresh pineapple.*

3 tablespoons butter or margarine
1 tablespoon olive oil
4 large chicken thighs
Salt to taste
2 medium onions, chopped
2 large garlic cloves, minced
1 cup long-grain rice
½ teaspoon ground cumin
½ teaspoon ground coriander
1 tablespoon chopped fresh gingerroot
⅛ teaspoon hot red pepper flakes
One 8-ounce can stewed tomatoes, mashed with a fork
½ cup peanut butter, blended with 1½ cups cold chicken broth
    into a smooth mixture
4 hard-boiled eggs, shells removed

1. In a heavy-bottomed casserole, over medium heat, heat the butter or margarine and oil, and evenly brown the chicken, seasoning with salt. Remove the thighs, and stir in the onions and garlic. Cook for 5 minutes, or until they are soft. Do not brown. Return the thighs to the pot and spoon the rice between them.

2. Blend the cumin, coriander, ginger, and hot red pepper flakes with the tomatoes and the peanut butter–broth mixture and spoon over the chicken and rice. Bring to a boil, cover, lower the heat, and simmer for 30 minutes, or until the thighs and rice are just tender.

3. Add the eggs to the pot, spooning the rice over them, cover, and cook for 5 minutes, or until the eggs are heated through.

*Serves 4*

# Lemon Rice with Curried Chicken

*Lemon Rice*

2 tablespoons butter or margarine
1 tablespoon olive oil
1 medium onion, finely chopped
2 cups long-grain rice
4½ cups water
1 teaspoon salt (optional)
3 tablespoons fresh lemon juice

*Curried Chicken*

¾ cup all-purpose flour
1 teaspoon sweet Hungarian paprika
2 tablespoons curry powder, or to taste (page 79)
1 teaspoon salt (optional)
3 whole chicken breasts, skinned, boned, and halved, and each
    half cut into halves crosswise
6 chicken thighs, skinned and boned
5 tablespoons butter or margarine
1 cup half-and-half
1 cup dry sherry
1¾ cups chicken broth
1 teaspoon Worcestershire sauce
Salt and freshly ground black pepper to taste
½ cup toasted blanched-and-slivered almonds

1. To prepare the lemon rice, melt the butter or margarine with the oil in a heavy saucepan over medium-high heat. Add the onion and cook for 3 minutes, or until it is soft and slightly golden. Do not brown. Add the rice and cook, stirring, for 2 minutes, or until it is well coated with the butter and oil.

2. Add the water, salt, and lemon juice and bring to a boil. Lower the heat, cover, and simmer for 25 minutes, or until the rice is tender and the liquid has been absorbed.

3. To prepare the curried chicken, combine the flour, paprika, curry powder, and salt in a clean paper or plastic bag. Add the chicken pieces and shake to coat them evenly.

4. In a large frying pan, heat the butter or margarine over medium-high heat and evenly brown the chicken. Add more butter or margarine if needed.

5. In a large measuring cup combine and blend the half-and-half,

sherry, broth, and Worcestershire sauce and pour the mixture over the chicken. Bring to a boil, lower the heat, cover, and simmer, stirring occasionally, for 30 minutes, or until the chicken is tender and the sauce has thickened. If the chicken seems to be getting tender before the sauce thickens, remove the cover from the pan. Taste for seasoning, adding salt and pepper if needed.

6. Serve with a border of the Lemon Rice, sprinkled with almonds.

*Serves 6*

# Rice and Chicken Oregano

4 tablespoons olive oil
4 chicken thighs
4 chicken drumsticks
Salt and freshly ground black pepper to taste
2 teaspoons dried oregano
2 medium onions, chopped
¼ cup dry vermouth
1 cup long-grain rice
2½ cups chicken broth

1. In a flameproof casserole, over medium heat, heat the oil. Sprinkle the chicken with salt, pepper, and oregano and brown it evenly. Remove the chicken. Preheat the oven to 350 degrees.

2. Add more oil to the casserole if necessary, and stir in the onions. Cook for 3 minutes.

3. Pour in the vermouth and cook, stirring well, scraping up the browned-on bits on the bottom of the pot.

4. Add the rice and stir to blend well.

5. Return the chicken to the pan and pour on the broth. Bring to a boil on top of the stove. Cover the casserole and bake for 40 minutes, or until the chicken and rice are tender and most of the liquid has been absorbed. It should be somewhat moist. Taste for seasoning, adding salt and pepper if needed.

*Serves 4*

# India's Rice

We can't claim to *know* India. But after six visits, we are absolutely convinced of one thing: Indians love rice and cook it in many interesting and exotic ways unknown to the Western world.

Two words jump out of India's remarkable rice repertoire: *pulao* and *biryani*. In pulaos, which are probably the most popular, the rice is first sautéed in ghee (butter from buffalo cream), and then steamed and spiced with a variety of ingredients added, varying in the different areas, ranging from the sumptuous to the simple.

Biryanis are fancier, offered to please and impress guests on special occasions. Often main courses, they are layered dishes (casseroles, if you will) alternating rice with various meats and vegetables, which are then baked. Before serving, the dishes are garnished with fried onion rings, eggs, nuts, raisins, or anything an imaginative host or hostess can dream up. We once had a biryani served with the gold-tinted coconut called *sajavat*.

## Chicken Biryani

1 cup plain yogurt
1 medium onion, grated
2 garlic cloves, minced
2 teaspoons grated fresh gingerroot
⅛ teaspoon ground cloves
½ teaspoon ground cardamom
⅛ teaspoon ground mace
¼ teaspoon ground cinnamon
2 tablespoons chopped fresh parsley leaves
2 large chicken thighs, boned and cut into 2-inch pieces
1 large whole chicken breast, boned and cut into 2-inch pieces
Salt to taste
2 cups chicken broth
1 cup long-grain rice
½ teaspoon of powdered saffron, blended with ½ cup
   warm water
4 tablespoons (½ stick) butter or margarine

1. In a large bowl, combine and blend well the yogurt, onion, garlic, ginger, cloves, cardamom, mace, cinnamon, and parsley. Add the chicken and blend well to thoroughly coat the pieces. Cover and marinate in the refrigerator for 3 to 4 hours, turning 2 or 3 times. Remove from the refrigerator 1 hour before cooking.

2. Transfer the chicken mixture to a saucepan. Bring to a boil, cover, lower the heat, and simmer for 20 minutes, or until the chicken is very nearly tender. Taste for seasoning, adding salt if needed.

3. While the chicken is cooking, bring the broth to a boil in another saucepan. Stir in the rice, cover, lower the heat, and simmer for 15 minutes. The rice should be quite al dente. Taste before seasoning, as the broth may have supplied enough.

4. Preheat the oven to 350 degrees. In a 2-quart casserole, arrange a layer of half of the chicken and a layer of half of the rice on the chicken, sprinkling each layer lightly with the saffron blend. Repeat. Dot the top layer of rice with the butter or margarine. Cover the casserole with aluminum foil and then with its cover. Bake for 25 minutes, or until the chicken and rice are tender.

*Serves 4*


# Castilian Arroz con Pollo

*Castilian Rice with Chicken*

Two 3-pound chickens, cut into serving pieces (Do not use the
  backs or wing tips; save them for making stock.)
All-purpose flour for dredging
¼ cup olive oil
Salt and freshly ground black pepper to taste
4 shallots, finely chopped
2 garlic cloves, minced
2 cups long-grain rice
3 cups chicken broth
3 large ripe tomatoes, peeled, seeded, and chopped, or 2 cups
  canned tomatoes, broken up

1 bay leaf
3 whole cloves
¼ teaspoon powdered saffron, dissolved in a little broth
½ cup Madeira
1 cup partially cooked fresh peas or defrosted frozen peas
½ cup coarsely chopped pimiento
3 tablespoons chopped broadleaf (Italian) parsley leaves

1. Lighly dredge the chicken parts in the flour, shaking off any excess. Preheat the oven to 375 degrees.

2. In a large flameproof casserole, heat the oil over medium heat. Add the chicken, cooking as many pieces as you can at a time, until they are evenly browned. Season with salt and pepper. Remove from the pot as they brown and reserve.

3. Add the shallots and garlic to the pot and cook until soft, about 5 minutes. Do not brown. Stir in the rice and cook for 2 minutes, stirring to coat the rice well. Add a little more oil if the chicken has absorbed all the fat.

4. Pour in the broth and cook, stirring, scraping up the browned-on bits on the bottom of the pot.

5. Add the tomatoes, bay leaf, cloves, saffron, and Madeira. Return the chicken pieces to the pot, mixing them in with the rice. Bring to a boil on top of the stove. Cover and bake for 25 minutes. Fluff the rice with a metal fork. Remove and discard the bay leaf and cloves. Taste for seasoning, adding salt and pepper if needed.

6. Stir in the peas and pimiento and bake for 10 minutes longer, or until the rice and chicken are tender and most of the liquid has been absorbed. If the liquid is absorbed before the rice is tender, add a small amount of hot broth and continue to bake.

7. Sprinkle with the parsley and serve from the casserole.

*Serves 6 to 8*

# Deviled Chicken with "Greek" Rice in
# Pepper Cups

*The French like to offer more or less plain chicken with fancy little side dishes of baked red peppers filled with rice that they call* Riz à la Grecque, *although the Greeks probably never saw the rice. But it's a nifty presentation.*

### *"Greek" Rice*

8 medium red bell peppers, tops cut off and seeds and white ribs
   carefully removed, leaving the pepper shells intact
3 tablespoons olive oil
4 large shallots, chopped
1 cup long-grain rice
4 medium fresh mushrooms, coarsely chopped
½ cup diced Canadian bacon or ham
12 pitted dark plump Calamata olives, coarsely chopped
2½ cups chicken broth
½ cup tomato purée, blended with ½ cup water

### *Deviled Broiled Chicken*

2 chickens, weighing no more than 2½ pounds each
2 tablespoons olive oil
Seasoned salt
6 tablespoons fine fresh bread crumbs
1 teaspoon dry mustard
⅛ teaspoon cayenne
3 tablespoons butter or margarine

1. To prepare the pepper cups, parboil the peppers in boiling water for 5 minutes. Remove from the water and invert the peppers to drain thoroughly. Preheat the oven to 375 degrees.

2. In a flameproof casserole, over medium heat, heat the olive oil and cook the shallots for 3 minutes, or until they are soft. Do not brown. Stir in the rice and cook for 2 minutes, stirring to coat the rice well. Stir in the mushrooms, bacon or ham, olives, and broth. Bring to a boil, cover, and bake for 25 minutes, or until the rice is tender and the liquid has been absorbed.

3. Spoon the rice stuffing loosely into the peppers. Arrange them in a baking dish with a cover or in a casserole just large enough to

hold them snugly without crowding. Pour the tomato purée–water mixture around the peppers, cover, and bake for 30 minutes, or until the peppers are tender, basting 2 or 3 times (see Note).

4. Meanwhile, split the chickens into halves, cutting down the backbones. Remove the backbones and save them for soup. Breast side up, striking firmly, flatten the halves with the flat side of a cleaver. Raise oven temperature to 450 degrees.

5. Rub the outside of the chicken halves with the olive oil and seasoned salt. Place on a lightly oiled baking sheet or in shallow broiler-proof baking dish. Bake for 20 minutes, or until just tender.

6. Combine the bread crumbs, dry mustard, and cayenne together in a small bowl. Sprinkle the mixture evenly over the chickens and dot with flecks of butter or margarine.

7. Place under a preheated broiler (5 inches from the heat) for 10 minutes, or until the chickens are golden.

8. Serve each chicken half with 2 rice-stuffed peppers.

*Note:* If you do not have two ovens, you can prepare the peppers and bake them before you bake the chickens. The peppers can then be reheated in the oven while the chickens are in the broiler.

*Serves 4*

# Chicken and Sausage Risotto

*The Italians have almost as many interesting combinations of various foods with rice as they have with pasta. Here's one that we like that comes from the Veneto region.*

4 Italian sweet sausages, in their casings
6 tablespoons butter or margarine
2 tablespoons olive oil
1 medium onion, finely chopped
1 celery stalk, scraped and finely chopped
1 medium carrot, scraped and finely chopped
4 large chicken thighs, boned and the flesh cut into ½-inch-wide strips
Salt and freshly ground black pepper to taste
½ cup dry white wine
1 cup long-grain rice
2½ cups chicken broth
½ cup grated Asiago or Parmesan cheese

1. Prick the sausages with the point of a knife and poach them in boiling water for 10 minutes. Drain, quarter, and set aside.

2. In a large deep frying pan, over medium heat, heat half of the butter or margarine with the oil and cook the onion, celery, and carrot for 5 minutes, or until the onion is soft. Do not brown. Add the chicken strips and sausage and brown evenly, seasoning with salt and pepper. Pour in the wine, cover, and simmer for 20 minutes.

3. Stir in the rice, mixing it in well with a wooden fork. Stir in the broth. Bring to a boil, lower the heat, cover, and simmer for 20 minutes, or until the rice and chicken are tender and the liquid has been mostly absorbed. If the rice is not cooked when the liquid is absorbed, add a small amount of hot broth and continue cooking. The risotto should be slightly moist. Taste the seasoning, adding salt and pepper if needed.

4. Stir in the remaining butter or margarine (in small pieces) with a metal fork, fluffing the rice. Serve on a hot serving dish and pass the cheese at the table.

*Serves 4*

# Pollo con Arroz Verde

*Spanish Chicken with Green Rice in a*
*Mushroom-Sherry Sauce*

One 3-pound chicken, trussed
5 cups chicken broth
8 tablespoons (1 stick) butter or margarine
1 medium onion, chopped
1 cup long-grain rice
½ cup chopped broadleaf (Italian) parsley leaves
4 tablespoons all-purpose flour
¼ cup dry sherry
6 medium fresh mushrooms, sliced and cooked in
   3 tablespoons butter or margarine until brown but
   still firm
½ cup grated Asiago or Parmesan cheese

1. Put the chicken in a large deep pot. Pour in the broth and bring to a boil over high heat. Lower the heat, cover, and simmer the chicken until it is tender, about 45 minutes. Remove the chicken from the liquid and strain the broth. Reserve *all* of the broth, setting aside 3 cups for the sauce.

2. In a deep saucepan, over medium heat, melt 2 tablespoons of the butter or margarine. Add the onion and cook until it is soft, about 3 minutes. Do not brown. Stir in the rice and cook for 2 minutes, coating it well with the butter or margarine. Pour the broth that remained after the 3 cups were reserved for the sauce into a 2-cup measure. If it does not fill the cup, add enough water to make 2 cups of liquid. Add to the rice in the saucepan. Bring to a boil, lower the heat, stir with a wooden fork, cover, and simmer for 15 minutes, or until the liquid has been absorbed and the rice is barely tender, still quite al dente. Stir in 2 tablespoons of the butter or margarine and the parsley.

3. Remove the chicken meat from the bones, discarding the skin and bones. Preheat the oven to 375 degrees.

4. In a saucepan, over medium heat, melt the remaining 4 tablespoons of butter or margarine. Add the flour and cook, stirring into a smooth paste. Gradually stir in the reserved 3 cups of chicken broth and cook, stirring into a smooth, slightly thickened sauce. Stir in the sherry and mushrooms.

5. Arrange the rice in a smooth layer in a buttered baking dish. Place the chicken meat on the rice and spoon the mushroom-sherry sauce over the chicken. Sprinkle the cheese on the sauce. Bake for 30 minutes, or until the top is golden and the sauce bubbling.

*Serves 4*

# Shanghai Stewed Chicken

4 large chicken drumsticks
4 large chicken thighs
½ cup rice wine or dry sherry
½ cup chicken broth
⅛ cup soy sauce
⅛ teaspoon hot red pepper flakes
¼ teaspoon ground ginger
¼ teaspoon ground coriander
4 garlic cloves, flattened with the broad side of a knife blade and peeled
2 teaspoons cornstarch, dissolved in 3 tablespoons cold water or chicken broth
4 cups hot cooked long-grain rice

1. In a large deep frying pan arrange the chicken parts in one layer. Combine the rice wine, broth, soy sauce, hot red pepper flakes, ginger, and coriander in a cup. Pour the mixture over the chicken. Drop in the garlic. Bring the liquid to a boil, lower the heat, cover, and simmer for 30 minutes, or until the chicken is tender.

2. Transfer the chicken to a hot dish and keep it warm. Stir the cornstarch into the liquid in the pan and cook until slightly thickened. Serve the chicken on a bed of hot rice with the sauce spooned over the chicken.

*Serves 4*

# Rice, Chicken, and Spinach Casserole

3 cups al dente–cooked long-grain rice
1 pound fresh spinach, cooked just until wilted, or two 10-ounce
  packages frozen leaf spinach, defrosted and well-drained
3 cups cooked chicken, cut into large bite-size pieces
3 tablespoons butter or margarine
3 tablespoons all-purpose flour
2 cups chicken broth
¼ cup Madeira
⅛ teaspoon ground nutmeg
Salt and freshly ground black pepper to taste

1. Preheat the oven to 350 degrees.

2. In a baking dish or casserole, arrange the rice in a smooth layer (do not pack it down). Top with a smooth layer of the spinach, and then with the chicken.

3. In a saucepan, over medium heat, melt the butter or margarine. Stir in the flour and cook, stirring, into a smooth paste. Gradually add the broth and cook, stirring into a smooth, medium-thick sauce. Stir in the Madeira, nutmeg, salt, and pepper.

4. Spoon the sauce over the chicken and bake, uncovered, until bubbly and slightly golden, about 25 minutes.

*Serves 4*

# Rice Tetrazzini

3 tablespoons butter or margarine
3 tablespoons all-purpose flour
2½ cups half-and-half
Salt and freshly ground black pepper to taste
½ teaspoon ground nutmeg
1 egg white, beaten
1½ cups al dente–cooked long-grain rice
1 cup grated Asiago or Parmesan cheese
2 cups cubed cooked turkey or chicken (the breast is classic)
8 small fresh mushrooms, quartered and cooked in 2 tablespoons
    butter or margarine for 2 minutes
One 10-ounce package frozen chopped spinach, defrosted and
    drained

1. In a saucepan, over medium heat, melt the butter or margarine. Stir in the flour, stirring into a smooth paste. Gradually add the half-and-half, stirring into a smooth, thickened sauce. Season with salt, pepper, and nutmeg. Remove from the heat and stir in the egg white. Reserve. Preheat the oven to 400 degrees.

2. In a large bowl, combine and blend well the rice and half of the cheese. Thoroughly, but carefully, stir in the turkey pieces, mushrooms, and spinach.

3. Arrange the rice-turkey mixture in a buttered casserole. Pour the sauce over it and sprinkle with the remaining cheese. Bake, uncovered, for about 15 minutes, or until bubbling and golden.

*Serves 4*

# Rice Croquettes with Pojarski Côtelettes

*We like these recipes so much that we're coupling them as a dinner suggestion.*

*Croquettes used to be quite difficult to master until we discovered this method after a dozen attempts. It's not easy to keep the croquette patties together (intact). Just "rice" cannot be listed in the ingredients. A clinging rice, short or medium grain, is a must, preferably California short-grain* rice. Also, with many of us today preferring lighter foods, keeping away from the deep-fried method as croquettes are usually cooked, we worked on a different approach. Much ado about croquettes? Perhaps. But they are delicious, different, and rarely served (a welcome change from potatoes or pasta), so perhaps this recipe will be a find for some, a discovery for others. It was for us.

This recipe makes approximately 20 "cutlets." (Cook whatever number you need, and freeze the remainder uncooked. They freeze exceptionally well.)

We like to serve this combination with puréed carrots.

*Rice Croquettes*

> 1 cup short-grain rice
> 2 cups water
> 1 teaspoon salt (optional)
> 3 tablespoons half-and-half
> 1 large egg, beaten
> 2 tablespoons minced fresh parsley leaves
> 4 tablespoons melted butter or margarine
> Freshly ground black pepper to taste
> ½ cup grated Asiago or Parmesan cheese
> Approximately 2 cups fine dry bread crumbs for dredging
> 4 tablespoons (½ stick) butter or margarine
> 3 tablespoons olive oil

*Pojarski Côtelettes*

> 6 slices white bread, crusts removed
> 2 cups chicken broth
> 8 tablespoons (1 stick) butter or margarine, melted
> 4 pounds skinned and boned chicken breasts, finely ground
> ½ pound lean pork, finely ground
> 2 medium eggs, beaten
> 1 teaspoon salt (optional)
> ½ teaspoon freshly ground black pepper
> 4 tablespoons dried dill
> All-purpose flour for dredging
> Butter or margarine and olive oil (amount depends on the
>     number of cutlets to be cooked)
> 1 pint sour cream

1. To prepare the rice croquettes, combine the rice, water, and salt in a saucepan. Bring to a boil, cover, lower the heat, and simmer for 25 minutes, or until the liquid has been absorbed and the

rice is very soft. Remove from the heat and cool. In a large bowl, combine and blend well with a metal fork the rice, half-and-half, egg, parsley, melted butter or margarine, pepper, and cheese. Refrigerate for 2 hours.

2. Remove from the refrigerator, and, using the "mud-pie" method, scoop up a handful of rice, sprinkle bread crumbs liberally on one side and then the other. Then remold the croquette with both hands, shaping it until the bread crumbs adhere to the outside. Place the croquettes on a large plate and refrigerate until ready to cook.

3. In a large frying pan, over medium heat, heat the 4 tablespoons of butter or margarine with the olive oil. Place the croquettes in the pan, not touching, and brown them evenly, carefully turning them with a spatula. As they become golden brown, they will be well-formed and intact. The croquettes can be browned while the côtelettes are in the oven in their last cooking stage. Serve immediately with the Pojarski Côtelettes.

4. To prepare the Pojarski Côtelettes, break up the bread and put it in a very large bowl. Stir in the chicken broth and melted butter or margarine. Using a large fork, stir in the chicken, pork, eggs, salt, pepper, and 2 tablespoons of the dried dill. With the fork, blend well. Cook a small patty to test the seasoning; then add more salt and pepper if needed. Form plump, oblong patties (not flattened like hamburgers), about 2 inches by 3 inches. Lightly dredge in the flour. Preheat the oven to 300 degrees.

5. In a large frying pan, over medium heat, heat 3 tablespoons of butter or margarine and 1 of olive oil. Cook 6 cutlets at a time, browning them evenly on both sides. Arrange in a single layer in a baking dish. Bake, uncovered, for 15 minutes.

6. Just before serving, heat the sour cream. Spoon it over the cutlets and sprinkle with the remaining dried dill.

*Serves 6 to 8*

# Boned Chicken Breasts with Scallioned Rice

1 tablespoon olive oil
8 tablespoons (1 stick) butter or margarine
2 large whole chicken breasts, split, skinned, and boned
Salt and freshly ground black pepper to taste
½ teaspoon ground cumin
¼ cup dry vermouth
1 cup long-grain rice
2 cups chicken broth
¼ cup dry white wine
6 whole scallions, trimmed and thinly sliced
2 celery stalks, scraped and thinly sliced
6 medium fresh mushrooms, sliced

1. In a frying pan, over medium heat, heat the oil and half of the butter or margarine. Evenly brown the chicken breasts, sprinkling them with salt, pepper, and cumin. Remove the breasts. Stir in the vermouth, mixing it with the browned-on bits on the bottom of the pan. Return the breasts to the pan, cover, lower the heat, and simmer for 15 minutes, or until the chicken is nearly tender. Remove from the heat.

2. In a large deep saucepan, melt the remaining butter or margarine. Stir in the rice, coating it well. Stir in the chicken broth and white wine. Bring to a boil, stir with a wooden fork, cover, lower the heat, and simmer for 15 minutes.

3. Stir in the scallions, celery, and mushrooms and push the chicken breasts into the rice-vegetable mixture. Cover the pan and cook for 8 minutes, or until the chicken and rice are tender. If liquid cooks off before the chicken and rice are tender, add a small amount of hot broth and continue cooking. Fluff the rice with a metal fork before serving.

*Serves 4*

# Cornish Game Hens Mole with Wild Pecan Rice

*Don't let this long list of ingredients deter you. This is not complicated, and it's rewarding. See the recipe for Pheasant with Wild Pecan Rice, page 105, for more about this rice.*

4 Cornish game hens, about 1 pound each, trussed
1 large whole onion
1 celery stalk, scraped and quartered
1 carrot, scraped and quartered
2 teaspoons salt (optional)
2 to 3 cups chicken broth
½ cup toasted, coarsely chopped almonds
1 tablespoon toasted sesame seeds
½ teaspoon ground aniseed
1 tortilla, or 1 slice toasted stale bread
½ cup raisins
½ square bitter chocolate, grated
1 tablespoon chili powder, or to taste
½ teaspoon ground cinnamon
⅛ teaspoon ground cloves
2 tablespoons olive oil
2 medium onions, chopped
2 garlic cloves, minced
2 tablespoons all-purpose flour
½ cup tomato purée
One 7-ounce package Wild Pecan Rice

1. Put the game hens with the whole onion, celery, carrot, and 1 teaspoon of the salt in a large pot. Barely cover with water. Bring to a boil, cover, and simmer for 15 minutes. Remove the birds; they will cook more later.

2. In a blender container, combine 1 cup of the chicken broth, the almonds, sesame seeds, aniseed, tortilla, raisins, chocolate, chili powder, cinnamon, and cloves and blend into a smooth purée.

3. In a large heavy pot, over medium heat, heat the olive oil and cook the chopped onions and garlic for 4 minutes. Lower the heat, stir in the flour, and blend well with the onions and garlic. Stir in the purée from the blender, mixing well. Simmer, stirring, for 2 minutes.

4. Stir in the tomato purée, 1 cup of the chicken broth, and the remaining teaspoon of salt if desired. Simmer, stirring occasionally, for 5 minutes, or until the sauce just begins to thicken.

5. Add the rice and the partially cooked game hens. Simmer, covered, for 25 minutes, or until the rice and birds are tender. If the sauce becomes too thick before the rice and birds are tender, add small amounts of hot broth to thin it.

*Note:* This dish is also served with plain boiled white rice, but we like this version where the rice is cooked with the birds, making the sauce doubly delicious.

*Serves 4*


## Cornish Game Hens Nested in Wild and Long-Grain Rice

*For this we prefer squabs to Cornish hens, but those baby pigeons are hard to come by and very expensive. However, get them if you can.*

6 tablespoons butter or margarine
4 scallions, trimmed and chopped
¾ pound chicken livers, trimmed and quartered
Salt and freshly ground black pepper to taste
2 tablespoons Madeira
4 Cornish games hens, about 1 pound (or less) each
1 pint sour cream
1½ cups wild rice and long-grain rice combination, cooked according to package directions

1. In a frying pan, over medium heat, melt 3 tablespoons of the butter or margarine and cook the scallions for 5 minutes, or until they are soft. Do not brown. Add the livers and cook for 3 minutes. (They should be brown on the outside and quite pink on the inside.) Season with salt and pepper. Stir in the Madeira and cook, stirring, for 2 minutes.

2. Preheat the oven to 350 degrees.

3. Stuff the birds with the livers. Then truss them and rub them with the remaining butter or margarine. Sprinkle with salt and pepper. Place in a flameproof roasting pan just large enough to hold them. Bake, uncovered, for 30 minutes, basting well after 20 minutes. Coat the birds with half of the sour cream and bake for another 30 minutes, or until fork-tender. Transfer to a hot dish and remove the trussing cord.

4. Stir the remaining sour cream and the rice into the pan the birds roasted in, blending the rice into the juices and brown particles in the pan. Heat through over medium heat. Serve the birds, each on a nest of the rice.

*Serves 4*

## Indian Duck and Brown Rice

*India has also been called "Spiceland" and its cooking is firm testament to their wide and constant use.*

3 tablespoons butter or margarine
1 tablespoon olive oil
One 5- to 6-pound duckling, cut into serving pieces (discard the wing tips)
Salt and freshly ground black pepper to taste
4 medium onions, quartered
1 small fresh hot red pepper, quartered and seeded, or ¼ teaspoon hot red pepper flakes
½ teaspoon ground ginger
1 teaspoon ground turmeric
1 teaspoon ground coriander
¼ teaspoon ground cloves
¼ teaspoon ground cinnamon
3 cups chicken broth
1 cup long-grain brown rice
1 cup small green peas (defrosted frozen peas may be used)

1. Preheat the oven to 350 degrees.

2. In a large flameproof casserole, over medium heat, heat the butter or margarine with the oil and evenly brown the duck pieces, seasoning them lightly with salt and pepper. Remove the duck and skim the fat from the casserole.

3. Add the onions and red pepper to the casserole and cook for 5 minutes, or until the onion is golden. Do not brown.

4. Return the duck to the casserole and sprinkle it with the ginger, turmeric, coriander, cloves, and cinnamon. Pour in the chicken broth. Bring to a boil, cover, and bake for 45 minutes.

5. Stir in the rice and bake for 40 minutes. Stir in the peas and bake for 10 minutes, or until the duck and rice are tender. Serve the duck pieces over the rice and peas.

*Serves 4*

## Arroz con Pato Cervesa Inglesa

*Duck with Rice and Ale South American Style*

Juice of 4 limes
½ teaspoon ground coriander
1 teaspoon salt (optional)
⅛ teaspoon hot red pepper flakes, or to taste
One 5-pound duck, cut into serving pieces, trimmed of excess fat
3 tablespoons olive oil
Two 12-ounce bottles dark ale
1½ cups long-grain rice
½ cup finely chopped broadleaf (Italian) parsley leaves, blended
    with ½ cup finely chopped chives

1. In a large bowl, blend the lime juice, coriander, salt, and hot red pepper flakes. Add the duck pieces and turn several times to coat them evenly with the marinade. Cover and marinate at room temperature for 2 hours, turning several times.

2. In a deep heavy saucepan, over medium heat, heat the oil and evenly brown the duck. Drain the fat from the pan and pour in the

ale. Bring to a boil, cover, lower the heat, and simmer for 40 minutes, or until the duck is fork tender. Remove the duck and keep it warm in a 200-degree oven.

3. Stir the rice into the liquid in which the duck cooked. Bring to a boil, stir with a wooden fork, cover, lower the heat, and simmer for 20 minutes, or until the rice is tender and the liquid has been absorbed. If the liquid is absorbed before the rice is tender, add small amounts of hot water and continue cooking. Or, if the rice is tender and there is an excess of liquid, raise the heat and cook, uncovered, watching carefully so that the rice does not burn. With a metal fork, blend the parsley-chives mixture with the rice, tossing as you mix. Spread the rice on a hot serving dish and top with the duck.

*Serves 4*

# Roast Goose with Cranberry-Rice Stuffing

One 7-pound goose
Cranberry-Rice Stuffing (see following recipe)
3 tablespoons soft butter or margarine
1 teaspoon salt (optional)
½ teaspoon freshly ground black pepper
¼ teaspoon dried rosemary

1. Preheat the oven to 375 degrees.

2. Geese are quite fatty, so pierce the breast and thighs in several places with the sharp point of a knife so the fat will cook off. Lightly stuff the bird with the Cranberry-Rice Stuffing (the rice will expand as the bird cooks). Any extra stuffing can be put into a small baking dish, wrapped in foil, and baked with the bird. Place the bird on a rack in a deep roasting pan. This will prevent the goose from cooking in its fat.

3. Blend the butter or margarine, salt, pepper, and rosemary into a paste. Rub the bird with this paste.

4. Roast, uncovered, 19 minutes to the pound (about 2 to 2½ hours), or until fork-tender. Do not overcook as the bird will dry out. Baste occasionally with 2 or 3 tablespoonfuls of boiling water and siphon the fat from the pan. We use a bulb baster and find it efficient.

*Serves 4 to 6*

## Cranberry-Rice Stuffing

4 tablespoons (½ stick) butter or margarine
1½ cups whole cranberries, washed, picked over, and coarsely chopped
4 cups al dente–cooked wild rice
2 tablespoons superfine sugar, dissolved in 2 tablespoons warm water and 2 tablespoons brandy
4 scallions (white part only), minced
1 teaspoon salt (optional)
½ teaspoon freshly ground black pepper
¼ teaspoon ground nutmeg

In a deep saucepan, over medium heat, melt the butter or margarine. Stir in the remaining ingredients. Lower the heat and simmer, stirring with a metal fork, for 10 minutes.

*Makes approximately 5 cups*

# Partridge Tandoori with Wild Pecan Rice

*They can say all they want to about the Italian and Indian rices, but we think American Wild Pecan Rice (more about this rice in the recipe for Pheasant with Wild Pecan Rice, page 105) is superior to them all. It is especially good with this classic from India which we've adapted. Actually, to be authentic, the birds should be cooked in a tandoor, a four-foot, cylindrical clay oven buried in the ground. Wood, sometimes charcoal, is the fuel. When the fire is banked and the coals glowing, the heat in the oven becomes intense. These partridges would be tastier cooked tandoor fashion, as we've had them in New Delhi, but we've borrowed the sauce and some of the method, which produces good results.*

3 chukar partridges (sold at game farms and specialty markets), split and skinned
3 cups plain yogurt
½ cup fresh lime juice
¼ cup olive oil
4 garlic cloves, crushed
1½ tablespoons curry powder (page 79)
¼ teaspoon ground ginger
½ teaspoon ground cumin
¼ teaspoon ground coriander
One 7-ounce package Wild Pecan Rice
1 teaspoon salt (optional)
2 cups water

1. Cut two small slits in each leg and each breast of the partridges. Place the birds in a shallow glass dish or casserole large enough to hold the halves spread flat.

2. In a bowl, combine and blend well the yogurt, lime juice, olive oil, garlic, curry powder, ginger, cumin, and coriander. Spoon the mixture over the partridges, turning to coat evenly. Cover and marinate in the refrigerator for 4 hours. Remove from the refrigerator 1 hour before cooking. Discard the garlic. Reserve the marinade. Preheat the broiler.

3. Put the partridges on a rack in the broiler, over a drip pan, 4 inches from the heat. Broil for 20 minutes on each side, turning frequently to prevent burning, or until tender, basting with marinade.

4. While the birds are cooking, combine the rice, salt, and water in a saucepan. Bring to a boil over medium heat. Stir with a wooden fork, cover, lower the heat, and simmer for 20 minutes, or until the water has been absorbed and the rice is tender.

5. Spoon the marinade that has collected in the drip pan after basting the birds into the rice, tossing with a metal fork. Serve each partridge half on its own bed of spicy rice.

*Serves 6*

# Pheasant with Wild Pecan Rice

*We don't claim to have discovered Wild Pecan Rice, but we certainly feel as if we have. As we mentioned earlier, Wild Pecan Rice is neither wild nor flavored with pecans, but is a very flavorful unique American long-grain rice with a nutty aroma. It is grown only in the Acadian country of South Louisiana. We found it in several of the larger supermarket chains. It comes sealed in foil in 7-ounce brown boxes.*

One 7-ounce package Wild Pecan Rice
3 teaspoons salt (optional)
10 tablespoons (1¼ sticks) butter or margarine
1½ cups water
1 cup all-purpose flour
1 teaspoon dried thyme
Two 3-pound pheasants, cut into serving pieces
2 tablespoons olive oil
1½ cups chicken broth
1 cup light cream or half-and-half
½ cup Madeira
Juice of ½ lemon
Salt and freshly ground black pepper to taste
2 leeks, all of the white and some of the green part, well washed and finely chopped
2 tablespoons chopped broadleaf (Italian) parsley leaves

1. In a saucepan, stir in the rice, 1 teaspoon of salt, and 1 tablespoon of butter or margarine. Add the water, bring to a boil, stir with a wooden fork, cover, lower the heat, and simmer for 10 minutes. If the water hasn't been absorbed, drain and reserve the rice. Preheat the oven to 375 degrees.

2. Blend ¾ cup of the flour, remaining 2 teaspoons of salt, and thyme. Dredge the pheasants in the seasoned flour.

3. In a frying pan, over medium heat, heat 4 tablespoons of the butter or margarine with the olive oil, and evenly brown the pheasant pieces. Remove and reserve them.

4. Discard whatever fat remains in the pan. Over medium heat, melt the remaining 5 tablespoons of butter or margarine in the pan. Add the remaining ¼ cup of flour and cook, stirring into a smooth paste.

5. Lower the heat and gradually stir in the chicken broth, stirring into a smooth sauce. Stir in the cream or half-and-half, Madeira, and lemon juice. Simmer for 2 minutes. Taste and season with salt and pepper if necessary. Stir in the leeks and parsley and simmer for 1 minute.

6. In a 5-quart casserole, spread the rice in a smooth layer. Pour half of the sauce over the rice. Arrange the pheasants on top and cover with the remaining sauce. Cover and bake for 25 minutes, or until the rice and pheasants are tender. If the sauce becomes too thick before the pheasants and rice are tender, add small amounts of hot broth or water.

*Note:* Admittedly, this is an elegant dish for special occasions, but if you aren't a hunter or don't have generous hunter friends for the game dishes in this chapter, don't despair. Many specialty markets sell game of all kinds.

*Serves 6*

# Isle of Pines Quail Picante

*We had this dish on the Isle of Pines, which is just off the coast of Cuba, where we were quail shooting just a few weeks before Castro came to power.*

6 tablespoons butter or margarine
2 tablespoons olive oil
1 large onion, chopped
4 bobwhite quails, or 8 coturnix quails, or 4 Cornish game hens
    (about 1 pound each)
Salt to taste
6 medium ripe tomatoes, peeled, seeded, and chopped, or 3 cups
    drained canned tomatoes, chopped
½ cup dry red wine
½ teaspoon cayenne
1 bay leaf
¼ teaspoon dried thyme
½ cup pitted black olives, halved (Use the plump dark purple
    Calamata olives, if possible.)
½ cup pimiento-stuffed green olives
3 scallions (white part only)
3 hard-boiled eggs
½ cup raisins
½ cup toasted blanched almonds
3 cups hot cooked long-grain rice
3 tablespoons chopped fresh parsley leaves

1. In a deep heavy frying pan, over medium heat, heat 1 tablespoon of the butter or margarine and 1 tablespoon of the oil. Add the onion and cook until it is soft, about 5 minutes. Do not brown.

2. Add 2 tablespoons of the butter or margarine and the remaining oil to the pan and evenly brown the quails or game hens. Season them with salt.

3. Add the tomatoes, wine, cayenne, bay leaf, and thyme and simmer, covered, for 35 minutes, or until the birds are fork tender. Add the black olives and heat through. Remove and discard the bay leaf.

4. Chop the stuffed olives, scallions, eggs, raisins, and almonds together.

5. With a metal fork, stir the remaining butter or margarine (in

small pieces) and the chopped mixture into the hot rice. Stir with the fork over medium heat, until just heated through, fluffing up the mixture with the fork.

6. Mound the rice in the center of a hot serving dish and arrange the birds around it. Spoon the tomato sauce over the birds and sprinkle with the parsley.

*Serves 4*

# Rabbits with Olives, Anchovies, and Wild Pecan Rice

*We had this dish in Bologna, Italy. We continue to tell you where we enjoyed some of the dishes in this book to point up that rice is a world traveler. In Italy, of course, this was served with their Arborio rice. Our unique Wild Pecan Rice, we believe, is better. We have more to say about this rice in the recipe for Pheasant with Wild Pecan Rice on page 105.*

Two 3-pound rabbits, cut into serving pieces
Salt and freshly ground black pepper to taste
4 tablespoons (½ stick) butter or margarine
2 tablespoons olive oil
1 medium onion, minced
2 garlic cloves, minced
1 cup dry white wine
Juice of 1 lemon
2 cups chicken broth
1 teaspoon dried marjoram
One 7-ounce package Wild Pecan Rice
12 Italian black olives, pitted and sliced
One 2-ounce can flat anchovy fillets, rinsed in cold water, dried, and cut up

1. Season the rabbit pieces with salt and pepper. In a deep non-aluminum frying pan, over medium heat, heat 3 tablespoons of butter or margarine and the oil and evenly brown the rabbit. Remove and reserve.

2. Pour off all but 1 tablespoon of fat. If the rabbit has absorbed all the fat, add 1 tablespoon of butter or margarine. Stir in the onion and garlic and cook for 4 minutes, or until they are soft. Do not brown. Add the wine and lemon juice and simmer, uncovered, stirring to loosen the browned-on bits on the bottom of the pan, until the liquid has reduced by half, about 10 minutes.

3. Add the broth, marjoram, and rice and bring to a boil. Return the rabbit to the pan with the olives and anchovies. Lower the heat. Stir with a wooden fork, cover, and simmer for 25 minutes, or until the rabbit and rice are tender. If the liquid cooks off before the rice and rabbit are tender, add small amounts of hot broth or water.

*Serves 6*

## Rabbit and Rice à la Roannaise

*With little fat and much flavor, and mated with rice, rabbit offers a welcome menu change. Rabbits are available frozen in some supermarkets and fresh in some larger cities.*

1 cup long-grain brown rice
3 teaspoons salt (optional)
1 cup water
¾ cup all-purpose flour
½ teaspoon dried rosemary
1 teaspoon freshly ground black pepper
Two 3-pound rabbits, cut into serving pieces
Olive oil
6 medium white onions, chopped
3 garlic cloves, minced
2 cups chicken broth

1. In a saucepan, combine the rice, 1 teaspoon of the salt, and the water. Bring to a boil, stir with a wooden fork, cover, lower the heat, and simmer for 10 minutes. If the water hasn't been absorbed, drain and reserve the rice.

2. In a clean paper or plastic bag, combine the flour, rosemary,

remaining 2 teaspoons of salt, and pepper. Add the rabbit pieces and shake them until they are evenly coated with the seasoned flour. In a frying pan, over medium heat, heat ¼ cup olive oil and evenly brown the rabbit.

3. In a casserole, make a smooth layer of the partially cooked rice. Arrange the rabbit on top of the rice. Preheat the oven to 350 degrees.

4. In the frying pan in which the rabbit cooked, stir in the onions and garlic, adding more oil if necessary. Cook over medium heat until the onions and garlic are soft. Gradually stir in the broth, scraping the botton of the pan to loosen the browned-on bits. Simmer until the onion sauce is smooth and golden. Taste for seasoning, adding salt and pepper if needed.

5. Pour the onion sauce over the rabbit and rice, cover, and bake for 30 minutes, or until the rabbit and rice are tender. If the sauce becomes too thick before the rabbit and rice are tender, add small amounts of hot broth or water. Serve right from the casserole.

*Serves 6*

# Rabbit Stew with Brown Rice

*We had this in Parma with Italian Arborio rice, which is not available many places in the United States, so we've substituted brown rice, because we think it is nuttier and even better and easier to cook.*

4 tablespoons (½ stick) butter or margarine
2 tablespoons olive oil
2 rabbits (each weighing about 3 pounds), cut into serving pieces
Salt and freshly ground black pepper to taste
3 large shallots, chopped
Leaves from 2 celery stalks, chopped
2 garlic cloves, minced
½ teaspoon crushed dried rosemary
1 cup chopped prosciutto or Canadian bacon
1 cup dry red wine

4 medium ripe tomatoes, peeled, seeded, and chopped
3 cups beef broth
1½ cups long-grain brown rice
3 tablespoons chopped broadleaf (Italian) parsley leaves

1. Preheat the oven to 350 degrees.
2. In a large flameproof casserole, heat the butter or margarine and oil over medium heat. Evenly brown the rabbit pieces, a few at a time, seasoning them with salt and pepper. Add more butter or margarine and oil if needed.
3. Add the shallots, celery leaves, garlic, rosemary, prosciutto, and wine. Cook until the wine has mostly evaporated.
4. Stir in the tomatoes, broth, and rice. Bring to a boil, cover, and bake for 40 minutes, or until the rabbit and rice are tender and the liquid has been mostly absorbed. If the liquid has been absorbed before the rice and rabbit are tender, add a small amount of hot broth and continue cooking. Serve right from the casserole with the parsley sprinkled over.

*Serves 6 to 8*

# Rice-Stuffed Turkey Thighs

4 medium-size turkey thighs, boned
2 tablespoons extra-virgin olive oil
4 large shallots, finely chopped
1 celery stalk, scraped and finely chopped
Salt and freshly ground black pepper to taste
3 tablespoons brandy
¼ teaspoon thyme and ¼ teaspoon tarragon, combined
2 cups cooked short- or medium-grain rice
Paprika

1. Enlarge the cavity of the thighs with a knife, being careful not to cut through.
2. In a frying pan, heat the oil over medium heat. Add the shal-

lots and celery to the pan and cook for 5 minutes, or until they are soft. Do not brown. Season with salt and pepper. Remove from the heat and stir in the brandy, thyme and tarragon, and rice, blending well. Preheat the oven to 450 degrees.

3. Stuff each thigh with a quarter of the mixture. Arrange, skin side up, in a shallow baking dish just large enough to hold the stuffed thighs snugly. Brush with the oil and sprinkle lightly with salt, pepper, and paprika. Bake for 7 minutes. Lower the oven temperature to 350 degrees and bake for 35 minutes, or until fork-tender.

*Serves 4*

# Brown Rice with Turkey Giblets

*We had this dish for lunch one day in Louisiana, and found it so surprisingly tasty that we often prepare it. There is no problem with what to do with versatile turkey or chicken livers, but most of us are baffled when it comes to gizzards and hearts. Here's one answer.*

4 tablespoons (½ stick) butter or margarine
3 medium onions, chopped
1 pound turkey (or chicken) hearts and gizzards, trimmed and diced
Salt and freshly ground black pepper to taste
¼ teaspoon ground nutmeg
1 cup long-grain brown rice
3 cups chicken broth
Bouquet garni made of 1 bay leaf, 3 sprigs fresh parsley, and 3 sprigs celery leaves tied in cheesecloth
¼ teaspoon dried thyme
3 tablespoons chopped fresh parsley leaves

1. Preheat the oven to 350 degrees.
2. In a deep flameproof casserole, over medium heat, melt the butter or margarine. Add the onions and giblets and cook for 10

minutes, seasoning with salt, pepper, and nutmeg. Stir in the rice, coating it well.

3. Pour in the broth and add the bouquet garni and thyme. Bring to a boil, cover, and bake for 45 minutes, or until the liquid has been absorbed and the giblets and rice are tender. Discard the bouquet garni. Sprinkle with the parsley before serving.

*Serves 4*

## Turkey and Rice Suprême with Italian Green Beans

3 tablespoons butter or margarine
2 medium onions, chopped
½ pound small fresh mushrooms, halved, or, if larger, quartered
Salt and freshly ground black pepper to taste
1 cup long-grain rice
1 tablespoon curry powder, or to taste (page 79)
1½ cups chicken broth
2 cups bite-size pieces cooked turkey
1 cup diced cooked ham
¼ cup chopped fresh parsley leaves
One 10-ounce package frozen Italian green beans, cooked half of
   the time indicated on the package and well drained
6 tablespoons dry sherry
1 cup half-and-half

1. In a saucepan, over medium heat, melt the butter or margarine and cook the onions for 5 minutes, or until they are soft. Do not brown. Add the mushrooms and cook for 2 minutes. Season with salt and pepper.

2. Stir in the rice and curry powder and cook for 2 minutes. Pour in the broth and bring to a boil. Stir with a wooden fork, cover, lower the heat, and simmer for 10 minutes.

3. Stir in the turkey, ham, and parsley. Taste for seasoning, adding salt and pepper if needed. Preheat the oven to 350 degrees.

4. Spoon half of the rice mixture into a casserole in an even layer. Arrange the beans over it in an even layer. Then spoon on the remaining rice mixture. Combine the sherry and half-and-half and pour the mixture over the rice. Bake for 30 minutes, or until the rice is tender and the liquid has been mostly absorbed.

*Serves 4 to 6*

# Venison and Wild Pecan Rice Bourguignonne

*Two items make this an unusual dish to offer guests: the venison—and the Wild Pecan Rice. We have special words on this rice in the Pheasant with Wild Pecan Rice recipe on page 105.*

   2 tablespoons extra-virgin olive oil
   8 medium fresh mushrooms, sliced medium thick
   2 pounds boneless venison steak, cut into 2-inch cubes
   2 tablespoons all-purpose flour, blended with 1 teaspoon dry
      mustard
   1 tablespoon sugar
   1½ teaspoons salt (optional)
   ¼ teaspoon dried thyme
   1 bay leaf
   4 whole black peppercorns, crushed
   ¾ cup beef broth
   1½ cups dry red wine
   12 small white onions, root ends scored
   One 7-ounce package Wild Pecan Rice or long-grain rice
   2 cups water

   1. In a large heavy pot, heat the oil over medium heat. Cook the mushrooms in the oil for 2 minutes. Remove with a slotted spoon and reserve.
   2. Add the venison cubes to the pot and brown evenly over medium heat. Add the flour and mustard mixture. Stir in the sugar, ½ teaspoon of the salt, thyme, bay leaf, and the peppercorns. Pour

in the beef broth and wine. Stir, cover, and simmer for 1 hour, stirring frequently.

3. Stir in the onions and simmer for 30 minutes, or until the venison and onions are tender. Add the mushrooms. Remove and discard the bay leaf. Taste for seasoning, adding salt and pepper if needed.

4. While the venison is cooking, combine the rice, remaining 1 teaspoon of salt, and water in a saucepan. Stir well with a wooden fork. Bring to a boil, stir with a wooden fork, lower the heat, cover, and simmer for 20 minutes, or until the water has been absorbed and the rice is tender.

5. Spread the hot rice onto warm individual plates and serve topped with the venison stew. Save some red wine to sip with this special dish.

*Serves 4*

# 6
# Rice with Meat and Variety Meats

It's a thousand-year-old story. The Chinese drop a few pieces of pork into a huge bowl of rice and feed a family a "meat meal."

We didn't have to travel to China to witness that magic act. We saw it in Lake Charles, Louisiana, where Jack was interviewing Paul Faulk, a noted duck-and-goose-calling champion, for a column he was writing.

It was bayou country, and for lunch we motorboated out to the goose caller's mother's home in the marshlands. Her house was so close to the water that it looked like an odd boat moored among the bulrushes. This is fish and shellfish country, so we expected a gumbo or jambalaya, but were pleasantly surprised.

We sat down to that region's famous dish of black beans and rice, but just before we dipped our forks into it, that lady dolloped atop it a few slices of a remarkable spicy sausage that she had left over from a batch she had made.

This was yet another example of the fact that the mating of any kind of meat with rice is one of the most graceful in the food world.

# Munich Meat-Pot

1½ pounds beef round steak, thinly sliced
All-purpose flour for dredging
2 tablespoons butter or margarine
2 tablespoons olive oil
Salt and freshly ground black pepper to taste
3 medium onions, sliced
12 ounces dark ale
1 cup beef broth
¼ teaspoon cayenne
1 tablespoon dark or light brown sugar
3 small turnips, scraped and cut into ¼-inch-thick slices
3 cups al dente–cooked long-grain rice

1. With a meat mallet, pound the steak to tenderize it (or have your butcher do it). Cut it into 1-inch-wide strips.

2. Lightly dredge the strips of meat in the flour, shaking off any excess.

3. In a large heavy frying pan, over medium-high heat, heat the butter or margarine and oil. Evenly brown the beef, seasoning it with salt and pepper. Lower the heat, add the onions, and cook for 4 minutes.

4. Add the ale, broth, cayenne, and brown sugar. Stir well. Bring to a boil, cover, lower the heat, and simmer for 15 minutes. Add the turnips and cook for 15 minutes, or until the beef and turnips are just tender and the sauce has thickened.

5. Stir in the rice and cook for 5 minutes to heat through. Taste for seasoning, adding salt and pepper if needed.

*Serves 6*

# Burgundian Beef and Rice

½ pound lean salt pork, blanched in boiling water for 10 minutes, dried, and cut into ½-inch cubes
2 tablespoons olive oil
3 pounds lean beef (chuck or top or botton round), cut into 1½-inch cubes
Salt and freshly ground black pepper to taste
24 tiny white onions, root ends scored
1 garlic clove, minced
1 cup white Burgundy wine
3 tablespoons brandy
Approximately 3 cups beef broth
Bouquet garni made of 2 sprigs parsley, several celery leaves, ¼ teaspoon dried thyme, and 1 bay leaf tied in cheesecloth
2 tablespoons tomato paste
2 tablespoons butter or margarine
1 cup long-grain rice

1. In a frying pan, over medium heat, cook the salt pork cubes in the olive oil until they are golden brown and crisp. With a slotted spoon transfer them to a flameproof casserole.

2. Add the beef to the frying pan (do not crowd it) and brown it evenly, sprinkling it lightly with salt and pepper. As the beef browns, transfer it to the casserole. Add the onions and garlic to the frying pan and cook until they are slightly golden. Do not brown. With a slotted spoon transfer them to the casserole. Preheat the oven to 350 degrees.

3. Pour off any fat remaining in the pan. Pour in the wine and brandy and heat, stirring, to scrape up the browned-on bits in the bottom of the pan. Pour into the casserole. Pour enough broth into the casserole to just cover the meat. Add the bouquet garni and tomato paste. Bring to a boil on top of the stove, cover, and bake for 1½ hours, or until the beef is almost tender. If the liquid in the casserole has cooked off, add more hot broth or water, in order to have 2½ cups of liquid.

4. In the frying pan in which the beef was browned, melt the butter or margarine. Add the rice and cook, stirring, until the rice is well coated. Remove the casserole from the oven, stir in the rice, return to the oven, and bake, covered, until the beef and rice are

tender and most of the liquid has been absorbed, about 25 minutes. Taste for seasoning, adding salt and pepper if needed. Discard the bouquet garni before serving.

*Serves 6*

# Stufato

### *Rice and Beef Casserole*

3 tablespoons olive oil
2 pounds lean beef chuck, cut into ½-inch cubes
Salt and freshly ground black pepper to taste
2 medium onions, chopped
1 garlic clove, minced
½ cup chopped prosciutto or other ham
3 large ripe tomatoes, peeled, seeded, and chopped, or one
    1-pound can tomatoes, drained and chopped
½ cup dry red wine
Approximately 1½ to 2 cups beef broth
3 cups al dente–cooked long-grain rice
1 cup grated Asiago or Parmesan cheese

1. Preheat the oven to 350 degrees.
2. In a flameproof casserole, heat the olive oil over medium heat and lightly brown the beef cubes, adding more oil if needed. Season lightly with salt and pepper.
3. Add the onions, garlic, and prosciutto and cook for 5 minutes, stirring occasionally. Add the tomatoes and wine and cook, uncovered, for 10 minutes. Pour in enough of the beef broth to just cover the meat. Bring to a boil, cover, and bake for 45 minutes, or until the beef is almost tender. Taste for seasoning, adding salt and pepper if needed. Lower the oven temperature to 325 degrees.
4. Using a slotted spoon, remove the beef from the casserole and arrange half of it in a deep baking dish. Smooth a layer of half of the rice over the beef and sprinkle with half of the cheese. Repeat,

using the remaining beef and rice. Spoon the sauce in the casserole over the top layer of rice; then sprinkle with the remaining cheese.

5. Bake, uncovered, for 30 minutes, or until the beef is tender and the liquid has been mostly absorbed.

*Serves 4 to 6*

# Baked Beef and Rice

3 tablespoons butter or margarine
1 tablespoon olive oil
1 large onion, finely chopped
2 celery stalks, scraped and finely chopped
1½ pounds lean ground beef (chuck, top, or bottom round)
2 tablespoons honey
1½ teaspoons salt (optional)
½ teaspoon freshly ground black pepper
1 teaspoon chili powder
1½ cups long-grain rice, cooked in water for 10 minutes and drained
One 1-pound can tomatoes with their liquid (Break the tomatoes up with your hands.)
1 cup beef broth, heated

1. Preheat the oven to 350 degrees.

2. Over medium heat, in a large frying pan, heat the butter or margarine and oil. Add the onion, celery, and beef and cook until the beef has lost its pink color. Stir in the honey, salt, pepper, chili powder, rice, tomatoes with their liquid, and the beef broth. Taste for seasoning, adding salt and pepper if needed.

3. Transfer to a baking dish and bake for 45 minutes, or until the rice is tender and most of the liquid has been absorbed.

*Serves 6*

# San Antonio Rice Hash

3 tablespoons butter or margarine
2 tablespoons olive oil
6 medium onions, chopped
2 green bell peppers, seeds and ribs removed, chopped
2 pounds chopped beef chuck
One 1-pound 12-ounce can tomatoes, chopped, with their liquid
1 cup long-grain brown rice
1 tablespoon chili powder
1 tablespoon salt (optional)
Beef broth (optional)

1. Preheat the oven to 350 degrees.
2. In a flameproof casserole, over medium heat, heat the butter or margarine and oil. Add the onions and green peppers, and cook for 10 minutes, or until they are soft. Do not brown.
3. Add all remaining ingredients, except the broth, and blend well.
4. Bake, covered, for 40 minutes, or until the rice is tender and most of the liquid has been absorbed. If the rice is almost tender and there is excess liquid, remove the top and continue cooking. If the rice is not yet tender enough and the liquid has been absorbed, add a small amount of hot beef broth and continue cooking. Taste for seasoning, adding salt and pepper if needed.

*Serves 6*

# Cocido with Wild Pecan Rice

*In our kitchen hang several unusual hand-carved wooden spoons that we collected from Spanish field hands and farmers. They range from an ornately carved one, which is twice as broad as an open hand, to a delicately scrolled one the size of a serving spoon. The large one is used to dip into the boiled dinner that we detail here, and serve as the bowl for the small spoon. This system is used when Spaniards eat from the* cocido *pot while working in the field. An older woman usually tends it, keeping the lunch warm by burning straw under the blackened pot. The wooden spoons are handmade. Intricate designs and secret symbols are carved on them by the peasants. The spoons are highly prized by them—and by us. So is their boiled dinner.*

2 pounds beef bones
3 pounds beef brisket
6 quarts water
1 tablespoon salt (optional)
1 teaspoon freshly ground black pepper
3 whole onions, each nailed with 2 cloves
1½ pounds lean smoked ham
8 to 10 *chorizos* (Spanish sausages) or any highly seasoned
    smoked pork sausage
3 pounds chicken, cut into 8 to 10 serving pieces
4 or 5 leeks (white part and some of the light green part), washed
    well under cool running water and cut into halves lengthwise
8 to 10 small carrots, scraped
2 garlic cloves, peeled
1 medium cabbage, trimmed and cut into 8 to 10 wedges
8 to 10 small potatoes
One 16-ounce can chick-peas, drained
1½ cups hot cooked Wild Pecan Rice
4 tablespoons chopped fresh parsley leaves

1. Put the beef bones, beef brisket, water, salt, pepper, and onions into a very large deep pot. Bring to a boil, lower the heat, and simmer, partially covered, for 1 hour, skimming any scum from the top.

2. Add the ham and sausages. Simmer for 30 minutes. Add the chicken and simmer for 30 minutes.

3. Add the leeks, carrots, garlic, cabbage, and potatoes. Simmer, partially covered, for 30 minutes, or until the meats and vegetables are fork tender. If the chicken and vegetables are tender before the meats are, remove them and return them to the pot just before serving. Stir in the chick-peas and simmer for 10 minutes. Remove and discard the onions and bones. Taste for seasoning, adding salt and pepper if needed.

4. Do not spoon out of the pot as the field hands do. But serve

just the broth in individual bowls with the Wild Pecan Rice stirred in, sprinkled with parsley.

5. After the exceptional rice soup, present the meats (sliced), whole sausages, and chicken on a large hot serving dish, surrounded by the vegetables.

*Serves 8 to 10*

# Blanquette de Veau in a Rice Ring

*See page 57 for a note on preparing rice rings.*

*Here's a saucy classic French country dish that demands a rice ring. Prepare the rice ring while the veal simmers in its pot, in the second stage of preparation. Remember to use short- or medium-grain rice for the ring. The French usually use the breast of veal cut into 1-inch pieces with bone for this dish, but we prefer the shoulder.*

*We surround the ring with a green vegetable, often Brussels sprouts.*

3 pounds boneless veal shoulder, cut into pieces 1 inch square
    and ½ inch thick
4 medium white onions, each nailed with a whole clove
3 celery stalks with leaves, scraped and cut into ¼-inch slices
2 medium carrots, scraped and cut into ¼-inch pieces
1 bay leaf
½ teaspoon dried thyme
1 teaspoon salt (optional)
5 cups chicken broth, or enough to completely cover the veal
18 small white onions, root ends scored
24 small firm fresh mushrooms, halved
3 tablespoons butter or margarine
3 tablespoons all-purpose flour
Salt and freshly ground black pepper to taste
3 egg yolks
½ cup half-and-half
Juice of ½ lemon
Rice ring (see recipes on pages 158 and 160)

1. In a deep heavy pot, blanch the veal in boiling water for 10 minutes. Drain the veal and rinse it with warm water. Return the veal to the pot and add the onions with the cloves, celery, carrots, bay leaf, thyme, salt, and broth. Cover, bring to a boil, lower the heat, and simmer for 1¼ hours, or until the veal is fork tender. (This is the time when the rice ring can be prepared.)

2. Remove the veal with a slotted spoon and transfer it to a bowl. Strain the broth, discarding the bay leaf, and return it to the pot. Simmer the onions in the broth for 8 minutes, or until they are tender but still intact. With a slotted spoon, transfer the onions to the bowl with the veal. Cook the mushrooms in the broth for 2 minutes. With a slotted spoon transfer them to the bowl with the veal.

3. Raise the heat under the pot of broth and reduce the liquid to about 2½ cups. In a large saucepan, over medium heat, melt the butter or margarine. Add the flour and cook, stirring into a smooth paste. Gradually add the hot broth, stirring into a medium-thick, smooth sauce. Season with salt and pepper.

4. Add the veal, onions, and mushrooms to the sauce and place over low heat to warm through.

5. In a bowl, beat the egg yolks with the half-and-half and lemon juice. Just before spooning the blanquette into the rice ring, stir in the egg yolk–half-and-half–lemon juice mixture. Cook over low heat, stirring, until thickened. Do not boil or the eggs will curdle.

6. Ladle the blanquette into the rice ring. If the ring cannot accommodate the entire blanquette, serve the remainder in a bowl.

*Serves 6*

# Risotto Milanese with Osso Buco

*Osso Buco*

Six 3-inch-thick meaty pieces veal shanks, cut from the center,
  with marrow
All-purpose flour for dredging
2 tablespoons butter or margarine
3 tablespoons olive oil
Salt and freshly ground black pepper to taste
⅛ teaspoon crushed dried rosemary
2 medium onions, finely chopped
1 garlic clove, minced
1 large ripe tomato, peeled, seeded, and finely chopped
1 large carrot, scraped and cut into ¼-inch dice
1 large celery stalk, scraped and cut into ¼-inch dice
1½ cups dry white wine
1 cup chicken broth
Gremolata (page 129)

*Risotto Milanese*

8 tablespoons (1 stick) butter or margarine
1 medium onion, finely chopped
1 garlic clove, minced
2 cups long-grain rice
4½ cups chicken broth
½ cup dry white wine
¼ teaspoon powdered saffron, dissolved in 1 or 2 tablespoons
  chicken broth
1 cup grated Asiago or Parmesan cheese
¼ cup finely chopped broadleaf (Italian) parsley leaves
Salt and freshly ground black pepper to taste

1. To prepare the osso buco, dredge the shanks lightly in the flour. In a flameproof casserole just large enough to hold the shanks snugly in a standing position, heat the butter or margarine and oil over medium heat, and brown the shanks evenly, sprinkling them with salt and pepper. Add more oil if needed. Preheat the oven to 325 degrees.

2. Stand the shanks upright in the pot so the bone and marrow are showing; this will prevent the marrow from falling out. Sprinkle the rosemary and vegetables around them and pour the wine

and broth over all. Bring to a boil on top of the stove; cover and bake for 1½ hours, or until the veal is very tender.

3. To prepare the risotto Milanese, melt 4 tablespoons of the butter or margarine in a saucepan over medium heat. Add the onion and garlic and cook for 5 minutes, or until they are soft. Do not brown. Add the rice and cook for 2 minutes, stirring. Pour in the broth, wine, and saffron. Bring to a boil, stir with a wooden fork, cover, lower the heat, and simmer for 20 minutes, or until the rice is tender and almost all of the liquid has been absorbed. If the liquid has been absorbed before the rice is cooked, add a small amount of hot broth and continue cooking. If the rice is cooked and there is excessive liquid in the pan, raise heat, remove the cover, and cook off most of the liquid. The rice should be slightly al dente and moist.

4. With a metal fork, stir in the cheese, the remaining butter or margarine (in small pieces), and the parsley, fluffing up the rice. Taste for seasoning and add salt and pepper if needed. The broth may have supplied enough.

5. Serve the rice on a large hot serving dish with the shanks arranged on the rice and the Gremolata sprinkled on the shanks.

*Note:* Put small spoons or forks at each place so the marrow can be removed from the shanks and eaten. Shops do sell marrow spoons.

*Serves 6*

## Gremolata

In a small bowl, using a fork, mix 1 minced garlic clove with 3 tablespoons finely chopped broadleaf (Italian) parsley leaves and the grated rind of 1 lemon.

# Escalopes de Veau à l'Estragon

5 tablespoons butter or margarine
2 tablespoons olive oil
2 medium onions, chopped
2 pounds veal, cut into 2-inch squares, ½ inch thick, beaten
    between sheets of wax paper with a mallet to a ¼-inch thickness
Salt and freshly ground black pepper to taste
A whole onion, nailed with 3 whole cloves
1½ cups long-grain rice
3 to 4 cups chicken broth
3 tablespoons chopped fresh tarragon, or 3 teaspoons dried
    tarragon
4 tablespoons chopped fresh parsley leaves

1. Over medium heat, in a flameproof casserole, heat 2 table-spoons of the butter or margarine and 1 tablespoon of the oil. Add the chopped onions and cook for 5 minutes, or until they are soft. Do not brown.

2. Add the remaining butter or margarine and oil and heat. Add the veal and brown evenly, adding more butter or margarine and oil if needed. Season with salt and pepper. Add the whole onion with the cloves, cover, and cook for 20 minutes, turning the veal after 10 minutes. If the bottom of the pot starts getting too brown add a small amount of broth. Remove and discard the whole onion. Preheat the oven to 375 degrees.

3. Mix in the rice. Pour in enough broth to cover (about 3 cups). Add 1 tablespoon of fresh tarragon (or 1 teaspoon of dried). Bring to a boil on top of the stove; then bake, covered, for 25 minutes, or until the rice and veal are tender and most of the liquid has been absorbed. However, the dish should be slightly moist. If the liquid is absorbed before the rice and veal are tender, add a small amount of hot broth and continue to cook. Taste for seasoning, adding salt and pepper if needed. Stir in the parsley and remaining tarragon and serve right from the casserole.

*Serves 6*

# Lamb and Rice Stew

6 tablespoons butter or margarine
3 tablespoons olive oil
3 pounds lean lamb from the leg, cut into 1-inch cubes
Salt and freshly ground black pepper to taste
4 large leeks (including some of the light green part), well
    washed and cut into ½-inch pieces
½ cup tomato purée
½ cup dry vermouth
3 cups beef broth
½ teaspoon dried oregano
¼ teaspoon ground cinnamon
1½ cups long-grain rice
1 garlic clove, minced

1. Over medium heat, in a frying pan, heat 3 tablespoons of the butter or margarine and 2 tablespoons of the olive oil. Brown the lamb evenly, seasoning it lightly with salt and pepper; transfer the lamb to a flameproof casserole.

2. Heat 1 tablespoon of the butter or margarine and the remaining oil in the frying pan. Add the leeks and cook for 5 minutes. Combine the tomato purée and vermouth and pour the mixture into the pan. Simmer for 1 minute, stirring and scraping up the browned-on bits in the pan. Pour the leeks and liquid into the casserole. Add the broth, oregano, and cinnamon and bring to a boil. Lower the heat, cover and simmer for 30 minutes.

3. Melt the remaining butter or margarine in the frying pan and add the rice and garlic. Cook for 2 minutes, stirring. Transfer the rice to the casserole with the lamb. Cover and cook for 25 minutes, or until the rice and lamb are tender and most of the liquid has been absorbed. If the liquid is absorbed before the rice and lamb are tender, add a small amount of hot broth and continue cooking. If they are cooked and there seems to be too much liquid, remove the cover, raise the heat, and cook off the excess, being careful not to burn the rice.

*Serves 6*

# Brodetto

### *Italian Lamb and Rice Casserole*

1 cup dry white wine
3 cups water
1½ teaspoons salt (optional)
¾ teaspoon freshly ground black pepper
5 tablespoons chopped broadleaf (Italian) parsley leaves
6 ripe plum tomatoes, peeled, seeded, and chopped, or one
    1-pound can imported Italian plum tomatoes, drained
    and chopped
2 medium onions, chopped
1 bay leaf
½ teaspoon dried oregano
¼ teaspoon dried rosemary
2 pounds boneless lamb, cut into large bite-size pieces
1 cup long-grain brown rice
4 large eggs
½ cup grated Asiago or Parmesan cheese
1 pound fresh peas, shelled (about 1 cup), cooked in water to
    cover until just tender, almost al dente, or the same amount of
    frozen peas, defrosted

1. Preheat the oven to 350 degrees.

2. In a flameproof casserole, combine the wine, water, 1 teaspoon salt, ½ teaspoon pepper, 3 tablespoons of the parsley, tomatoes, onion, bay leaf, oregano, rosemary, and lamb. Bring to a boil on top of the stove, cover, and bake in the oven for 45 minutes. Stir in the rice, cover, and bake for 35 minutes, or until the lamb and rice are almost tender. The rice should be al dente, as the lamb and rice will cook further. Check the dish as it cooks. If it seems dry, add more hot water. It should be moist but not soupy. Remove and discard the bay leaf.

3. Beat together the eggs, remaining parsley, cheese, ½ teaspoon salt, and ¼ teaspoon pepper.

4. Stir the peas into the egg-cheese mixture. Pour this over the rice and lamb and bake, uncovered, for about 25 minutes, or until the eggs are set and the lamb and rice are tender.

*Serves 4 to 6*

# Stuffed Leg of Lamb

4 tablespoons (½ stick) butter or margarine
4 lamb kidneys (or chicken livers), trimmed and coarsely
   chopped
2 tablespoons brandy
1 garlic clove, minced
2 medium onions, finely chopped
¾ cup long-grain rice
¼ cup of pignoli or broken-up walnuts
¼ cup currants
3 tablespoons finely chopped fennel leaves
½ teaspoon ground allspice
¼ teaspoon ground cinnamon
1½ cups beef broth
Salt and freshly ground black pepper to taste
5- to 6-pound leg of lamb, boned
1 medium carrot, scraped and chopped
¼ teaspoon cayenne
1 teaspoon dried rosemary
½ cup water

1. In a frying pan, over medium-high heat, melt 2 tablespoons of the butter or margarine and cook the kidneys until they are brown on the outside but still very pink inside. Stir in the brandy and quickly cook it off. Transfer the kidneys to a bowl.

2. In a saucepan, heat the remaining butter or margarine over medium heat. Cook the garlic and half of the onions for 5 minutes, or until they are soft. Do not brown. Add the rice, nuts, currants, fennel, allspice, and cinnamon and cook, stirring, for 1 minute. Pour in the broth. Bring to a boil, lower the heat, stir with a wooden fork, cover, and simmer for 15 minutes, or until the liquid has been absorbed. The rice should still be quite al dente. If necessary, drain before it becomes too soft. Taste for seasoning, and add salt and pepper if needed. The broth may have supplied enough. Combine the rice mixture with the kidneys and mix well.

3. Flatten the leg of lamb, skin side down, with a meat mallet or the broad side of a knife blade. Sprinkle with salt and pepper. Spread the kidney-rice stuffing over the meat, not quite to the edge. Roll and tie to keep the stuffing intact.

4. Preheat the oven to 400 degrees.

5. Sprinkle the carrot, remaining onion, cayenne, and rosemary on the bottom of a roasting pan or casserole just large enough to hold the lamb snugly. Set lamb on top and sprinkle lightly with salt and pepper. Pour in ½ cup of water. Bake, uncovered, for 1½ hours, or until fork tender. If necessary, add more water to the pan as the lamb cooks.

*Note:* To test lamb for degree of doneness, insert a narrow-bladed knife deeply into the lamb. If the juice runs pink, it is medium-rare; if the juice runs yellow, it is well-done.

*Serves 6*

# Lamb Meatball Pulao

*While in the planning stages of an involved trip to India, where we would stay for several months in various cities and the jungles, Leela Nadhan, from the Government of India Tourist Office, visited our home in Washington, Connecticut. This is one dish she prepared, using the ingredients we had at hand. She was accustomed to first soaking and then washing the rice, but we pointed out that this wasn't necessary with American rice, that the method, in fact, washed away the important nutrients.*

2½ cups chicken broth
1 cup long-grain rice
½ pound ground lean lamb
⅛ teaspoon hot red pepper flakes
1½ teaspoons salt (optional)
⅛ teaspoon ground nutmeg
½ teaspoon ground cumin
½ teaspoon ground coriander
1 egg, beaten
10 tablespoons (1¼ sticks) butter or margarine
1 tablespoon olive oil
2 medium onions, chopped
½ teaspoon ground cinnamon

1 teaspoon light brown sugar
½ teaspoon ground turmeric
½ teaspoon chili powder
1 small red bell pepper, cored, seeded, and chopped
1 large onion, thinly sliced

1. In a saucepan, bring the chicken broth to a boil. Stir in the rice, cover, lower the heat, and simmer for 20 minutes, or until the rice is tender and the liquid has been absorbed. Reserve.

2. In a large bowl, combine and blend well (hands are good for this) the lamb, hot red pepper flakes, 1 teaspoon of the salt, nutmeg, cumin, coriander, and the egg. Form into very small meatballs (about ½ inch in diameter). In a large frying pan, over medium heat, heat 2 tablespoons of the butter or margarine and the olive oil. Brown the meatballs evenly; then remove and reserve them.

3. In the same frying pan, over medium heat, add 2 tablespoons of butter or margarine and cook the chopped onions with the cinnamon for 3 minutes. Add the brown sugar and cook, stirring, for 1 minute. Do not burn. Stir in the turmeric, chili powder, ½ teaspoon of salt, and the chopped red pepper, and cook for 5 minutes. Do not burn. With a metal fork, stir in the rice, fluffing it up and blending well. Preheat the oven to 350 degrees.

4. In a casserole, arrange half of the rice mixture in a smooth layer. Do not pack down. Arrange the meatballs on the rice in a layer, using all of them. Then arrange the remaining half of the rice on the meatballs in a smooth layer. Do not pack down. Dot with 2 tablespoons of the butter or margarine and bake for 15 minutes.

5. Meanwhile, in a frying pan, over medium heat, melt the remaining butter or margarine (at least 4 tablespoons) and cook the sliced onion until it is crisp, about 6 minutes. Do not let it burn. Drain on paper towels. Garnish the rice casserole with the crisp onion slices.

*Serves 4*

# Greek Meatballs with Piquant Sauce

3 slices white bread, with crusts trimmed, soaked in milk
1 pound ground lean lamb
½ cup short- or medium-grain rice
1 egg, beaten
1 medium onion, finely chopped
1 garlic clove, minced
¼ cup minced fresh parsley leaves
5 fresh mint leaves, minced
½ teaspoon ground cumin
Salt and freshly ground black pepper to taste
All-purpose flour for dredging
4 cups beef broth
Piquant Sauce (see below)

1. Squeeze the milk from the bread and break up the bread. In a large bowl, combine the bread with all of the remaining ingredients, except the flour, beef broth, and Piquant Sauce. Mix well with a large fork or your hands. Shape into 1-inch-diameter balls or into 1-by-1½-inch cylinders. Dredge lightly in the flour.

2. In a large deep frying pan, heat the broth to a simmer. With a slotted spoon, lower the balls into the liquid, cover, and simmer for 45 minutes, turn when half of the time has elapsed. Don't crowd. Cook in two pans if necessary.

3. Remove the meatballs from the cooking liquid with a slotted spoon and transfer them to a serving dish. Serve with the Piquant Sauce spooned over them.

*Serves 4*

## Piquant Sauce

2 tablespoons butter or margarine
2 tablespoons minced shallots or onion
2 tablespoons all-purpose flour
1 cup beef broth, heated
2 tablespoons white vinegar

½ cup bottled chili sauce
1 small sour pickle, minced
Salt and freshly ground black pepper to taste

In a saucepan, over medium heat, melt the butter or margarine. Add the shallots and cook until they are soft and slightly golden. Stir in the flour, blending well. Gradually stir in the broth, simmering and stirring until the sauce is smooth and thickened. Stir in the vinegar, chili sauce, and pickle. Taste and season with salt and pepper if necessary.

*Makes about 1½ cups*


## Middle Eastern Lamb and Rice with Apricots

*The Arab countries like to pair lamb with apricots, and, of course, rice. Few dishes are served without it. They have complicated ways of cooking rice, washing, then soaking, and cooking with a cloth under the cover of the pot, but we're staying with the American method, as it is easy, surefire, and equally delicious.*

6 tablespoons butter or margarine
1½ cups long-grain rice
2½ cups water
1 teaspoon salt (optional)
1½ pounds boneless lamb (from the leg), cut into 1½-inch cubes
2 garlic cloves, minced
Salt and freshly ground black pepper to taste
¼ teaspoon ground nutmeg
1 teaspoon ground cumin
1 cup dried apricots, cut into halves
2 tablespoons currants

1. In a saucepan, over medium heat, melt 2 tablespoons of the butter or margarine. Stir in the rice and cook for 2 minutes. Add the 2½ cups of water and the teaspoon of salt. Bring to a boil, lower

the heat, stir with a wooden fork, cover, and simmer for 15 minutes, or until the rice is tender, but still somewhat al dente, and most of the liquid has been absorbed.

2. In a large heavy frying pan, over medium heat, melt the remaining butter or margarine and brown the lamb evenly. Add more butter if needed. Add the garlic and season with salt, pepper, nutmeg, and cumin. Cook for 5 minutes. Then just barely cover with water and simmer, covered, for 20 minutes. Add the apricots and currants and cook, covered, for 20 minutes, or until the lamb is just tender. Taste for seasoning, adding salt and pepper if needed.

3. Preheat the oven to 350 degrees.

4. In a casserole, arrange alternating layers of rice, with any of the liquid it cooked in, and the lamb mixture, with its sauce, ending with a layer of rice. Cover and bake for 15 minutes, or until bubbling and thoroughly heated. Serve from the casserole.

*Serves 6*

# Baked Shoulder Lamb Chops and Brown Rice

4 lean ¾-inch-thick shoulder lamb chops, trimmed
All-purpose flour for dredging
2 tablespoons olive oil
4 tablespoons (½ stick) butter or margarine
2 medium onions, chopped
1 garlic clove, minced
6 tablespoons Madeira
3 cups beef broth
2 sprigs fresh parsley
¾ cup long-grain brown rice
Salt and freshly ground black pepper to taste

1. Preheat the oven to 325 degrees.

2. Dredge the lamb chops with flour, shaking off any excess. Over medium heat, in a flameproof casserole just large enough to hold the chops snugly in a single layer, heat the oil and 2 tablespoons of the butter or margarine. Brown the chops on both sides. Remove

from the pan. Add the onions and garlic and cook for 5 minutes, or until they are soft. Do not brown. Stir in the Madeira and cook for a minute or two, stirring up the browned-on bits in the bottom of the pan. Pour in the broth. Return the chops to the pan and add the parsley sprigs. Bring to a boil, cover, and bake for 1 hour.

3. In a saucepan, melt the remaining butter or margarine. Add the rice and cook, stirring, for 2 minutes. Add to the casserole. Cover and cook for 40 minutes, or until the lamb and rice are tender. If the liquid evaporates before they are done, add more hot beef broth and continue cooking. The dish should not be too dry. Taste for seasoning, adding salt and pepper if needed. Remove and discard the parsley before serving.

*Serves 4*

# Arnaki Rizi

### *Greek Lamb with Rice*

5- to 6-pound leg of lamb, wiped dry with a paper towel
3 garlic cloves, cut into halves lengthwise
Juice of 1 lemon, blended with ¼ cup of olive oil
1 teaspoon dried oregano
1 teaspoon dried mint
Salt and freshly ground black pepper to taste
2 medium onions, coarsely chopped
2 cups beef broth
¼ cup dry white wine
1½ cups long-grain rice
3½ cups water
½ teaspoon salt (optional)
1 cup tomato juice

1. Preheat the oven to 450 degrees.
2. Make 6 incisions in the lamb and insert a piece of garlic in each. Rub the lamb with the lemon juice–oil mixture. Place in a roasting pan or flameproof casserole just large enough to hold it snugly. Sprinkle with the oregano, mint, salt, and pepper. Sprinkle

the onions around the lamb and pour in ½ cup of the broth and the wine. Roast, uncovered, for 20 minutes, basting every 5 minutes. Lower the oven temperature to 350 degrees and cook for 40 to 60 minutes, depending on how rare or well done you like lamb. It will cook more later.

3. While the lamb is roasting, cook the rice in the 3½ cups of water with the ½ teaspoon of salt, simmering for 8 minutes. Drain well.

4. Remove the roasting pan from the oven and quickly (to prevent spattering) pour in the tomato juice and the remaining broth. Bring to a boil on top of the stove, stir in the rice, return to the oven, and bake for 15 minutes, or until the rice is tender and most of the liquid has been absorbed. If the liquid cooks off before the rice is tender, add a small amount of hot broth and continue to bake. Serve the lamb sliced over the rice.

*Note:* To test the lamb for degree of doneness, insert a narrow-bladed knife deeply into the lamb. If the juice runs pink, it is medium-rare; if the juice runs yellow, it is well-done.

*Serves 6*

# Pork and Chicken Andaluz

1 cup dry red wine
2 tablespoons red wine vinegar
1 medium onion, finely chopped
1 garlic clove, minced
1 teaspoon salt (optional)
½ teaspoon freshly ground black pepper
2 teaspoons ground cumin
1 bay leaf
1 pound lean pork, cut into strips ½ by ½ by 1½ inches
6 chicken thighs
One 1-pound can plum tomatoes, chopped, with their liquid
12 pimiento-stuffed olives, quartered
1 cup long-grain rice
Salt and freshly ground black pepper to taste
3 tablespoons chopped fresh parsley leaves

1. In a large bowl, combine and blend well the wine, vinegar, onion, garlic, salt, pepper, cumin, and bay leaf. Add the pork and chicken, stir, or mix with your hands to coat all well. Cover and marinate at room temperature for 1 to 2 hours, turning once or twice.

2. Preheat the oven to 350 degrees.

3. Transfer the meat with its marinade to a flameproof casserole. Mix in the tomatoes, olives, and rice. Bring to a boil on top of the stove. Cover and bake for 1 hour, or until the chicken, pork, and rice are tender and the rice has absorbed most of the liquid. If the liquid is absorbed before the meats and rice are tender, add a small amount of hot water and continue cooking. Taste for seasoning, adding salt and pepper if needed. Sprinkle with parsley and serve from the casserole.

*Serves 6*

## Pork Chops and Brown Rice Luau

*This has the Polynesian touch of coupling pork with pineapple.*

6 slices canned pineapple, liquid reserved
12 whole cloves
4 tablespoons (½ stick) or more butter or margarine
1 tablespoon olive oil
6 loin pork chops, ½ inch thick, trimmed
Salt and freshly ground black pepper to taste
½ cup diced green bell peppers
1 large onion, finely chopped
2 celery stalks, scraped and finely chopped
1 cup long-grain brown rice
2½ cups chicken broth
1 bay leaf
Dark or light brown sugar

1. Arrange the pineapple slices in a shallow dish. Stud each slice with 2 cloves and pour on the pineapple liquid. Cover and let stand at room temperature until ready to use.

2. In a large flameproof casserole, heat 2 tablespoons of the butter or margarine with the olive oil over medium-high heat and brown the chops evenly, adding more butter or margarine and oil if needed. Sprinkle the chops with salt and pepper. Remove and reserve. Preheat the oven to 350 degrees.

3. In the same pot, melt the remaining 2 tablespoons of butter or margarine. Add the green pepper, onion, and celery and cook for 5 minutes. Stir in the rice and cook for 2 minutes, stirring, until the rice is well coated with fat. Add the broth and bay leaf. Bring to a boil. Lay the browned chops on the rice. Cover tightly and bake for 1 hour, or until the chops and rice are tender and the liquid has been mostly absorbed. If they are not tender before the liquid has cooked off, add a small amount of hot broth or water and continue to bake. Remove the bay leaf.

4. Remove the cloves from the pineapple slices and arrange the slices over the chops. Sprinkle lightly with brown sugar and bake, uncovered, for about 10 minutes, or until the sugar has melted and formed a glaze.

*Serves 6*


# Hong Kong Pork and Lime Rice


4 loin pork chops, 1 inch thick, boned and trimmed of all fat,
    then beaten between sheets of wax paper with a mallet to a
    ¼-inch thickness
1 lime
⅓ cup soy sauce
⅔ cup fresh lime juice
2 egg whites
1 teaspoon salt (optional)
1 tablespoon cornstarch
⅓ cup corn oil, approximately
2 medium carrots, scraped and cut into julienne
1 small red bell pepper, cored, seeded, and cut in half lengthwise,
    then into ¼-inch strips
1 celery stalk, scraped and cut into ¼-inch diagonal slices

4 whole scallions, trimmed, cut into 2-inch lengths, and then cut
   lengthwise into julienne
1 cup chicken broth
2 tablespoons white vinegar
2 tablespoons dark or light brown sugar
1 tablespoon cornstarch, dissolved in 1 tablespoon cold water
3 cups cooked long-grain rice
Salt and freshly ground black pepper to taste


1. Put the pork chops in a single layer in a glass dish. Grate the rind from the lime and set aside. Combine and blend the soy sauce with half the lime juice and pour the mixture over the pork. Turn to coat. Cover and marinate in the refrigerator for 2 hours and at room temperature for 1 hour, turning several times and spooning the marinade over the pork.

2. Combine the egg whites, salt, and cornstarch and beat well. Dip the chops into the egg white mixture, coating evenly.

3. In a large frying pan, over medium heat, heat 3 tablespoons of the corn oil and brown the pork evenly; then cook until it is tender, turning, about 20 minutes. Add more oil if needed. Remove the pork and cut crosswise into ½-inch-wide strips. Reserve and keep warm.

4. If any oil remains in the pan, pour off all but about 1 tablespoon. If not, add 1 tablespoon of oil and cook the carrots, pepper, celery, and scallions for 2 minutes, or until they are crisp-tender (more crisp than tender), stirring. Add the broth, bring to a boil, and cook for 2 minutes.

5. In a small stainless steel or porcelain-lined saucepan, combine the vinegar and remaining lime juice and bring to a boil. Lower the heat, add the sugar, and simmer, stirring for 1 minute to dissolve the sugar. Stir in the cornstarch-water blend. Add to the vegetables and bring to a boil. Lower the heat and cook just until the sauce has thickened.

6. Stir the grated lime rind and rice into the vegetables with a metal fork and cook long enough to heat through. Taste for seasoning, adding salt and pepper if needed.

7. To serve, evenly spoon the rice-vegetable mixture onto a large hot serving dish and top with the strips of pork.

*Serves 6*

# Hungarian Rice-Stuffed Pork Chops

5 tablespoons butter or margarine
1 medium onion, minced
1 small celery stalk, scraped and minced
½ cup short- or medium-grain rice
¾ cup chicken broth
1 tablespoon finely chopped fresh parsley leaves
¼ cup golden raisins, halved
⅛ teaspoon each ground mace, sage, and thyme
Salt and freshly ground black pepper to taste
6 center-cut loin pork chops, 1 inch thick, with a pocket cut for
    stuffing
2 tablespoons olive oil
¾ cup chicken broth or dry white wine
1 cup sour cream
2 teaspoons Hungarian paprika

1. In a saucepan, over medium heat, melt 2 tablespoons of the butter or margarine. Add the onion and celery and cook until they are soft. Do not brown. Stir in the rice and cook for 2 minutes. Pour in ¾ cup broth or white wine and add the parsley. Bring to a boil, lower the heat, cover, and simmer for 10 minutes, or until the rice is quite al dente and the liquid has been absorbed. Remove from the heat and stir in the raisins, mace, sage, and thyme and blend well. Taste for seasoning and add salt if needed.

2. Season the chops lightly with salt and pepper. Stuff without packing and secure with toothpicks or small skewers. In a large frying pan, over medium-high heat, heat the remaining butter or margarine and the olive oil and carefully brown the chops on both sides. Add ¾ cup chicken broth or white wine, cover, and simmer for 40 minutes, or until the chops are tender. Transfer to a hot serving dish and keep warm.

3. If there is more than ½ cup of liquid in the pan, turn up the heat to reduce it to that amount. Stir in the sour cream and paprika and heat, stirring, without boiling. Spoon the sauce over the chops.

*Serves 6*

# Pork Crown with Orange Rice

*Here's a party dish we discovered in Spain. Crown roasts, dramatic and different, call for a number of dinner guests as spectators at the carving match. Thus, have your butcher create one with about 16 chops to serve 8: 1 large chop per serving, seconds, if desired.*

1 crown roast of pork, made up of 16 ribs
1 tablespoon salt (optional)
½ teaspoon freshly ground black pepper
¼ teaspoon ground cinnamon
2 tablespoons butter or margarine
3 medium onions, chopped
½ teaspoon ground cumin
½ cup golden raisins
½ cup fresh orange juice
¼ cup dry sherry
6 cups hot cooked long-grain rice
2 tablespoons grated orange rind
3 large navel oranges, peeled and sectioned, with all
   membranes removed

1. Preheat the oven to 350 degrees.
2. Sprinkle the pork with 2 teaspoons of the salt, all of the pepper, and the cinnamon. Cover the ends of the bones with aluminum foil and put the roast in a roasting pan. Roast, uncovered, for 30 to 40 minutes a pound (about 3½ to 4 hours), or until fork tender but not dry, basting every 20 minutes with the pan juices.
3. When the pork is nearly cooked, melt the butter or margarine in a frying pan over medium heat. Add the onions and cook for 5 minutes, or until they are soft. Do not brown. Stir in the remaining salt, the cumin, raisins, orange juice, and sherry and simmer, covered, for 5 minutes. With a metal fork stir in the hot cooked rice and 1 tablespoon of the grated orange rind, tossing and fluffing well to blend.
4. Remove the roast from the oven and stand it on a large hot serving dish. Fill the center with the orange rice, spooning any remaining rice around the roast. Sprinkle with the remaining orange rind and garnish with the orange sections.

5. Carve at the table. Each serving of pork should be lavishly accompanied by orange rice and orange sections.

*Serves 8*

# New Orleans Skillet Pork Chops and Rice

2 tablespoons butter or margarine
1 tablespoon olive oil
1 medium onion, coarsely chopped
1 large celery stalk, scraped and chopped
4 pork chops, ½ inch thick
Salt and freshly ground black pepper to taste
1½ cups water
2 tablespoons dark or light brown sugar
2 cups tomato sauce, homemade or canned
1 cup long-grain rice
½ teaspoon fennel seeds

1. In a large heavy, deep frying pan, over medium heat, heat the butter or margarine and oil. Add the onion and celery and cook for 2 minutes, or until they are slightly soft.

2. Add the chops to the frying pan. Season with salt and pepper and brown evenly. Remove and reserve.

3. Stir the water, brown sugar, and 1½ cups of the tomato sauce into the pan. Heat, stirring and scraping up the browned-on bits in the bottom of the pan. Bring to a boil and stir in the rice and fennel seeds.

4. Return the chops to the pan, spooning the sauce and rice over them. Cover tightly and cook over medium-low heat for 30 minutes. Pour on the remaining tomato sauce, cover, and cook for 10 minutes, or until the rice and chops are tender. Taste for seasoning, adding salt and pepper if needed.

*Serves 4*

# Pork Chops with Wined Brown Rice

*One of the assets of brown rice, besides its nutty flavor, is that it mates exceptionally well with baked meats, cooking in about the same time.*

2 tablespoons butter or margarine
1 tablespoon olive oil
4 loin pork chops, ¾ inch thick
Salt and freshly ground black pepper to taste
4 red bell pepper rings
4 thick slices Bermuda onion
¾ cup long-grain brown rice
1 cup dry red wine
1 cup chicken broth

1. In a large frying pan, over medium heat, heat the butter or margarine and oil. Season the chops lightly with salt and pepper. Brown them evenly. Preheat the oven to 350 degrees.

2. Place chops in a flameproof casserole just large enough to hold them snugly in one layer. Top each with a pepper ring and an onion slice. Sprinkle the rice around and between the chops. Combine the wine and broth and pour the mixture over all. Bring to a boil on top of the stove, cover, and bake for 1 hour, or until the chops and rice are tender and liquid has been absorbed. If the liquid cooks off before the chops and rice are tender, add more hot broth and continue cooking.

*Serves 4*

# Arroz com Chourico e Paio

*Portuguese Rice Stew with Sausage and Ham*

2 medium onions, chopped
¼ pound *chourico* (garlic sausage), skin removed and the meat
  chopped
¼ pound lean pork sausage meat
¼ pound cooked ham, chopped
2 garlic cloves, minced
2 teaspoons ground cumin
¼ teaspoon cayenne, or to taste
1 cup long-grain rice
2½ cups beef broth
Salt and freshly ground black pepper to taste

1. In a heavy saucepan, over medium heat, cook the onions for 5 minutes. Do not brown. Stir in the garlic sausage, pork sausage meat, ham, garlic, cumin, and cayenne. Simmer, stirring and breaking up the sausage meat with a fork, for 15 minutes.

2. Stir the rice and beef broth into the pan with the sausage and ham. Bring to a boil, stir with a wooden fork, lower the heat, cover, and simmer for 20 minutes, or until the rice is tender and most of the liquid has been absorbed. Taste for seasoning, adding salt and pepper if needed. The broth may have supplied sufficient seasoning.

*Serves 4*

# Glazed Ham and Rice Loaf

2 tablespoons butter or margarine
1 large onion, finely chopped
1 garlic clove, minced
1 pound ground cooked ham
1 pound ground lean pork

1½ cups cooked short- or medium-grain rice
1 cup fine fresh bread crumbs
1 cup milk
3 eggs, beaten
Dark or light brown sugar
1 teaspoon dry mustard
Horseradish Sauce (see following recipe)

1. In a frying pan, over medium heat, melt the butter. Add the onion and garlic and cook for 5 minutes, or until soft. Do not brown. Preheat the oven to 350 degrees.

2. In a bowl, combine the onion, garlic, ham, pork, rice, bread crumbs, milk, and eggs, and blend well with a fork. Loosely pack into a buttered loaf pan. Smooth over the top with the back of a fork and coat it with a thin, even layer of brown sugar; then sprinkle on the dry mustard.

3. Set in a pan of hot water and bake for 1½ hours. Pour off the fat collected in the pan and let sit for 10 minutes before transferring to a serving dish and slicing. Serve with the Horseradish Sauce.

*Serves 6*

## Horseradish Sauce

3 tablespoons freshly grated horseradish or well-drained bottled
  horseradish
½ cup heavy cream, whipped
¼ cup mayonnaise
Salt and freshly ground white pepper to taste

Combine and blend all ingredients well.

# Italian Sausage and Rice Pie

1 pound Italian sausage meat
6 eggs, lightly beaten
2 cups cooked short- or medium-grain rice
1 cup grated Asiago or Parmesan cheese
¼ pound mozzarella, diced

1. In a frying pan, over medium heat, cook the sausage, stirring and breaking it up with a wooden fork, for 15 minutes, or until it loses all pink color. With a slotted spoon transfer it to a bowl. Preheat the oven to 350 degrees.
2. Add all the other ingredients to the sausage and blend well. Spoon into a well-buttered baking dish 10½ inches square by 2½ inches deep, and bake for 40 minutes, or until golden brown and set.

*Serves 4*

# Rice Planters' Risotto

*This is a favorite of those who work in the rice paddies of Lombardy, Italy.*

2 tablespoons olive oil
5 Italian sweet sausages (about 1½ pounds), casings removed
2 medium onions, chopped
⅛ teaspoon ground cinnamon
3 tablespoons butter or margarine
4 cups hot cooked long-grain rice (cooked in beef broth)
½ cup grated Asiago or Parmesan cheese
Salt and freshly ground black pepper to taste

In a large frying pan, over medium heat, heat the oil and cook the sausage and onions, breaking up the sausage with a fork as it cooks. Blend in the cinnamon and cook for 20 minutes, or until the sausage is thoroughly cooked, stirring frequently. Add the butter or margarine and stir until it is melted. With a metal fork, blend in the rice and cheese, fluffing up the rice. Taste for seasoning before adding salt and pepper, as the beef broth and cheese may have supplied enough. Spoon into a hot serving dish.

*Serves 4*

# Rice Arrabiata

## *Raging Rice*

*This is a dish we have eaten in Rome several times. Depending upon the amount of hot pepper in the sausages, it can raise you right out of your seat. The Romans always add extra crushed hot red pepper flakes. We don't. With a salad, this makes an excellent lunch.*

2 tablespoons olive oil
2 medium white onions, finely chopped
8 lean Italian hot sausages, casings removed
½ cup dry red wine
1 cup long-grain rice
2½ cups beef broth
½ cup grated Asiago or Parmesan cheese
¼ teaspoon hot red pepper flakes
Salt to taste

1. In a large heavy, deep frying pan, over medium heat, heat the oil and cook the onions for 5 minutes, or until they are soft. Do not brown. Stir in the sausage meat, breaking it up with a wooden fork as you brown it. Add the wine and simmer until most of the wine has evaporated.

2. Stir the rice and beef broth into the pan. Bring to a boil, stir with a wooden fork, cover, lower the heat, and simmer for 20 minutes, or until the rice is tender and the liquid has been absorbed.

3. With a metal fork, stir in the grated cheese, fluffing the rice as you do. Add the red pepper and salt if needed.

*Serves 4*

# Rice with Black Beans and Sausage

1 pound Italian hot sausages, cut into ¼-inch-thick slices
2 tablespoons olive oil (optional)
1 medium poblano pepper, cored, seeded, and diced
1 garlic clove, minced
2 medium onions, chopped
½ cup tomato purée
½ teaspoon salt (optional)
½ teaspoon dried thyme
⅛ teaspoon hot red pepper flakes, or to taste
1½ cups chicken broth
3 cups al dente–cooked long-grain rice
One 1-pound can black beans (available in supermarkets),
    drained

1. If the sausages appear to be fatty do not use the oil, but if they seem very lean, heat the oil in a deep frying pan and evenly brown the slices over medium heat. Remove them, drain on paper towels, and reserve.

2. Add the pepper, garlic, and onions to the frying pan and cook for 5 minutes, or until they are soft. Do not brown.

3. Stir in the tomato purée, salt, thyme, hot red pepper flakes, and broth. Bring to a boil and stir in the rice and beans, blending well. Fluff the rice with a metal fork, and place the sausage slices on top. Cover the pan and cook for 5 minutes. Remove from the heat and let sit, covered, for 10 minutes, or until the liquid has been absorbed. Taste for seasoning, adding salt and pepper if needed. The broth may have supplied enough.

*Serves 4*

# Herbed Lamb Kidneys with Rice

12 lamb kidneys
1 cup chopped fresh parsley leaves
1 tablespoon chopped fresh tarragon, or 1 teaspoon dried
1 small onion, minced
⅔ cup soft butter or margarine
2 teaspoons Worcestershire sauce
Salt and freshly ground black pepper to taste
½ cup dry sherry
4 cups hot cooked long-grain rice

1. Remove the membranes from the kidneys; then cut them into halves lengthwise and remove the fatty knob inside. Wash the kidneys and pat them dry with paper towels. Preheat the broiler.

2. Combine the parsley, tarragon, onion, butter or margarine, Worcestershire sauce, salt, and pepper and blend well into a paste.

3. With one-third of the butter paste, coat the bottom of a shallow baking pan just large enough to hold the halved kidneys snugly, placed side by side.

4. Arrange the kidneys, cut side up, in the baking pan. Dot the kidneys with the remaining butter paste. Sprinkle with sherry. Broil for 5 minutes on one side; turn, spoon the pan sauce over, and broil for 3 to 5 minutes, or until brown on the outside and pink inside. Do not overcook or they shrink and toughen.

5. Spoon a mound of rice onto each plate. Arrange the kidneys around the rice and spoon the sauce over the rice and kidneys.

*Serves 4*

# Louisiana "Dirty Rice"

*This dish originated with the Cajuns in the Lake Charles bayou country.
We had it in the bayou home of our goose-hunting guide whose mother
gave us the recipe by demonstration.*

5 tablespoons butter or margarine
1 tablespoon olive oil
1 large onion, finely chopped
1 garlic clove, minced
1 large green bell pepper, seeded, cored, and finely chopped
1 celery stalk, scraped and finely chopped
½ pound chicken gizzards and hearts, trimmed and finely
   chopped
½ pound chicken livers, trimmed and coarsely chopped
Salt and freshly ground black pepper to taste
1 cup long-grain brown rice
2½ cups chicken broth
⅓ cup chopped fresh parsley leaves

1. In a deep saucepan, over medium heat, heat 2 tablespoons of
the butter or margarine and the oil. Add the vegetables and cook
for 10 minutes, or until they are soft. Do not brown. Add the gizzards and hearts and cook for 5 minutes. Add the livers and cook
until they are no longer pink but still tender (about 5 minutes) and
most of the liquid in the pan has cooked off. Do not overcook the
giblets as they will toughen. Season with salt and pepper.

2. In another saucepan, heat the remaining butter or margarine.
Stir in the rice and cook for 2 minutes, stirring, to coat it well. Add
the broth, bring to a boil, cover, lower the heat, and simmer for 40
minutes, or until the rice is tender and the liquid has been
absorbed.

3. Add the rice to the vegetable-giblet pan with half of the parsley
and mix with a metal fork, fluffing the rice. Mound on a hot serving
dish and sprinkle on the remaining parsley.

*Serves 4 to 6*

# Pennsylvania Dutch Rice with Knockwurst and Beans

6 knockwurst
12 ounces beer
1 tablespoon white vinegar
2 teaspoons dark or light brown sugar
4 tablespoons (½ stick) butter or margarine
1 medium onion, finely chopped
½ of a green bell pepper, seeds and ribs removed, finely chopped
Salt and freshly ground black pepper to taste
One 15-ounce can red kidney beans, drained
1½ cups long-grain rice, cooked al dente
½ cup fine fresh bread crumbs

1. In a saucepan, over medium-low heat, simmer the knockwurst in the beer for 15 minutes. Remove and reserve the knockwurst. Raise the heat and reduce the beer to ¾ cup. Add the vinegar and sugar and simmer, stirring, just long enough to melt the sugar. Cut the knockwurst into ½-inch slices and return them to the saucepan.

2. In a frying pan, over medium heat, melt 2 tablespoons of the butter or margarine. Add the onion and green pepper, season with salt and pepper, and cook for 5 minutes. Do not brown. Preheat the oven to 400 degrees.

3. In a bowl combine all the ingredients except the bread crumbs and remaining butter or margarine, and mix carefully with a metal fork. Taste for seasoning, adding salt and pepper if needed. Spoon into a buttered 13½-by-8¾-by-1¾-inch baking dish. Cover with the bread crumbs and dot with the remaining butter or margarine.

4. Bake for 15 minutes, or until the crumbs are golden and the dish is heated through.

*Serves 6*

# Calf's Brains with Caper and Lemon Sauce

*We have two favorites here: the most delicate of the variety meats, and the nutty Wild Pecan Rice, which offers, as the best of rices do, a nice counterpoint to the somewhat tart sauce. Check the recipe for Pheasant with Wild Pecan Rice, page 105, for more on this rice.*

3 calf's brains (about 1½ pounds)
4 tablespoons white vinegar
1 teaspoon salt (optional)
Freshly ground black pepper
All-purpose flour for dredging
12 tablespoons (1½ sticks) butter or margarine
2 tablespoons olive oil
3 tablespoons fresh lemon juice
3 tablespoons rinsed and drained capers
3 tablespoons chopped broadleaf (Italian) parsley leaves
4 cups hot cooked Wild Pecan Rice

1. Soak the brains in cold water for 2 hours. Drain and rinse. Soak again in fresh cold water with 2 tablespoons of the vinegar for 1 hour. Clean the brains, removing the membranes and blood spots. Place in a saucepan and cover with boiling water. Add the remaining 2 tablespoons of vinegar and salt and simmer for 15 minutes. Remove from the heat, drain, and dry.

2. Cut the brains lengthwise into ½-inch-thick slices. Sprinkle with salt and pepper. Dredge lightly in the flour, shaking off any excess so they are just dusted.

3. In a frying pan, over medium heat, heat 6 tablespoons of the butter or margarine with the olive oil until the butter or margarine bubbles. Cook the brains until golden on both sides (add more butter or margarine and oil if needed, in addition to that listed above).

4. In a saucepan, over medium heat, melt the remaining 6 tablespoons of the butter or margarine, stir in the lemon juice, capers, and parsley. Blend well.

5. Arrange the hot rice in a smooth layer on individual plates and top with the brain slices, spooning the caper sauce over both the brains and rice.

*Serves 6*

# Tripe with Wild Pecan Rice

*See page 57 for a note on preparing rice rings. And check the recipe for Pheasant with Wild Pecan Rice on page 105 for more information on this unusual rice. One thing for sure, no European or Asian rice can compare with it for flavor and cooking ease.*

*As this is written, tripe, along with squid, is coming into favor with those who continue to search for something "new." Actually, tripe is an old European favorite that still graces menus there—and here. We found this recipe in Spain.*

*Tripe is the stomach lining of a cow, one of four, each having its own market name. The one we favor, the second stomach, is called "honeycomb tripe," which makes a surprisingly tasty dish.*

3 pounds fresh white veal honeycomb tripe
3 tablespoons olive oil
3 tablespoons chopped pork
2 garlic cloves, minced
1 lemon, cut into 1-inch slices, seeds removed
One 1-pound 12-ounce can imported Italian plum tomatoes, mashed
½ teaspoon dried oregano
1 bay leaf
2 teaspoons salt (optional)
½ teaspoon freshly ground black pepper
¼ teaspoon hot red pepper flakes
One 7-ounce package Wild Pecan Rice
1 tablespoon butter or margarine
2 cups water

1. Wash the tripe carefully in water four different times. Place in a large pot, pour in 4 quarts of water, cover, and simmer for 3 hours, or until it is tender. Pour off the water twice during the cooking, replacing with fresh hot water. Drain the tripe well, cool, and cut it into ½-by-2-inch strips.

2. In a deep saucepan, over medium heat, heat the olive oil and sauté the pork and garlic for 5 minutes. Add the lemon slices, tomatoes, oregano, bay leaf, 1 teaspoon of the salt, black pepper, hot red pepper flakes, and the tripe. Simmer, uncovered, for 25 minutes. Discard the lemon slices and bay leaf.

3. While the tripe is cooking, combine the rice, the remaining 1 teaspoon of salt, the butter or margarine, and water in a saucepan

over medium heat. Bring to a boil and stir with a wooden fork. Cover, lower the heat, and simmer for 20 minutes, or until the rice is tender and the water has been absorbed.

4. Spoon a bed of rice on individual hot dishes and top with generous portions of the tripe and its sauce.

*Serves 6*

# Rice Ring with Saged Chicken Livers

*See page 57 for a note on preparing rice rings.*

6 tablespoons butter or margarine
2 large shallots, or 1 small white onion, minced
2 cups short- or medium-grain rice
4½ cups chicken broth
½ cup minced fresh parsley leaves
Saged Chicken Livers (see following recipe)

1. Melt 2 tablespoons of the butter or margarine in a saucepan over medium heat. Add the shallots and cook for 2 minutes, or until they are soft. Do not brown. Stir in the rice and cook for 2 minutes. Stir in the broth. Bring to a boil, lower the heat, stir with a wooden fork, cover, and simmer for 20 minutes, or until the rice is tender and the liquid has been absorbed. Stir in the remaining butter or margarine and parsley.

2. Pack the rice into a 6-cup ring mold coated with butter or margarine, set in a pan of hot water that comes halfway up the mold, and place in a preheated 350-degree oven for 15 minutes. Carefully run a knife blade around the inside of the mold and turn out the rice onto a large hot serving dish.

3. Fill the center with the Saged Chicken Livers. Serve any remaining livers in a hot serving dish. If desired, arrange your vegetable around the rice ring.

*Serves 6*

# Saged Chicken Livers

5 tablespoons butter or margarine
2 large shallots, or 1 small white onion, minced
1½ pounds chicken livers, trimmed, washed, and thoroughly dried
All-purpose flour for dredging
1 tablespoon olive oil
Salt and freshly ground black pepper to taste
1 cup coarsely chopped prosciutto or other cooked ham
¼ cup brandy
¼ cup chicken broth
¾ cup half-and-half
2 tablespoons chopped fresh sage, or 1 teaspoon dried, crumbled
    leaf sage

1. Over medium heat, in a large frying pan, melt 2 tablespoons of the butter or margarine. Add the shallots and cook for 2 minutes, or until they are soft. Do not brown. With a slotted spoon transfer the shallots to a bowl.

2. Dredge the livers in the flour, shaking off any excess. Heat the remaining butter or margarine and the olive oil in the frying pan over medium-high heat. Add the livers and brown them evenly, leaving them slightly pink inside. Season with salt and pepper. Transfer to the bowl with the shallots. Add the prosciutto to the pan and cook for 1 minute. With the slotted spoon transfer to the bowl with the shallots.

3. Pour the brandy into the frying pan and cook, over medium-high heat, until half has evaporated. Stir in the broth and half-and-half. Cook, stirring and scraping the bottom of the pan to release the browned-on bits, until reduced and thickened. Return the shallots, livers, and prosciutto to the pan, stir in the sage, and heat through. Taste for seasoning, adding salt and pepper if needed.

# Rice Ring with Sweetbreads Véronique

*See page 57 for a note on preparing rice rings. The sweetbreads can be blanched before you start preparing the rice ring; then the sauce can be made while the rice ring is baking.*

3 tablespoons butter or margarine
1 medium onion, finely chopped
2 cups short- or medium-grain rice
4 cups chicken broth
2 eggs, beaten
1 cup milk
3 tablespoons melted butter or margarine
1 cup grated Fontina or Gruyère cheese
½ cup finely chopped fresh parsley leaves
Salt and freshly ground black pepper to taste

1. In a saucepan, over medium heat, melt the 3 tablespoons of butter or margarine. Add the onion and cook for 3 minutes, or until it is soft. Do not brown. Add the rice and cook for 2 minutes, stirring. Pour in the broth and bring to a boil. Lower the heat, stir with a wooden fork, cover, and simmer for 20 minutes, or until the liquid has been absorbed. Cool slightly. Blend in the eggs, milk, the melted butter or margarine, cheese, and parsley. Taste before adding salt and pepper as the broth may have supplied enough salt. Preheat the oven to 350 degrees.

2. Spoon the rice into an 8-cup mold that has been coated with butter or margarine, and set in a pan of hot water that comes halfway up the sides of the mold. Bake for 45 minutes, or until set. Carefully run a knife blade around the inside of the rice ring. Turn the ring out onto a hot serving dish.

3. Fill it with the sweetbreads and grapes. If the ring doesn't accommodate all of the filling, serve what's remaining in a hot serving bowl.

*Serves 4*

# Sweetbreads Véronique

2 pairs veal sweetbreads
2 tablespoons fresh lemon juice
3 tablespoons butter or margarine
3 tablespoons all-purpose flour
1 cup milk
½ cup Madeira
1 cup half-and-half
One 8½-ounce can seedless white grapes, drained
Salt to taste

1. Soak the sweetbreads in cold water for 1 hour. Carefully pull off any membrane that comes off easily. Soak again in cold water with 1 tablespoon of lemon juice for another hour. Remove the remaining membrane and the tissue connecting the lobes.

2. In a saucepan, cover the sweetbreads with water. Add 1 tablespoon of lemon juice and bring to a boil. Lower the heat and simmer for 15 minutes. Do not overcook. (They should be fairly firm but not hard.) Plunge into cold water for a few minutes, drain well, and cut into bite-size cubes. Set aside.

3. In a saucepan, over medium heat, melt the butter or margarine. Add the flour and cook, stirring into a smooth paste. Gradually add the milk, wine, and ½ cup of the half-and-half, and cook, stirring into a smooth, medium-thick sauce. Stir in the sweetbreads, grapes, and 1 tablespoon of lemon juice and heat through. Taste and add salt if needed. Just before serving, stir in the remaining half-and-half and heat for 1 minute.

# Rice Ring with Kidneys and Scrambled Eggs

*This makes a unique brunch or late-breakfast offering.*

2 veal kidneys
8 tablespoons (1 stick) butter or margarine
2 tablespoons all-purpose flour
1½ cups chicken broth
⅛ cup Madeira
Salt and freshly ground black pepper to taste
¼ teaspoon ground mace
8 eggs, lightly beaten in a bowl
½ cup half-and-half
Rice ring (see recipes on pages 158 and 160)

1. Remove the membranes from the kidneys; then cut the kidneys into thin slices, removing the fatty nugget from the center.

2. In a frying pan, over medium-high heat, melt 4 tablespoons of the butter or margarine. Cook the kidneys, turning, until they are barely golden, about 4 minutes. Sprinkle on the flour and stir.

3. Lower the heat and pour in the broth and Madeira. Add the salt, pepper, and mace and cook for 10 minutes, or until the sauce thickens. Do not overcook or the kidneys will toughen. They should be slightly pink inside.

4. Melt the remaining butter or margarine in a frying pan over medium heat and scramble the eggs, adding salt and pepper. When the eggs begin to set, stir in the half-and-half and cook until it is blended with the eggs. Cook to whatever degree of firmness you prefer, but do not overcook. The eggs should be moist.

5. Turn the rice ring out onto a large hot serving dish. Fill the center with the kidneys and their sauce. Spoon the eggs around the ring.

*Serves 4 to 6*

# 7

# Rice with Vegetables

We were driving from New Delhi to the Nilgiri Hills, the "Blue Mountains" in the south of India, accompanied by a government of India tourist officer, R. Ramaswamy. He, like many others in India, was a vegetarian.

Late one afternoon we stopped for dinner. We ordered a crusty-moist *tandoori* chicken; he had a vegetable cutlet surrounded with lime rice. This day Ramaswamy said, somewhat vehemently, "If it weren't for rice, I think I'd give up this diet!"

We knew what he meant. During the two weeks we spent with him, he'd have a vegetable cutlet with most of his meals, but he would always have a side dish of rice, usually a different rice combination. He often toyed with the vegetable cutlet and gulped the rice, each time mixed with different vegetables. A favorite of his and ours was rice with lentils, *Kitcheri*.

Rice mates zestfully with vegetables of all kinds. Two surprises for us were rice with cabbage in Germany and rice and parsnips in Hungary. With its flexibility and remarkable range, rice has a way of continually surprising. Sometimes, as with the dish of peas with rice, Risi e Bisi, it sounds like a song and tastes like a poem. Rice is one of those rare foods—a poem you eat.

# Rice Parma

12 tender fresh asparagus stalks
4 tablespoons (½ stick) butter or margarine
1 cup long-grain rice
2½ to 3 cups beef broth
1 cup fresh shelled peas or frozen, defrosted
1 cup finely diced prosciutto
½ cup grated Parmesan cheese


1. Snap off the tough ends of the asparagus and peel the stems. Cut the stems into ¾-inch pieces.

2. Separate the scaly tips and cook them in salted boiling water until crisp-tender. Set aside and keep warm.

3. Heat 2 tablespoons of the butter or margarine in a saucepan. Add the rice and cook, stirring, for 2 minutes, to coat well. Add 2½ cups of the broth, bring to a boil, stir with a wooden fork, lower the heat, cover, and simmer for 10 minutes.

4. With a wooden fork, stir in the fresh peas and the asparagus stems. Cover and simmer for 5 minutes. If using defrosted frozen peas, add them at this time and simmer for 3 minutes. Stir in the prosciutto and simmer for 5 minutes, or until the rice and vegetables are tender and most of the liquid has been absorbed. If it seems too dry, add a small amount of hot broth. It should be moist, but not soupy.

5. With a metal fork, stir in the remaining butter or margarine and half of the cheese. Garnish with the asparagus tips. Serve the remaining cheese at the table.

*Serves 4*

# Rice with Cannellini Beans Cacciatore

2 tablespoons olive oil
1 large onion, finely chopped
1 celery stalk, scraped and finely chopped
2 large ripe tomatoes, peeled, seeded, and chopped, or 2 cups
    canned imported Italian plum tomatoes, drained and chopped
Salt and freshly ground black pepper to taste
¼ teaspoon dried crumbled leaf sage
¼ teaspoon dried rosemary
2 cups cooked white beans, or a 1-pound can, drained
3 cups cooked long-grain rice
3 tablespoons butter or margarine, cut into small pieces
½ cup grated Asiago or Parmesan cheese

1. In a saucepan, over medium heat, heat the oil and cook the onion and celery for 5 minutes, or until they are soft. Do not brown. Add the tomatoes, salt, pepper, sage, and rosemary. Cover, lower the heat, and simmer for 30 minutes, or until the sauce begins to thicken.

2. Stir in the beans, rice, butter or margarine, and cheese. Cook for 5 minutes, stirring with a metal fork several times, to heat through. Taste for seasoning, adding salt and pepper if needed.

*Serves 4 to 6*

# Black Beans and Rice, Cuban Style

1 cup dried black beans
1 green bell pepper, halved and seeded, half left intact,
   the other half chopped
2 medium onions, 1 left whole and nailed with 2 whole
   cloves, the other finely chopped
1 bay leaf
¼ teaspoon dried oregano
5 tablespoons olive oil
1 teaspoon sugar
2 tablespoons light rum, or 2 tablespoons white
   wine vinegar
Salt and freshly ground black pepper to taste
1 garlic clove, minced
1 cup long-grain rice
2 cups hot water
1 teaspoon salt (optional)
3 tablespoons butter or margarine, cut into small pieces
1 ripe but firm avocado, peeled and cut into 6 wedges
1 lemon, cut into 6 wedges, seeds removed

1. Pick over the beans and rinse several times. Soak in cold water
for 5 hours. Drain and put the beans with the green pepper half,
the onion with the cloves, bay leaf, oregano, and 2 tablespoons of
the olive oil in a heavy saucepan. Barely cover with cold water.
Bring to a boil, lower the heat, and simmer, partially covered, for
2 hours, or until the beans are cooked but still somewhat firm and
can be mashed against the side of the pan. If the liquid cooks off
before the beans are cooked, add small amounts of *hot* water (cold
water will harden them). Remove and discard the green pepper
half, the onion with the cloves, and the bay leaf. Mash 2 or 3 tablespoonfuls of the beans against the side of the pot. Stir in the sugar,
rum, salt, and pepper.

2. In a frying pan, over medium heat, with the remaining olive
oil, cook the chopped green pepper, chopped onion, and garlic for
5 minutes, or until they are soft. Do not brown. Add the rice and
cook, stirring, for 1 minute. Transfer to the bean pot. Stir in the hot
water and the salt with a wooden fork. Bring to a boil, stirring, to
prevent burning. Cover, lower the heat, and simmer for 20 minutes, or until the rice is tender and the liquid has been absorbed.

Taste for seasoning, adding salt and pepper if needed. Stir in the butter or margarine.

3. Transfer to a hot serving bowl and garnish with the avocado and lemon wedges.

*Serves 6*

# Rice and Broccoli with Three Cheeses

2 tablespoons butter or margarine
1 garlic clove, minced
1½ cups long-grain rice
3 cups chicken broth
Salt and freshly ground black pepper to taste
1-pound bunch broccoli
⅛ cup crumbled blue cheese, at room temperature
⅛ cup small cubes of Monterey Jack cheese, at room temperature
3 tablespoons soft butter or margarine
1½ cups half-and-half, heated
¼ cup grated Asiago or Parmesan cheese
½ cup additional warm half-and-half, if needed

1. In a saucepan, over medium heat, melt the 2 tablespoons of butter or margarine. Add the garlic and cook for 1 minute, or until it is soft. Do not brown. Stir in the rice and cook for 2 minutes, coating well with the butter or margarine. Pour in the broth. Bring to a boil, lower the heat, stir with a wooden fork, cover, and simmer for 15 minutes. The rice should be quite al dente and the liquid absorbed. Taste and add salt and pepper if needed.

2. Trim the broccoli, dividing the florets and peeling the stems. Cut the stems into ½-inch diagonal pieces. Cook the stem pieces in boiling water for 2 minutes. Add the florets and cook for 2 minutes, or until they are crisp-tender (more crisp than tender as they will cook more later). Drain and set aside.

3. With a fork, mash the blue cheese and Monterey Jack with the

3 tablespoons of soft butter or margarine into a semismooth paste. Preheat the oven to 350 degrees.

4. Arrange half of the rice in a loose, smooth layer in a well-buttered shallow baking dish. Do not pack down the rice. Dot with half of the cheese paste. Arrange all of the broccoli pieces on the rice. Dot with the remaining cheese paste. Spoon on the remaining rice in a smooth, loose layer. Pour over the half-and-half. It should seep down through the layers. If it does not come to the top of the rice, add more half-and-half. But it should not cover the rice. Sprinkle on the grated cheese.

5. Bake for 30 minutes, or until the top is golden and most of the liquid has been absorbed.

*Serves 6 to 8*


# German Rice and Cabbage

*Here's that vegetable-rice surprise we found in Munich. It makes a neat side dish when served with ham.*

    4 tablespoons extra-virgin olive oil
    2 medium onions, chopped
    2 garlic cloves, minced
    One 8-ounce can tomato sauce
    1 cup chicken broth
    2 cups shredded cabbage
    ½ teaspoon crushed caraway seeds
    Salt to taste
    ¼ teaspoon hot red pepper flakes, or to taste
    3 cups very al dente–cooked rice
    ¼ cup grated Emmenthal or Gruyère cheese

1. In a deep pan, over medium heat, heat the 4 tablespoons of olive oil. Add the onions and garlic to the pan and cook until they are soft. Do not brown. Stir in the tomato sauce, chicken broth, and cabbage, and sprinkle on the caraway seeds, salt, and hot red pep-

per flakes. Cover and simmer for 15 minutes, or until the cabbage is tender.

2. Blend in the rice and cook, covered, until most of the liquid has been absorbed. Transfer to a hot serving dish and serve with the cheese sprinkled on top. The hot rice will melt the cheese.

*Serves 4 to 6*

## Cabbage Dolmas

1 large head (at least 3 pounds) cabbage
2 tablespoons butter or margarine
5 tablespoons olive oil
1 medium onion, finely chopped
1 garlic clove, minced
¾ pound ground lamb, beef, or veal
¼ teaspoon ground cinnamon
½ teaspoon ground cumin
½ teaspoon dried oregano
Salt and freshly ground black pepper to taste
1 medium ripe tomato, peeled, seeded, and chopped,
    or 2 tablespoons tomato purée or sauce
1 cup quite al dente–cooked rice
1 medium onion, thinly sliced
1 large carrot, scraped and thinly sliced
1 lemon, thinly sliced, seeds and ends discarded
⅔ cup tomato purée or tomato sauce
1½ cups beef broth

1. Trim any imperfect leaves from the cabbage and cut out whatever part of the core you can, but leave the head intact. Immerse it in boiling water and parboil for 5 minutes. Allow it to sit in the water for another 5 minutes. Remove, drain, and cool. Carefully remove the outer leaves. You'll need at least 12 large leaves. If you can, remove and stuff more, as they are even tastier as leftovers. If necessary, return the cabbage to the hot water so the leaves can be easily removed. Divide the leaves into halves, cutting along the tough spine and discarding the spine.

2. In a frying pan, over medium heat, heat the butter or margarine with 3 tablespoons of the olive oil. Add the chopped onion and garlic and cook for 5 minutes, or until they are soft. Do not brown. Add the meat and cook, breaking it up with a fork until it is just slightly pink. Stir in the cinnamon, cumin, oregano, salt, pepper, and tomato. Raise the heat and cook until most of the liquid has cooked off. Mix in the rice. Preheat the oven to 350 degrees.

3. Spread the cabbage leaves out on a large work surface and place a tablespoonful of the rice-meat mixture on each. Roll them into neat cylinders by folding the sides over the filling and then rolling away from you. Fastening them with toothpicks will help hold them together.

4. Coat the bottom of a shallow baking dish with the remaining oil. Arrange the sliced onion, carrot, and lemon on the bottom of the baking dish. As you roll the leaves arrange them, seam side down, snugly side by side on top of the lemon slices. Bake for 10 minutes.

5. Blend the tomato purée with the broth and heat to a boil. Pour the mixture over the cabbage rolls. Cover and return to the oven for 45 minutes, or until the cabbage is tender. Baste 2 or 3 times during cooking. Transfer the rolls to a hot serving dish and spoon the sauce over.

*Serves 4*

# Baked Rice and Cauliflower

1 medium head (1 pound or more) firm white
   cauliflower
1½ cups water
⅔ cup medium-grain rice
½ teaspoon salt (optional)
8 tablespoons (1 stick) butter or margarine
1 small onion, finely chopped
Fine fresh bread crumbs
2 cups Béchamel Sauce (see below)
6 tablespoons grated Asiago or Parmesan cheese
Salt and freshly ground black pepper to taste

1. Break the cauliflower into florets. Score the stems of each floret. Cook in boiling water for 10 minutes, or until they are crisp-tender. Drain.

2. Bring the 1½ cups of water to a boil in a saucepan. Add the rice and salt and bring to a boil again. Stir with a wooden fork, lower the heat, cover, and simmer for 15 minutes, or until the liquid has been absorbed.

3. In a frying pan, over medium heat, melt 4 tablespoons of the butter or margarine. Cook the onion until it is soft and golden but not brown. Add the rice. Cook, stirring, for 2 minutes. Preheat the oven to 350 degrees.

4. Coat a deep 2-quart baking dish with butter or margarine. Sprinkle the bottom and sides with bread crumbs. Shake out any excess. Arrange layers of the rice and cauliflower. Spoon some sauce and sprinkle cheese on each layer and dot with 2 tablespoons butter or margarine. Season with salt and pepper.

5. Sprinkle bread crumbs on top and dot with the reserved 2 tablespoons of butter or margarine. Bake for 30 minutes, or until the top is golden and the sauce bubbling.

*Serves 4 to 6*

## Béchamel Sauce

3 tablespoons butter or margarine
3 tablespoons all-purpose flour
2 cups milk, heated
Salt and freshly ground black pepper to taste
¼ teaspoon ground nutmeg
⅛ teaspoon cayenne

1. In a saucepan, over medium heat, melt the butter or margarine. Add the flour and cook, stirring into a smooth paste.

2. Gradually stir in the milk and cook, stirring constantly, into a smooth, medium-thick sauce. Season with salt, pepper, nutmeg, and cayenne.

# Rice Garbanzos

*We like this with broiled hamburgers that have been topped with nuggets of blue cheese before broiling.*

3 tablespoons butter or margarine
2 tablespoons olive oil
1 small green bell pepper, cored, seeded, and diced
3 whole scallions, trimmed and finely chopped
1 cup long-grain rice
2½ cups chicken broth
One 1-pound can chick-peas
Salt and freshly ground black pepper to taste
Juice of 1 lemon

1. In a saucepan, over medium heat, warm the butter or margarine and oil. Stir in the green pepper and scallions. Cook, stirring, for 5 minutes. Do not brown. Stir in the rice and chicken broth. Bring to a boil, stir with a wooden fork, cover, lower the heat, and simmer for 20 minutes, or until the rice is tender and the liquid has been absorbed.

2. Drain the liquid from the can of chick-peas, saving half of it. In a saucepan, combine the chick-pea liquid, the chick-peas, salt, pepper, and lemon juice. Blend and simmer for 10 minutes.

3. Spoon the hot chick-peas with the liquid over the cooked rice. Taste for seasoning, adding salt and pepper if needed. Cover and allow to sit for 5 minutes before serving.

*Serves 6*

# Cucumber Rice

*This is an excellent accompaniment to fish, especially salmon.*

2 medium firm cucumbers, peeled, cut lengthwise, seeds scooped
    out and discarded, then diced
1 small onion, minced
2 tablespoons chopped fresh dill
½ pint sour cream
Salt and freshly ground black pepper to taste
3 cups hot cooked long-grain rice

1. In a bowl, blend the cucumbers, onion, dill, sour cream, salt,
and pepper.
2. Spoon the hot rice into a serving dish, crown with the cucumber mixture and serve.

*Serves 4 to 6*

# Neapolitan Rice and Eggplant

3 tablespoons butter or margarine
1 medium onion, finely chopped
1½ cups long-grain rice
2½ to 3 cups chicken broth
Salt to taste
2 eggplants (each about 1 pound), peeled and cut into ½-inch
    slices
All-purpose flour for dredging
½ cup olive oil
Freshly ground black pepper to taste
2½ cups tomato sauce, preferably homemade
½ pound mozzarella, thinly sliced
1 cup grated Asiago or Parmesan cheese
1 teaspoon dried basil

1. In a deep saucepan, melt the butter or margarine over medium heat and cook the onion for 3 minutes, or until it is soft. Do not brown. Add the rice and cook, stirring, for 2 minutes. Pour in 2½ cups of the broth. Bring to a boil, cover, lower the heat, and simmer for 15 minutes, or until the liquid has been absorbed and the rice is just al dente. If the rice is too underdone, add a small amount of hot broth and continue to cook. However, the rice should be quite al dente.

2. Lightly salt each slice of eggplant. Arrange slices in 2 or 3 equal stacks on several layers of paper towels; place on top of the stacks a plate with a weight on it to allow the moisture to drain off. After 30 minutes, pat the slices dry with paper towels, lightly dredge in flour. Heat 4 tablespoons of the oil in a large frying pan, over medium heat, and brown the eggplant slices on both sides, adding more oil as needed. Lightly season with pepper and additional salt if necessary. Drain the browned slices on paper towels. Preheat the oven to 350 degrees.

3. Coat the bottom of a large baking dish with some of the tomato sauce. Arrange a layer of one-third of the eggplant slices on the sauce, then a layer of half the rice. Cover lightly with some of the tomato sauce, a layer of mozzarella, then sprinkle with grated cheese and basil. Repeat the process, ending with a layer of eggplant, sauce, and grated cheese on top. Bake for 30 minutes, or until bubbling and golden. Allow to sit for a few minutes before serving.

*Serves 6 to 8*

# Risotto with Fennel

3 small firm heads fennel
2 tablespoons olive oil
5 tablespoons butter or margarine
2 garlic cloves, halved
1 medium onion, chopped
Salt and freshly ground black pepper to taste
1 cup long-grain rice
2½ cups chicken broth
1 cup grated Asiago or Parmesan cheese

1. Trim the fennel, cutting off the tops and discarding the tough outer leaves, leaving just the firm white bulb. Cut into halves lengthwise and thinly slice each half crosswise.

2. In a saucepan, over medium heat, heat the oil and 2 tablespoons of the butter or margarine. Add the garlic. Cook until it is golden, then discard it. Add the onion and fennel, season lightly with salt and pepper, and cook for 3 minutes, or until the fennel is just beginning to get soft but is still quite crisp.

3. Stir in the rice and cook for 1 minute, coating the grains with the butter or margarine and oil. Pour in the broth. Bring to a boil, lower the heat, cover, and simmer for 20 minutes, or until the rice is tender and the liquid has been absorbed. If the liquid is absorbed and the rice is still not cooked, add a small amount of hot broth and continue cooking; or if the rice is cooked but still liquidy, remove the cover, raise the heat, and cook until the liquid evaporates, being careful not to burn the rice. Taste for seasoning, adding salt and pepper if needed.

4. Stir in the remaining butter or margarine (in small pieces) and half of the cheese. Let sit for 2 or 3 minutes. Pass the remaining cheese at the table.

*Note:* This can also be prepared with broccoli instead of fennel.

*Serves 4 to 6*

# Kitcheri

## *Indian Rice with Lentils*

*This is served everywhere in India, sort of their French fried potatoes. It is often offered with poultry or meat. For the majority of poor, however, it is a main dish, because the lentils are very nourishing. There are several versions. This, we believe, is the most popular.*

6 tablespoons butter or margarine
3 medium onions, thinly sliced
2 garlic cloves, minced
1½ cups long-grain rice
1 cup dry lentils (preferably orange), well washed, then soaked in
    cold water for 6 hours, and well drained
½ teaspoon salt (optional)
1 teaspoon ground turmeric
½ teaspoon ground ginger
⅛ teaspoon ground cinnamon
3 cups chicken broth
Salt and freshly ground black pepper to taste

1. In a large frying pan, over medium heat, melt 4 tablespoons of the butter or margarine and cook the onions for 5 minutes, or until they are deep golden in color but not brown. Remove with a slotted spoon and drain on paper towels. Set aside.

2. Melt the remaining butter or margarine in a saucepan and stir in the garlic, rice, and lentils. Cook, stirring, for 4 minutes. Stir in ½ teaspoon salt, turmeric, ginger, and cinnamon, blending well. Pour in the chicken broth and bring to a boil. Lower the heat, stir with a wooden fork, cover, and simmer for 20 minutes, or until the liquid has been absorbed and the rice and lentils are tender. If the rice and lentils are tender and there is still too much liquid, raise the heat, remove the cover, and cook until the liquid has evaporated, being careful not to burn. If the liquid is absorbed before the rice and lentils are cooked, add a small amount of hot broth and continue to cook. Taste for seasoning, adding salt and pepper if needed. Serve garnished with the fried onions.

*Serves 4*

# Ricealeekie

6 tablespoons butter or margarine
1 medium onion, finely chopped
4 large leeks (white part only), cut into ¼-inch slices
1 cup long-grain rice
⅛ teaspoon dried tarragon
2½ cups beef broth
Salt and freshly ground black pepper to taste

1. Preheat the oven to 350 degrees.
2. In a flameproof casserole, over medium heat, melt 3 tablespoons of the butter or margarine. Add the onion and leeks and cook for 5 minutes, or until they are soft and golden. Do not brown.
3. Stir in the rice and cook for 2 minutes. Stir in the tarragon and the broth. Bring to a boil on top of the stove, stir, cover, and bake for 20 minutes, or until the rice is tender and the broth has been absorbed. Taste before adding salt and pepper as the broth may have supplied enough seasoning. Add the remaining butter or margarine and mix with a metal fork, fluffing up the rice.

*Serves 4 to 6*


# Mushroom Trifolati Risotto

*This technique, discovered in Milan, produces one of the most unusual of the risottos.*

2 tablespoons butter or margarine
1 cup long-grain rice
2 cups chicken broth
¼ cup olive oil
4 large garlic cloves, minced
½ pound medium fresh mushrooms, thinly sliced
Salt and freshly ground black pepper to taste
¼ cup dry white wine
Juice of 1 lemon
2 tablespoons chopped broadleaf (Italian) parsley leaves

1. In a saucepan, over medium heat, melt the butter or margarine. Stir in the rice and cook, stirring, for 2 minutes to coat the rice. Pour in the broth. Bring to a boil, lower the heat, cover, and simmer for 20 minutes, or until the rice is tender and the liquid has been absorbed.

2. Meanwhile, in a frying pan, over medium heat, heat the oil and cook the garlic for 5 minutes, or until it is soft, stirring. Do not brown. Stir in the mushrooms, sprinkle with salt and pepper, and cook for 3 minutes. Add the wine and cook for 1 minute. Stir in the lemon juice and parsley. Cook over medium-high heat for 2 minutes, or until most of the liquid has evaporated. Remove from the heat. Blend the mushroom mixture with the hot cooked rice, fluffing it with a metal fork. Taste for seasoning. Spoon into a hot serving dish.

*Serves 4*

# Louisiana Okra Rice

*Southerners are big on rice, with the people of Louisiana being the champions. They eat rice at least once a day, in interesting combinations.*

1 tablespoon extra-virgin olive oil
2 medium onions, chopped
1 garlic clove, minced
1 large poblano green pepper, or 1 green bell pepper, seeded and
   chopped
½ teaspoon salt (optional)
1 cup long-grain rice
2 cups chicken broth
2 medium ripe tomatoes, peeled, seeded, and chopped
1 cup sliced okra
Salt and freshly ground black pepper to taste

1. In a deep saucepan, over medium heat, heat the olive oil. Stir in the onions, garlic, and chopped pepper. Sprinkle on ½ teaspoon salt. Cook for 10 minutes.

2. Add the rice, blending well. Pour in the broth. Bring to a boil, lower the heat, cover, and simmer for 15 minutes.

3. With a metal fork, stir in the tomatoes and okra, fluffing up the rice. Cover and simmer for 5 minutes, or until the rice is tender and the liquid has been absorbed. Remove from the heat and let stand for 5 minutes. Taste for seasoning, adding salt and pepper if needed. Fluff up the rice before serving.

*Serves 4*

## Parsnips and Brown Rice Hungarian Style

*Serve hot with meat or fowl. In Rost, Hungary, this was served to us with poached fresh ham.*

2½ cups water
1 cup long-grain brown rice
6 tablespoons butter or margarine
1 teaspoon salt (optional)
4 medium (about 1 pound) parsnips, peeled
2 medium onions, chopped
Salt and freshly ground black pepper to taste

1. In a saucepan, bring the water to a boil. Add the rice, 2 table-spoons of the butter or margarine, and 1 teaspoon salt, blending well. Cover, lower the heat, and simmer for 45 minutes, or until the rice is tender and the liquid has been absorbed.

2. While the rice is simmering, cook the parsnips in salted boiling water, then drain and mash them.

3. In a small saucepan, over medium heat, melt the remaining butter or margarine, and cook the onions for 8 minutes, or until they are golden. Do not brown.

4. With all the ingredients hot, combine and blend well the rice, mashed parsnips, and the onions with their butter or margarine. Taste for seasoning, adding salt and pepper if needed.

*Serves 4*

# Rice Piselli

*Here's a tasty Roman number, which again proves that rice is as versatile as pasta—maybe more so.*

*We enjoyed this dish with a delicious and tender scaloppine of turkey breast that the Romans prepare better than anyone.*

1 cup long-grain rice
2 medium ripe tomatoes, peeled, seeded, and finely chopped
2 medium onions, finely chopped
4 medium fresh mushrooms, sliced
1 cup dry red wine
1 cup chicken broth
½ teaspoon salt (optional)
¼ teaspoon freshly ground black pepper
3 tablespoons butter or margarine
1 cup small fresh green peas, cooked and drained, or use frozen
   tiny peas, cooked according to package directions
½ cup grated Asiago or Parmesan cheese

1. In a large saucepan, combine the rice, tomatoes, onions, and mushrooms. Stir in the wine, broth, salt, and pepper and blend well. Bring to a boil, lower the heat, cover, and simmer for 25 minutes, or until the liquid has been absorbed and the rice is tender.

2. With a metal fork, stir in the butter or margarine and peas, also fluffing up the rice. Taste for seasoning, adding salt and pepper if needed. Sprinkle with the cheese and serve immediately, piping hot.

*Serves 4*

# Risi e Bisi

*Rice and Peas*

4 tablespoons (½ stick) butter or margarine
4 scallions, trimmed and finely chopped
2 cups long-grain rice
½ cup dry white wine
4 cups chicken broth
1 tablespoon olive oil
2 cups small fresh green peas, or one 10-ounce package frozen
   tiny peas, defrosted
1 teaspoon sugar
½ cup water
Salt and freshly ground black pepper to taste
4 medium-thin slices prosciutto or other lean cooked ham, cut
   into small squares
¾ cup grated Asiago or Parmesan cheese

1. In a saucepan, over medium heat, melt 2 tablespoons of the butter or margarine. Add half of the scallions and cook for 2 minutes, or until they are soft. Do not brown. Stir in the rice and cook, stirring, for 2 minutes, coating the rice with the butter or margarine. Pour in the wine and the broth. Bring to a boil, lower the heat, cover, and simmer for 20 minutes, or until the rice is al dente and the liquid has been absorbed. If the rice is not cooked before the liquid is absorbed, add more hot broth and continue cooking. If the rice is cooked and the liquid has not been absorbed, remove the cover, raise the heat, and cook until the liquid has evaporated, being careful not to burn the rice.

2. While the rice is cooking, heat the oil in another saucepan and sauté the remaining scallions for 5 minutes, or until the scallions are soft. Add the peas, sugar, and ½ cup of water. Sprinkle with salt and pepper. Cover and, if the peas are fresh, cook for 10 minutes; if they are frozen and defrosted, cook for 5 minutes, or until they are just tender. Remove with a slotted spoon and, with a metal fork, mix into the rice along with the ham, cheese, and remaining butter or margarine (in small pieces). Taste for seasoning, adding salt and pepper if needed. Fluff up the rice before serving.

*Serves 6 to 8*

# Italian Stuffed Green Peppers

4 large firm green bell peppers
3 tablespoons butter or margarine
1 medium onion, finely chopped
1 garlic clove, minced
½ pound Italian sausage meat
1 cup long-grain rice
1 cup tomato juice
2 cups beef broth
½ teaspoon dried thyme
3 tablespoons chopped broadleaf (Italian) parsley leaves
¼ cup grated Asiago or Parmesan cheese
Salt and freshly ground black pepper to taste
Four ¼-inch slices mozzarella, about 3 inches in diameter

1. Cut a thin slice from the top of each pepper. Remove the seeds and white ribs. Drop into boiling water and blanch for 5 minutes. Remove, invert, and drain well.

2. In a frying pan, over medium heat, melt the butter or margarine. Add the onion and garlic and cook for 3 minutes, or until they are soft. Do not brown. Add the sausage meat and cook for 7 minutes, breaking it up with a fork. Add the rice and cook for 1 minute, stirring. Combine the tomato juice and broth. Pour 2 cups of the juice-broth mixture into the rice. Add the thyme and parsley and bring to a boil. Lower the heat, stir with a wooden fork, cover, and simmer for 15 minutes. The rice should be quite al dente and the liquid absorbed. If the rice is al dente before the liquid has been absorbed, remove the cover, raise the heat, and cook off the liquid, being careful that the rice does not burn. Remove from the heat and stir in the grated cheese. Taste for seasoning, adding salt and pepper if needed. The broth may have supplied enough seasoning. Preheat the oven to 350 degrees.

3. Heap the stuffing into the peppers. If any remains it can be spooned into the baking dish alongside the peppers. Arrange the peppers in a baking dish just large enough to hold them. Pour the remaining juice-broth mixture around them and bake for 25 minutes. Remove from the oven and lay a slice of mozzarella over each pepper. Return to oven and bake for 10 minutes, or until the cheese melts and is golden. Serve with the sauce spooned over.

*Serves 4*

# Riz à la Basquaise

*Rice Pilaf with Sweet Pepper*

2 tablespoons butter or margarine
1 cup long-grain rice
2½ cups chicken broth
3 tablespoons olive oil
2 medium onions, chopped
1 garlic clove, minced
1 large red bell pepper, seeded, white ribs removed, and coarsely
   chopped
Salt and freshly ground black pepper to taste
1 tablespoon white vinegar

1. In a saucepan, over medium heat, melt the butter or margarine. Add the rice and cook, stirring, for 2 minutes to coat the rice
well. Add the broth. Bring to a boil, stir with a wooden fork, lower
the heat, cover, and simmer for 20 minutes, or until the rice is tender and the liquid has been absorbed.

2. In a frying pan, heat the oil and add the onions, garlic, and
pepper. Cook for 7 minutes, or until they are soft. Do not brown.

3. Combine the rice and vegetables and mix well, fluffing with a
metal fork. Taste for seasoning, adding salt and pepper if needed.
The broth may have supplied enough seasoning. With a metal fork,
stir in the vinegar.

*Serves 4*

# Jalapeño Rice

4 tablespoons (½ stick) butter or margarine (Mexicans use lard,
   but we prefer the flavor of butter or margarine.)
1½ cups long-grain rice
1 large onion, chopped
3 garlic cloves, minced
3 small jalapeño peppers, seeded and diced
1 teaspoon ground coriander
⅛ teaspoon ground cinnamon
2 tipe tomatoes, peeled, seeded, and chopped
3 cups beef broth
Salt to taste

1. In a flameproof casserole, over medium heat, melt the butter
or margarine and add the rice, blending it well. Cook for 2 minutes,
stirring. Add the onion, garlic, peppers, coriander, and cinnamon,
blending well. Cook for 5 minutes. Preheat the oven to 350 degrees.

2. Stir in the tomatoes. Pour in the broth and bring to a boil.

3. Cover and bake for 20 minutes. Lower the oven temperature
to 300 degrees, uncover, and cook for 10 minutes. Fluff up the rice
with a metal fork. Taste before adding salt, as the broth may supply enough. At this point, the liquid should be absorbed and the
rice tender. If not, return to the oven and continue baking. If the
rice is tender but liquid still remains, cook, uncovered, on top of
the stove until the liquid evaporates, being careful that the rice
doesn't burn. Fluff up the rice with a metal fork before serving.

*Note:* Mexicans sometimes add a cup of briefly sautéed minced beef
and stir it in during the last 10 minutes of cooking.

*Serves 4 to 6*

# Peppered Rice

*For some reason, peppers of all kinds—hot, mild, sweet—are "in" right now. We like them, too, but not the way they are being used to excess, especially when they overwhelm delicate foods. The pepper sauce in this dish, for instance, would not be appropriate spooned over fish, which some cooks are in the habit of doing, because it would obliterate the delicate flavor of the fish. However, it is excellent on rice, which can hold its own with any flavor competition, making a snappy side dish for a bland entrée.*

2½ cups water
1 cup long-grain rice
1 teaspoon salt (optional)
3 tablespoons butter or margarine
2 tablespoons olive oil
5 whole scallions, trimmed and chopped
2 garlic cloves, chopped
1 medium poblano pepper, cored, seeded, and chopped
1 medium red bell pepper, cored, seeded, and chopped
2 tablespoons chopped jalapeño pepper
1 teaspoon dried thyme
Salt to taste

1. In a saucepan, bring the water to a boil. Stir in the rice and 1 teaspoon of salt. Cover, lower the heat, and simmer for 20 minutes, or until the rice is tender and the liquid has been absorbed. Reserve the rice and keep it warm.

2. In another saucepan, over medium heat, heat the butter or margarine and oil. Stir in all the vegetables, sprinkle with thyme and salt, and cook for 5 minutes. Cover, lower the heat, and simmer for 15 minutes, or until the vegetables are tender.

3. Purée the vegetables in a blender container or food processor. Return to the saucepan and heat through.

4. Spoon the warm rice into a hot serving dish and stir in the hot pepper purée to your taste, fluffing up the rice with a metal fork.

*Serves 4*

# Iraqi Rice with Potato Crust

*This makes an excellent accompaniment to tender slices of pink roast lamb.*

3 tablespoons butter or margarine
1½ cups long-grain rice
2 cups boiling water
1½ teaspoons salt (optional)
3 medium potatoes, peeled and very thinly sliced
6 tablespoons melted butter or margarine
2 garlic cloves, minced
½ cup toasted blanched almonds, chopped

1. In a saucepan, over medium heat, melt the 3 tablespoons of butter or margarine. Stir in the rice and cook for 1 minute. Add the water and 1 teaspoon of the salt, cover, lower the heat, and simmer for 10 minutes. Remove from the heat and drain. Reserve the rice.

2. In a large bowl, toss the potato slices with half of the melted butter or margarine and the remaining salt. In a heavy-bottomed pot with a tight-fitting cover, arrange the potato slices overlapping (using all the butter or margarine in which they were tossed) in 2 or 3 layers covering the bottom of the pot. Sprinkle with the garlic. Evenly spoon the half-cooked rice on top of the potatoes and garlic, and spoon the remaining melted butter or margarine over the rice.

3. Cover the pot with aluminum foil, and then with the cover. Cook over very low heat for 45 minutes, or until the rice is tender. Sprinkle with the almonds, gently stirring them into the rice with a metal fork. Be careful not to touch the bottom potato layer while you fluff the rice.

4. Serve on warm plates with spoons of rice side-by-side with a scoop of the crisp garlic-potatoes.

*Serves 4 to 6*

# Potatoes and Rice

*The potato is probably our most popular vegetable, but rice is closing in on it fast. We discovered this unique coupling of the two winners in Frankfurt.*

7 tablespoons butter or margarine
½ cup long-grain rice
2 medium potatoes, peeled and cut into ½-inch cubes
1 cup water
½ teaspoon salt (optional)
¼ teaspoon freshly ground black pepper
½ teaspoon ground allspice
3 whole scallions, trimmed and thinly sliced

1. In a saucepan, over medium heat, melt 2 tablespoons of the butter or margarine. Add the rice and cook, stirring, for 1 minute. Add the potatoes and water and stir in the salt, pepper, and allspice. Bring to a boil, lower the heat, cover, and simmer for 15 minutes, or until the rice and potatoes are tender and the liquid has been absorbed.

2. In a frying pan, melt 2 tablespoons of the butter or margarine. Cook the scallions for about 2 minutes, or just until they are crisp-tender. With a metal fork, mix them and the remaining butter or margarine (in small pieces) with the rice and potatoes, fluffing as you mix. Taste for seasoning, adding salt and pepper if needed.

*Serves 4*

# Rice and Sauerkraut Bake

*This was served with roast pork at the elegant Schloss Fuschl near Salzburg, Austria.*

2½ cups water
1 teaspoon salt (optional)
1 cup long-grain rice
4 tablespoons grated sharp Cheddar cheese
2 tablespoons chopped broadleaf (Italian) parsley leaves
½ teaspoon freshly ground black pepper
3 tablespoons butter or margarine
1 large onion, chopped
2½ pounds sauerkraut, well drained
1 teaspoon caraway seeds
1 cup milk
3 eggs

1. In a saucepan, bring the water to a boil. Stir in the salt and rice. Cover, lower the heat, and simmer for 20 minutes, or until the rice is tender and the liquid has been absorbed. If the rice is cooked before the liquid is absorbed, remove the cover, raise the heat, and cook until the liquid evaporates, being careful that the rice does not burn. If the liquid is absorbed and the rice is not yet tender, add a small amount of hot water and continue cooking. Stir in the cheese, parsley, and pepper with a metal fork. Reserve.

2. In a deep saucepan, over medium heat, melt the butter or margarine. Cook the onion for 5 minutes, or until it is soft. Do not brown. Stir in the sauerkraut and caraway seeds, blending well. Sauté for 15 minutes. Preheat the oven to 350 degrees.

3. Lightly butter a casserole and alternate layers of sauerkraut and rice, starting and ending with a layer of sauerkraut.

4. In a small bowl, beat the milk and eggs together and pour the mixture over the sauerkraut. Bake, uncovered, for 25 minutes, or until the top is set and golden.

*Serves 6*

# Spanakorizo

*In Athens, the old section of the city is an area called the* **Plaka.** *It is filled with gay tavernas and the throbbing music of the guitarlike bouzoukis, making it popular with tourists and Greeks alike. We had this rice dish in one of the little restaurants there, oddly enough, with a highly spiced ground lamb dish that we think is Turkish,* **kadm budu** *(lady's thigh).*

2 tablespoons olive oil
4 whole scallions, trimmed and chopped
2 pounds fresh spinach, washed, drained, and finely chopped
1½ cups long-grain rice
3 cups tomato juice
6 ripe plum tomatoes, peeled, seeded, and chopped
1 teaspoon salt (optional)
¼ teaspoon freshly ground black pepper
½ teaspoon ground cinnamon

1. In a large heavy saucepan, over medium heat, heat the oil. Add the scallions and cook for 3 minutes. Make an even layer of the spinach over the scallions. Cover with an even layer of the rice.

2. In a bowl, blend the tomato juice, tomatoes, salt, and pepper and spoon the mixture over the rice. Sprinkle with the cinnamon. Bring to a boil, then turn the heat very low, cover, and simmer for 20 minutes, or until the rice is tender. Remove from the heat and let sit, covered, for 10 minutes before serving.

*Serves 6*

# Brown Rice and Spinach

4 tablespoons olive oil
4 large shallots, chopped
2 garlic cloves, minced
1 cup long-grain brown rice
2 medium ripe tomatoes, peeled, seeded, and diced
Salt and freshly ground black pepper to taste
2½ cups water
Two 10-ounce packages fresh spinach, trimmed, washed,
     drained, and chopped

1. In a deep saucepan, over medium heat, heat the olive oil and cook the shallots and garlic for 5 minutes, or until they are soft. Do not brown.

2. Stir in the rice and cook for 2 minutes, stirring. Add the tomatoes, salt, pepper, and water. Bring to a boil, cover, lower the heat, and simmer for 35 minutes.

3. Quickly stir in the spinach, cover again, and cook for 10 minutes, or until the rice is tender and the liquid has been absorbed. Fluff up with a metal fork. If the liquid is absorbed before the rice is tender, add more hot water and continue cooking. If the rice is cooked before the liquid is absorbed, remove the cover, raise the heat, and cook until the liquid evaporates, being careful not to burn the rice.

*Serves 4*

# Riso al Forno

2 cups al dente–cooked long-grain rice (It should be quite firm.)
One 1-pound can imported Italian plum tomatoes, chopped,
     liquid reserved
1 medium onion, sliced
Salt and freshly ground black pepper to taste
3 tablespoons butter or margarine

1. Preheat the oven to 350 degrees.

2. In a buttered baking dish, combine and blend well all the ingredients except the butter or margarine.

3. Dot with the butter or margarine and bake, uncovered, for 30 minutes, or until bubbling and most of the liquid has been absorbed.

*Serves 4*

# Tomatoes Antalya Irfan

*We enjoyed these tomatoes when they were served to us with calf's liver at Antalya, called the Turkish Riviera. The chef gladly gave us the recipe, but asked that his first name be attached. It is.*

6 medium firm ripe tomatoes
Salt and freshly ground black pepper to taste
2 tablespoons olive oil
1 medium onion, finely chopped
1 garlic clove, minced
1 cup long-grain rice
½ teaspoon ground turmeric
⅛ teaspoon ground cinnamon
½ teaspoon dried oregano
1½ cups chicken broth
¼ cup dry white wine
3 tablespoons finely chopped broadleaf (Italian)
    parsley leaves
½ cup pignoli
¼ cup tomato purée
¼ cup additional olive oil
½ cup additional chicken broth

1. Cut a thin slice from the stem ends of the tomatoes. Remove the seeds and center pulp, leaving firm shells. Discard the seeds and chop the pulp and the tops (peel the tops before chopping).

Sprinkle the inside of the tomatoes with salt and pepper and invert to drain.

2. In a saucepan, over medium heat, heat the 2 tablespoons of olive oil. Add the onion and garlic and cook for 2 minutes, or until they are soft. Do not brown. Stir in the rice and cook for 2 minutes, coating with the oil. Stir in the turmeric, cinnamon, and oregano. Pour in 1½ cups chicken broth and wine and bring to a boil. Lower the heat, cover, and simmer for 10 minutes, or until the liquid has been absorbed and the rice is al dente. If the rice is not cooked before the liquid has been absorbed, add more hot broth and continue cooking. If the rice is cooked and the liquid has not been absorbed, remove the cover, raise the heat, and cook off the liquid, being careful not to burn the rice. Taste and season. Add the chopped tomato pulp and tops. Preheat the oven to 350 degrees.

3. Stir the parsley and pignoli into the rice, mixing with a metal fork. Fill the tomato shells with the rice mixture, dividing it equally. Place the stuffed tomatoes in a baking dish just large enough to hold them snugly. If there is too much filling, spoon it around the tomatoes.

4. Combine the tomato purée, ¼ cup olive oil, and ½ cup chicken broth and pour the mixture around the tomatoes. There should be about ½ inch of liquid in the bottom of the pan. Bake for 20 minutes (basting 2 or 3 times), or until the rice is tender.

*Serves 6*

# Stuffed Tomatoes Creole Style

6 medium firm ripe tomatoes
Salt to taste
3 tablespoons butter or margarine
1 medium onion, finely chopped
1½ cups al dente–cooked long-grain rice
1 cup shelled and deveined shrimp, cut into cubes slightly
    smaller than ½ inch
½ cup cooked corn kernels
¼ teaspoon cayenne
3 tablespoons bread crumbs

1. Cut a thin slice from the stem ends of the tomatoes. Remove the seeds and center pulp, leaving firm shells. Discard the seeds and chop the pulp and the tops (peel the tops before chopping). Sprinkle the inside of the tomatoes with salt and invert to drain.

2. Melt the butter or margarine over medium heat in a frying pan. Add the onion and cook for 3 minutes, or until it is soft. Do not brown. Combine the rice, shrimp, corn, onion, cayenne, and additional salt to taste, and stir with a fork. Add the chopped tomato pulp and tops. Preheat the oven to 400 degrees.

3. Divide the stuffing equally and fill the tomatoes, mounding it if necessary. Cover the tops with bread crumbs. Arrange the stuffed tomatoes in a baking dish just large enough to hold them snugly. Pour ½ cup water into the baking dish and bake, uncovered, for 20 minutes, or until the tops are golden and the rice stuffing heated through. At this time the shrimp should be pink.

*Serves 6*

# Risotto Estivo

## *A Summertime Risotto*

2 tablespoons butter or margarine
2 tablespoons olive oil
4 whole scallions, trimmed and cut into ¼-inch lengths
2 celery stalks, scraped and coarsely chopped
1½ cups long-grain brown rice
3½ cups chicken broth
4 ripe but firm plum tomatoes, peeled, seeded, and coarsely
    chopped
1 bay leaf
1 cup shelled fresh peas, cooked al dente, or frozen, defrosted
¼ pound small fresh mushrooms, sliced and cooked in 3
    tablespoons of butter or margarine until brown but still firm
½ cup chopped broadleaf (Italian) parsley leaves
5 fresh basil leaves, chopped
Salt and freshly ground black pepper to taste
¼ pound prosciutto, cut into slivers
1 cup grated Asiago or Parmesan cheese

1. In a large saucepan, over medium heat, heat the butter or margarine and oil. Add the scallions and celery and cook for 6 minutes, or until they are slightly soft. Do not brown.

2. Stir in the rice and cook for 2 minutes, stirring to coat the rice well with the fat. Add the broth, tomatoes, and bay leaf. Bring to a boil, lower the heat, stir with a wooden fork, cover, and simmer for 35 minutes, or until the rice is al dente and most of the liquid has been absorbed. The rice should be moist but not soupy. Remove and discard the bay leaf.

3. Stir in the peas, mushrooms, parsley, and basil and cook for 3 minutes, or to heat through. Taste for seasoning, adding salt and pepper if needed. The broth may have supplied enough.

4. Remove from the heat and stir in the prosciutto and half of the cheese with a metal fork, fluffing up the rice. Pass the remaining cheese at the table.

*Serves 6 to 8*

# Risotto Legumi Misti

## *Rice with Mixed Vegetables*

2 tablespoons extra-virgin olive oil
2 medium onions, chopped
2 garlic cloves, minced
2 medium parsnips, scraped and diced
2 medium carrots, scraped and diced
2 small (about 1 by 4 inches) zucchini, cut into ½-inch slices
2 cups fresh (or frozen) baby lima beans
1½ cups long-grain rice
3½ cups beef broth
Salt to taste
¼ teaspoon hot red pepper flakes
1 cup grated Romano cheese

1. In a large saucepan, heat the oil over medium heat. Stir the onions, garlic, parsnips, carrots, zucchini, and lima beans into the pot. Cook for 15 minutes, stirring occasionally. Do not brown.

2. Stir in the rice, broth, salt, and hot red pepper flakes. Bring to a boil, stir with a wooden fork, lower the heat, cover, and simmer for 20 minutes. Remove from the heat and let sit for 5 minutes, covered. The rice should be slightly al dente and moist, but not soupy. Taste for seasoning, adding salt and pepper if needed.

3. Sprinkle the rice and vegetables with half of the cheese. Toss with a metal fork, fluffing up the rice. Serve the remaining cheese at the table.

*Serves 6 to 8*

# Armenian Rice-Stuffed Zucchini

*These go very nicely with slices of pink roasted leg of lamb.*

4 zucchini, about 2½ by 6 inches
3 tablespoons olive oil
2 medium onions, finely chopped
1 garlic clove, minced
Salt and freshly ground black pepper to taste
3 cups al dente–cooked long-grain rice (cooked in chicken broth)
6 medium fresh mushrooms, chopped
2 tablespoons minced broadleaf (Italian) parsley leaves
5 fresh mint leaves, minced
½ teaspoon ground cumin
½ cup grated Asiago or Parmesan cheese
One 1-pound 12-ounce can imported Italian plum tomatoes
½ cup beef broth

1. Cut the zucchini into halves lengthwise; scoop out the pulp, leaving a shell about ¼ inch thick. Lightly salt the zucchini shells and invert them on paper towels to drain. Chop one-third of the pulp and discard the remainder. In a frying pan, over medium heat, heat the oil and cook the onions, garlic, and zucchini pulp for 5 minutes, or until the onion is soft, seasoning with salt and pepper. Remove from the heat and blend in the rice, mushrooms, parsley, mint, cumin, cheese, and 2 of the canned tomatoes, chopped.

2. Preheat the oven to 375 degrees.

3. Place the zucchini halves in a baking dish or casserole just large enough to hold them snugly. Divide the rice mixture, mounding it in the shells. Chop the remaining tomatoes and blend them and their liquid with the beef broth. Season with salt and pepper. Spoon this mixture over and around the stuffed zucchini.

4. Tightly cover the baking dish with foil or the casserole with its cover and bake for 15 minutes. Baste with the sauce in the pan, return to the oven, and bake, covered, for 30 minutes, or until the zucchini shells are tender. Serve with the tomato sauce spooned over.

*Serves 4*

# Parsleyed Zucchini Rice

4 small (about 4 by 1½ inches) zucchini, cut into ¼-inch slices
3 tablespoons butter or margarine
1 small onion, finely chopped
1 garlic clove, minced
1 cup long-grain brown rice
1 bay leaf
2½ cups chicken broth
Salt and freshly ground black pepper to taste
¾ cup chopped broadleaf (Italian) parsley leaves
2 tablespoons fresh lemon juice
1 cup ricotta
½ cup grated Gruyère or Fontina cheese
¼ cup grated Asiago or Parmesan cheese

1. Cook the zucchini slices in just enough salted boiling water to cover until they are crisp-tender. Drain well.

2. In a saucepan, over medium heat, melt the butter or margarine. Add the onion and garlic and cook for 3 minutes, or until they are soft. Do not brown. Stir in the rice and cook for 1 minute, coating the rice well with the butter or margarine. Add the bay leaf and broth and bring to a boil. Stir with a wooden fork, lower the heat, cover, and cook for 40 minutes, or until the rice is tender but still slightly al dente and the liquid has been absorbed. Discard the bay leaf. Taste for seasoning, adding salt and pepper if needed. Preheat the oven to 350 degrees.

3. With a metal fork, mix the parsley and lemon juice with the rice.

4. Butter a shallow baking dish. Arrange the rice in a smooth layer on the bottom. Cover the rice with a layer of the ricotta and an overlapping layer of the zucchini slices. Sprinkle the zucchini with the grated cheeses and bake for 25 minutes, or until the cheese has melted and the dish is heated through.

*Serves 4 to 6*

# Zucchini Rice alla Parma

*Just about everything (except stuffing for poultry and some meats) that is rice to Italians is risotto. They like it soupy, not so soupy that it must be eaten with a spoon, but often a little too moist for our taste. But here's one we discovered in Parma (with, what else, Parmesan cheese!) that we often enjoy when that ubiquitous, do-everything zucchini is dominating our garden.*

3 tablespoons butter or margarine
2 tablespoons olive oil
3 slices *panchetti* (this is Italian bacon and delicious; but if you
    can't find it, use prosciutto), diced
2 medium onions, chopped
2 garlic cloves, minced
5 small (about 1 by 4 inches) zucchini, cut into ¼-inch slices
1½ cups long-grain rice
3 cups chicken broth
Salt and freshly ground black pepper to taste
½ cup grated Parmesan cheese

1. In a flameproof casserole, over medium heat, heat the butter or margarine and olive oil. Add the *panchetti* and cook for 5 minutes. Add the onions, garlic, and zucchini and cook, stirring, for 10 minutes. Preheat the oven to 350 degrees.

2. Stir in the rice, blending it with the vegetables. Add the broth and bring to a boil. Cover the casserole and bake for 25 minutes, or until the rice is tender and the liquid has been absorbed. Taste before seasoning, as the broth may have supplied enough. Fluff the rice with a metal fork and serve with a generous spoonful of the cheese on top of each portion.

*Serves 6*

# 8

# Rice Specialties
# and Side Dishes

One of our several idiosyncrasies regarding food is a dislike for the word *leftover*. Thus, we have no chapter on that category.

Instead, convinced that rice is surely the most versatile of all accompaniments, we offer the following recipes, with rice given a starring role. Even if it only has a walk-on part in the drama of dinner, rice usually steals the show.

We still remember a dinner for which we prepared a perfectly cooked whole fillet of beef and served it with its own delicious juices. With it we offered Riz Bourguignonne—rice with egg, wine, cream, and cheese. Remarks on the rice ran around the table among our guests, but the fillet was not commented on at all.

# Chinese Eight-Jewel Rice

*Other than several simple versions of fried rice, the Chinese do not do anything spectacular with rice, except eat it—about three times a day. But it usually is a side dish, to be mixed by the diner with other foods, or simply eaten as an accompaniment. There is nothing wrong with this technique. In fact, the Chinese know more about eating and cooking rice than anyone. But we're partial to this fancier version that we discovered in Hong Kong. Either a wok or frying pan can be used to cook this dish. The finest Chinese cooks we know, the Wah Chins, don't even own a wok.*

3 tablespoons safflower oil
4 eggs, beaten
4 whole scallions, trimmed and cut into ½-inch lengths
2 lean loin pork chops (all fat removed), diced
½ cup diced smoked ham
½ chicken breast, boned and diced
4 water chestnuts, thinly sliced
4 large fresh mushrooms, thinly sliced
8 medium shrimp, shelled, deveined, and diced
4 cups cooked long-grain rice
1 tablespoon soy sauce, blended with 3 tablespoons chicken broth

1. In a wok or large frying pan, over medium heat, heat 1 tablespoon of the oil and lightly scramble the eggs until they are just barely set. Remove and set aside.

2. Add the remaining oil to the pan and, over medium heat, stir-fry the scallions for 20 seconds. Stir in the pork and stir-fry for 4 minutes. Add the ham, chicken, and water chestnuts. Stir-fry for 1 minute. Add the mushrooms and shrimp and stir-fry for 1 minute, or until the shrimp just turn pink.

3. Stir in the cooked rice and the soy sauce–chicken broth blend and stir-fry for 2 minutes, or until the rice is heated through. Return the scrambled eggs to the pan and carefully stir-fry for 30 seconds. Serve immediately.

*Serves 4 to 6*

# Apple-Time Rice

*This is a rice dish that we like to serve with pork or ham in October, when we can pick apples from our tree. It's unusual—and taste tempting.*

2 tablespoons butter or margarine
1½ cups long-grain rice
1 teaspoon salt (optional)
1 cup cranberry juice
2 cups unsweetened apple juice
2 tablespoons fresh lemon juice
2 teaspoons dark or light brown sugar
½ teaspoon ground cinnamon
1 tablespoon chopped raisins
2 small tart apples, peeled, cored, and coarsely chopped
2 whole small scallions, trimmed and cut into ¼-inch lengths
Salt and freshly ground black pepper to taste

1. In a saucepan, over medium heat, melt the butter or margarine. Stir in the rice and 1 teaspoon salt and cook, stirring, for 2 minutes to coat the rice. Add the cranberry, apple, and lemon juices and sugar, cinnamon, and raisins and bring to a boil. Stir with a wooden fork, lower the heat, cover, and simmer for 20 minutes, or until the rice is tender and the liquid has been absorbed.

2. Stir in the apples and scallions with a metal fork and heat through. Do not cook, as the apples and scallions should be crunchy counterpoints to the rice. Taste for seasoning, adding salt and pepper if needed.

*Serves 6 to 8*

# Arroz Alentejo

## *Portuguese Rice and Pea Pudding*

5 tablespoons butter or margarine
2 medium onions, chopped
1½ cups long-grain brown rice
3½ cups chicken broth
Salt and freshly ground black pepper to taste
One 10-ounce package frozen tiny peas, cooked slightly less than
  the package directs and drained
¼ pound smoked ham or prosciutto, minced
3 large eggs, beaten

1. In a saucepan, over medium heat, melt 3 tablespoons of the butter or margarine. Cook the onions for 5 minutes. Do not brown. Stir in the rice, coating it well with the butter or margarine.

2. Pour in the chicken broth and bring to a boil. Stir with a wooden fork, lower the heat, cover, and simmer for 35 minutes, or until the rice is al dente. Taste and season with salt (remember, the ham is salty, as is the broth) and pepper if needed. Remove from the heat. Preheat the oven to 400 degrees.

3. Stir the peas and remaining butter or margarine into the rice with a metal fork. Add the ham and beaten eggs, blending well.

4. Spoon into a buttered 8-inch-square by 2-inch-deep baking dish. Bake, uncovered, until the eggs are set, about 20 minutes.

*Serves 6*

# Avocado Rice

*We had this in Florida with pompano that had been baked in parchment; it was a delicious and exotic combination. We've also enjoyed a similar dish, served with broiled sea trout in the Bahamas, where mango was substituted for the avocado.*

2 cups water
½ cup unsweetened pineapple juice
1 cup long-grain rice
1 teaspoon salt (optional)
3 tablespoons butter or margarine, cut into small pieces
1 large ripe but firm avocado, peeled, coarsely chopped, and
    mixed with 2 tablespoons pineapple juice

1. In a saucepan, bring the water and pineapple juice to a boil. Stir in the rice and salt, cover, lower the heat, and simmer for 20 minutes, or until the rice is tender and the liquid has been absorbed.

2. With a metal fork, stir in the butter or margarine, then carefully blend in the avocado and cook for 1 or 2 minutes to heat through. Fluff up the rice with a metal fork before serving.

*Serves 4*

# Au Gratin Rice

*This is an excellent plate mate for a nice juicy piece of roast chicken.*

3 cups hot cooked, seasoned long-grain rice
1 cup grated Monterey Jack cheese with jalapeño pepper
2 tablespoons melted butter or margarine
½ cup fine dry bread crumbs
2 tablespoons grated Parmesan cheese

1. Preheat the oven to 350 degrees.

2. In a bowl, with a metal fork, toss the rice with half of the Monterey Jack cheese. Spoon evenly into a buttered baking dish. Sprinkle with the remaining cheese.

3. Bake, uncovered, for 10 minutes, or until the cheese melts.

4. With a fork, blend the butter or margarine, bread crumbs, and Parmesan cheese together. Sprinkle evenly on the rice dish. Return to the oven and bake until the crumbs are crusty.

*Serves 4*


# Bacon and Chives Toss-Up

*This is a taste-enlivening dish to serve with something simple, such as broiled fish.*

3 slices bacon, cooked until crisp and crumbled
3 cups cooked long-grain rice
3 tablespoons chopped fresh chives
4 tablespoons olive oil
Salt and freshly ground black pepper to taste
⅛ teaspoon hot sauce, or to taste

In a bowl, combine the bacon, rice, chives, and olive oil and toss. Taste and season with salt and pepper. Sprinkle on the hot sauce and toss again. Transfer to a saucepan and heat thoroughly on top of the stove, fluffing up the rice with a metal fork as you heat it.

*Serves 4*

# Bacon-and-Egg Fried Rice

3 eggs
½ teaspoon salt (optional)
2 tablespoons light vegetable oil
2 slices lean bacon, coarsely chopped
4 whole scallions, trimmed and chopped
4 cups cooked long-grain rice
2 tablespoons soy sauce
¼ teaspoon sugar
Salt and freshly ground black pepper to taste
3 tablespoons butter or margarine, cut into small pieces
½ cup cooked fresh or frozen tiny peas

1. Lightly beat the eggs and salt together. In a wok or deep frying pan, over medium heat, heat the oil. Add the bacon and cook for 2 minutes. Add the scallions and cook for 1 minute.

2. Pour in the eggs, covering the bottom of the pan, and cook until the eggs are almost set. Quickly stir the eggs into a coarse, soft scramble. With a metal fork quickly stir in the rice, soy sauce, and sugar. Heat through. Taste for seasoning before adding salt and pepper. Just before serving, stir in the butter or margarine and the peas.

*Serves 4*

# Deep-fried Rice Balls

*Serve as a hot hors d'oeuvre or to accompany a main course.*

2 cups cooked short- or medium-grain rice, seasoned with salt
    and pepper and blended with ½ cup grated Asiago or Parmesan
    cheese and ¼ cup soft butter
2 eggs, beaten in a large bowl
About twelve ½-inch cubes mozzarella
Fine dry bread crumbs for dredging
Vegetable oil for deep-frying

1. Mix the rice with the beaten eggs.
2. Scoop about 2 tablespoonfuls of the mixture into your hand,
push a cube of mozzarella into it, molding the rice around it into a
ball to enclose the cube. Holding the ball in your hand, sprinkle it
with bread crumbs until it is evenly covered. Pat the crumbs onto
the rice. Refrigerate the completed balls, not touching, for 1 hour
or more.
3. Heat the vegetable oil to 375 degrees, or until a 1-inch cube of
bread becomes golden brown in 40 to 50 seconds. Cook a few balls
at a time (lowering them into the hot fat with a slotted spoon), until
they are golden brown. Do not crowd them. Remove with a slotted
spoon and drain on a baking sheet lined with paper towels. The
rice balls may be kept warm in a 200-degree oven while the others
are being fried.

*Serves 4 to 6*

# Riz Bourguignonne

*This is a good accompaniment for beef bourguignonne.*

2 tablespoons butter or margarine
1 cup long-grain rice
2¼ cups water
1 teaspoon salt (optional)
Freshly ground black pepper to taste
1 egg, beaten
½ cup grated Gruyère cheese
¼ cup grated Asiago or Parmesan cheese
2 tablespoons dry white wine
¾ cup half-and-half
¼ cup fine fresh bread crumbs
2 tablespoons melted butter or margarine

1. In a saucepan, over medium heat, melt the 2 tablespoons of butter or margarine. Add the rice and cook, stirring, for 2 minutes. Stir in the water and salt. Bring to a boil, lower the heat, stir with a wooden fork, cover, and simmer for 20 minutes, or until the rice is al dente and the liquid has been absorbed. Remove from the heat. Taste and add salt and pepper if needed. Beat in the egg. Preheat the oven to 400 degrees.

2. Spread the rice in a 1½-inch layer in a shallow baking dish. Smooth the top but do not pack it down. Combine and blend the cheeses, wine, and half-and-half, and spoon the mixture over the rice. Sprinkle with the bread crumbs and melted butter or margarine. Bake for 15 minutes, or until golden.

*Serves 4 to 6*

# Fried Rice Cakes Italiano

8 tablespoons (1 stick) butter or margarine
2 cups cold leftover Risotto Milanese (page 128), mixed with 1
  beaten egg
¼ pound mozzarella, cut into small pieces

1. Over medium heat, melt 2 tablespoons of the butter or margarine in a small (4 to 5 inches in diameter), shallow frying pan. When hot, stir in one-quarter of the rice mixture. Mix it with the butter or margarine. Before it starts to cook, press with a spatula into a cake, covering the bottom of the pan. Continue to pat as it cooks. Shake the pan gently from time to time to keep the rice from sticking but do not break up the cake.

2. When the rice cake is golden brown on the underside, place a plate larger than the frying pan over the pan, turn the pan over so the rice cake falls onto the plate, browned side up. Slide the cake back into the pan, browned side up and pat it flat.

3. Put one-quarter of the mozzarella on the top, cover, and cook for 3 to 4 minutes to brown the bottom. Slide out onto a small hot serving plate (see Note). Cover and keep warm in a 250-degree oven while cooking the others. Serve each right on the hot plate on which you kept it warm.

*Note:* You'll need 4 small hot plates. This prevents the cakes from being broken up while being transferred from one plate to another.

*Serves 4*

# Rice with Four Cheeses

1 cup half-and-half
2 ounces Fontina cheese, cut into small cubes (less than ½ inch)
2 ounces Gouda cheese, cut into small cubes (less than ½ inch)
2 ounces mozzarella, cut into small cubes (less than ½ inch)
3 tablespoons butter or margarine, cut into small pieces
Freshly ground black pepper to taste
4 cups hot cooked long-grain rice
1 cup grated Asiago or Parmesan cheese

1. In a saucepan, over medium heat, heat the half-and-half just to a simmer. Remove from the heat and stir in the cubed cheeses.

2. Mix the butter or margarine and pepper with the rice, stirring and fluffing up with a metal fork.

3. Return the cheese sauce to the heat and heat until the cheese is very nearly melted, but the cubes still have some shape.

4. Place the rice in a hot serving bowl. Pour on the cheese sauce and mix with a metal fork. Serve the grated cheese at the table.

*Serves 6 to 8*


# Rice Dumplings

*These dumplings can be served with any stew.*

1 egg, beaten
½ cup milk
1½ cups sifted all-purpose flour
2½ teaspoons baking powder
1 teaspoon salt (optional)
¼ teaspoon ground nutmeg
1 cup cooked short- or medium-grain rice
2 tablespoons finely minced parsley leaves
2 tablespoons melted butter or margarine
Additional milk, if needed

1. In a large bowl, blend the egg and milk. Sift the flour two times, once before measuring and the second time with the baking powder, salt, and nutmeg, and add to the egg-milk bowl. With a metal fork, stir in the rice, parsley, and butter or margarine. Blend well. If the batter seems too heavy, add a small amount of milk. It should be just thick enough to hold its shape on a spoon.

2. Drop by tablespoonfuls onto barely simmering stew. Cover tightly and cook for 15 minutes. Test for doneness by inserting a toothpick. If it comes out clean, the dumplings are ready.

*Serves 6*

## Indian Egg Rice

*The Indian version of fried rice, which also has eggs, is softer than Chinese fried rice and has a different taste texture.*

1½ cups long-grain rice
1 teaspoon salt (optional)
⅛ teaspoon hot red pepper flakes
2 whole cloves
⅛ teaspoon ground nutmeg
3 cups boiling water
Salt and freshly ground black pepper to taste
4 tablespoons (½ stick) butter or margarine
1 large garlic clove, minced
4 eggs, beaten

1. In a saucepan, combine the rice, salt, hot red pepper flakes, cloves, and nutmeg. Stir in the boiling water. Over high heat, keep at a boil for 1 minute. Lower the heat, cover, and simmer for 20 minutes, or until the rice is tender and the liquid has been absorbed. Remove and discard the cloves. Taste for seasoning, adding salt and pepper if needed.

2. In a large deep frying pan, over medium heat, melt the butter

or margarine. Add the garlic and cook until it is soft. Do not brown. Stir in the eggs and cook, stirring, for 1 minute, or until they are set. Do not overcook. Blend in the hot, cooked rice. Remove from the heat and serve immediately.

*Serves 4*

# Turkish Egg-Sauced Rice

*This simple but extremely tasty dish was served in Istanbul with* shish kebab, *its usual accompaniment, but it is excellent with any meat or chicken dish. In fact, we also had it with swordfish, another specialty of that city.*

2½ cups beef broth
1 cup long-grain rice
Salt and freshly ground black pepper to taste
3 tablespoons soft butter or margarine
1 large egg yolk, carefully separated in order not to break one-
    half of the shell kept to serve it in

1. In a saucepan bring the broth to a boil. Slowly pour the rice into the broth, stirring and keeping the broth at a boil until all of the rice has been poured in. Lower the heat, cover, and simmer for 20 minutes, or until the rice is tender and the broth has been absorbed. Taste before adding salt and pepper, as the broth may have had enough.
2. With a metal fork, stir in the butter or margarine, fluffing up the rice. Spoon into a hot serving dish. Make a small depression in the center of the rice. Set the egg yolk in the shell in it. At the table, just before serving, remove the egg yolk from the shell and stir the yolk into the hot rice with a metal fork.

*Serves 4*

# Kasha-Rice Pilaf

3 tablespoons butter or margarine
1 cup buckwheat groats
1 cup long-grain rice
4½ cups beef broth
Salt and freshly ground black pepper to taste
½ teaspoon powdered saffron, or to taste
2 tablespoons melted butter or margarine
¼ cup fresh lemon juice

1. In a deep saucepan, over medium heat, melt the 3 tablespoons of butter or margarine. Add the buckwheat groats and rice and cook for 2 minutes, stirring, until they are well coated with the butter.

2. Pour in the broth, bring to a boil, and stir with a wooden fork. Lower the heat, cover, and simmer for 20 minutes, or until the grains are tender and the liquid has been absorbed. Taste for seasoning, adding salt and pepper if needed. The broth may have supplied enough.

3. With a metal fork, stir in the saffron, melted butter or margarine, and lemon juice, tossing to fluff.

4. Cover, place over high heat for 1 minute. Remove from the heat and let sit, covered, for 5 minutes before serving.

*Serves 6*

# Po Valley Rice Omelet

¾ cup cooked long-grain rice
½ cup grated Provolone
½ cup pepperoni cut into ¼-inch cubes
8 eggs
Salt and freshly ground black pepper to taste
3 tablespoons butter or margarine

1. In a bowl, blend the rice, Provolone, and pepperoni with a fork.

2. Beat the eggs in a bowl just long enough to mix the whites and yolks, then season lightly with salt and pepper.

3. In a large frying pan or omelet pan, over medium-high heat, melt the butter or margarine, being sure the entire bottom of the pan is coated. Pour the eggs into the pan and cook as for an omelet, lifting the cooked part of the eggs to allow the uncooked part to run under and shaking the pan when the bottom starts to set.

4. While the top is still moist, spoon the rice filling down the center of the omelet. Fold over and cook just long enough to heat the filling and melt the cheese. Or, if you prefer, cook individual omelets, using 2 or 3 eggs per person and divide the filling among the omelets.

*Serves 3 or 4*

# Madras Spicy Rice

*We were taught to make this simple but tasty Indian dish by the Nadhans, friends from Madras, who also taught us to make delicious vegetable and ground lamb cutlets. For this dish, they used the whole spices (obtainable in Indian and Middle Eastern grocery stores), but we find that the ground spices found in supermarkets also work fine. We like this rice with a simple, lightly seasoned fish or chicken dish.*

1½ cups long-grain rice
4 cups water
1 teaspoon salt (optional)
1 bay leaf
3 whole cloves
½ teaspoon ground cinnamon
1 teaspoon ground cardamom
3 tablespoons butter or margarine
2 teaspoons light brown sugar
1 teaspoon cumin seeds

1. In a large saucepan, combine the rice, water, salt, bay leaf, cloves, cinnamon, and cardamom. Stir well, then set aside.

2. In a small frying pan, over medium-low heat, melt the butter or margarine and stir in the sugar and cumin seeds, stirring until the sugar has caramelized, about 1½ minutes. Stir into the pan with the rice.

3. Bring the water in the rice pan to a boil, stir with a wooden fork, and cover. Lower the heat and simmer for 20 minutes, or until the rice is tender and the liquid has been absorbed. Let sit, covered, for 10 minutes. Taste for seasoning, adding salt and pepper if needed. Remove the cloves, if you can find them, and the bay leaf. Fluff up the rice with a metal fork before serving.

*Serves 4 to 6*

## Rice Pancakes

*These nifty little cakes are an excellent way to use leftover rice. They can be served as a breakfast cake with eggs or as a side dish for lunch or dinner.*

3 cups cooked short- or medium-grain rice
Salt to taste
3 medium eggs, beaten
2 slices bacon
2 tablespoons vegetable oil

1. Put the rice in a bowl and season it lightly with salt, then stir in the beaten eggs, blending well.

2. In a large frying pan, over medium heat, cook the bacon until it is crisp and golden brown. Drain on paper towels. Cool the bacon, then finely crumble it.

3. Blend the crumbled bacon with the rice-egg mixture. Heat the vegetable oil in the frying pan over medium heat. Drop heaping tablespoonfuls of the rice mixture into the hot oil, leaving a space

between each spoonful. With a spatula, flatten each spoonful of rice into a flat cake. Fry until crisp and golden; turn over and repeat. Serve immediately.

*Note:* Serve with apricot jam thinned with some lemon juice.

*Serves 4*

# Stir-fried Pepper Rice

3 tablespoons light vegetable oil
5 scallions, trimmed and cut into ½-inch slices, using all but the last inch of the dark green part
1 medium green bell pepper, seeded, cored, and cut into ½-inch slices
1 garlic clove, minced
One ¼-inch slice boiled or other cooked ham, cut into ½-by-1-inch strips
4 cups cooked long-grain rice
3 tablespoons soy sauce
1 egg, beaten
Salt to taste
½ cup chopped fresh coriander or fresh parsley leaves

In a wok or large deep frying pan, over medium heat, heat the oil. Stir in the scallions, green pepper, garlic, and ham, and cook for 2 to 3 minutes, stirring. Stir in the rice and soy sauce. Cook for 5 minutes, stirring, until heated through. Stir in the egg and cook just long enough to set the egg. Taste for seasoning, adding salt if needed. Stir in the coriander or parsley and serve.

*Serves 4*

# Small Fried Rice "Pies" with
# Gorgonzola Cheese Sauce

3 cups cooked, seasoned short- or medium-grain rice
1 whole egg and 1 egg yolk, beaten together in a large bowl
Fine fresh unseasoned bread crumbs for dredging
6 tablespoons butter or margarine
1½ cups half-and-half
½ cup crumbled Gorgonzola cheese
½ cup grated Asiago or Parmesan cheese

1. Add the rice to the bowl with the egg and mix well with a fork.

2. Form 6 neat patties approximately ¾ inch thick. Dredge in the bread crumbs.

3. In a large frying pan, over medium-high heat, melt 3 table-spoons of the butter or margarine. Cook the "pies" on one side until they are golden brown. Add the remaining butter or margarine to the pan and cook the "pies" on the other side until golden brown. Transfer to a hot serving dish and keep warm while making the sauce.

4. In a saucepan, over low heat, heat the half-and-half and cheeses, stirring, until the cheeses have melted and the sauce is reasonably smooth. Serve at the table to be spooned onto the "pies."

*Note:* The rice mixture can also be baked in well-buttered 3-inch tart tins. Sprinkle the top with the crumbs and dot with butter or margarine. Bake in a preheated 375-degree oven until they are golden on top. Run a knife around the inside edges of the tins to make it easier to turn them out.

*Serves 6*

# Greek Pilaf

*This is a dish we had on the Greek island of Lesbos. It was served with cold poached sea bass, which was dolloped with a nut sauce probably made from walnuts.*

4 tablespoons (½ stick) butter or margarine
1 cup long-grain rice
½ teaspoon salt (optional)
1 cup broken up (¼-inch pieces) vermicelli
2 medium onions, minced
2¼ cups chicken broth
¼ cup dry white wine
1 tablespoon tomato purée
Salt and freshly ground black pepper to taste

In a saucepan, over medium heat, melt the butter or margarine. Stir in the rice, coating it well with the butter or margarine. Stir in the salt, noodles, and onions. Combine the broth, wine, and tomato purée and add the mixture to the pan. Stir, bring to a boil, cover, lower the heat, and simmer for 20 minutes, or until the rice is tender and the liquid has been absorbed. Taste for seasoning before adding salt and pepper. Fluff up with a metal fork before serving.

*Note:* The Greeks place a towel over the pot, then replace the cover and let the rice sit for 5 minutes. This technique is supposed to make certain that all moisture is absorbed and each grain of rice is separate. But with U.S. parboiled rice, this is unnecessary.

*Serves 4 to 6*

# Roman Pilaf

*This dish, discovered in Rome, was not called a risotto. Why, we never discovered. The restaurant chef gave us the recipe, a confusing one that we believe we have clarified. The Italians cook rice differently, using a lot of water (usually after first soaking the rice) and a short cooking time. But, as we have stated, the recipes in this book are cooked with American rice, using our techniques.*

*In Rome, this was served to us with a delicious turkey breast cutlet, which was topped with ham and cheese—a dish created in that city.*

6 tablespoons butter or margarine
2 medium onions, chopped
2 garlic cloves, minced
1½ cups long-grain rice
½ teaspoon salt (optional)
Freshly ground black pepper to taste
⅛ teaspoon ground cinnamon
3½ cups chicken broth
⅛ cup golden raisins, halved
2 tablespoons chopped toasted almonds (see Note)

1. In a saucepan, over medium heat, melt 3 tablespoons of the butter or margarine and stir in the onions, garlic, rice, salt, pepper, and cinnamon. Cook for 5 minutes, stirring, blending the rice with the onions, garlic, and butter or margarine.

2. Stir in the broth and bring to a boil. Stir with a wooden fork, cover, lower the heat, and simmer for 20 minutes, or until the rice is just tender, al dente, and the liquid has been mostly absorbed. Taste for seasoning, adding salt and pepper if needed.

3. With a metal fork stir the remaining butter or margarine (in small pieces), the raisins, and almonds into the rice, fluffing it up.

*Note:* To prepare unblanched almonds, drop them into boiling water. Allow to stand for a minute or two, then drain and slip off the skins. Dry thoroughly and place in a shallow pan in a preheated 300-degree oven, turning frequently to avoid burning. They should be golden, not brown.

*Serves 4 to 6*

# Rice O'Brien

5 tablespoons butter or margarine
6 whole scallions, trimmed and chopped
1 medium green bell pepper, seeded, cored, and chopped
3 cups cooked long-grain rice
3 tablespoons chopped pimientos
Salt and freshly ground black pepper to taste

In a frying pan, over medium heat, melt 2 tablespoons of the butter or margarine. Add the scallions and green pepper and cook for 3 minutes, or until they are just crisp-tender. Blend in the rice, pimientos, and remaining butter or margarine (in small pieces). Season with salt and pepper. Heat through, fluffing up the rice with a metal fork.

*Serves 4*


# Turkish Pilaf Nuyam Yigit

*We've named this one after Turkish journalist Nuyam Yigit, who introduced it to us in Istanbul—along with the best piece of swordfish we've ever tasted.*

8 tablespoons (1 stick) butter or margarine
2 medium onions, chopped
1½ cups long-grain brown rice
3½ cups chicken broth
Salt and freshly ground black pepper to taste
⅛ cup golden raisins
⅛ cup pignoli or broken-up walnuts

1. In a saucepan, over medium heat, melt 3 tablespoons of the butter or margarine. Stir in half of the onions and cook for 3 minutes, or until they are soft. Add the rice and cook, stirring, for 2 minutes. Stir in the broth and bring to a boil. Lower the heat, cover,

and simmer for 35 minutes, or until the rice is al dente. Taste before adding salt and pepper.

2. Cook the raisins, remaining onions, and nuts separately, in 1 tablespoon of butter or margarine each, until the raisins are plump, the onions golden, and the nuts crisp. Using a metal fork, stir them into the rice along with the remaining butter or margarine. Set over low heat for 1 or 2 minutes, fluff up with a metal fork, and serve.

*Serves 6*

# Rice Pommarola

*We like to serve this as an accompaniment to broiled sirloin steak.*

1 cup tomato juice
2½ cups water
1 teaspoon salt (optional)
1½ cups long-grain rice
3 tablespoons butter or margarine
1 large ripe tomato, peeled, seeded, and chopped
3 fresh basil leaves, chopped

1. In a saucepan, bring the tomato juice and water to a boil. Stir in the salt and rice, cover, lower the heat, and simmer for 20 minutes, or until the rice is al dente and the liquid has been absorbed. With a metal fork, stir in the butter or margarine. Preheat the oven to 350 degrees.

2. With a metal fork, combine and blend the rice, tomato, and basil. Lightly spoon into a well-buttered casserole. Bake, uncovered, for 10 minutes.

*Serves 4 to 6*

# Rijsttafel

The most popular dish of Holland isn't Dutch, it's Indonesian, originating in that former possession of the Netherlands. We don't suppose that Dutch families are big on *rijsttafel* (pronounced RYE-stah-ful), the "rice table," but visitors are always taken to a restaurant that serves it. When we were in Amsterdam, we had it six times in one week (out of politeness we didn't say we'd had the menu), and each restaurant had a different version. It's sort of an Eastern smorgasbord. Thus, one can set a rice table limited only by the imagination. At one restaurant in Amsterdam, forty items were offered to be spread upon hot rice, which is evenly layered on large individual warm plates (which become the base or "table") on which the sauced food and condiments are spooned or sprinkled.

Classically, a rice table is laid with at least twenty dishes, which are chosen to offer a variety and, at the same time a taste symphony, of different flavor textures, always with a *saté*, sort of an Oriental shish kebab, of pieces of broiled pork, beef, or chicken; a heavily spiced fish dish; vegetables fried with rice, shrimp, and pieces of chicken; and always a very hot curry. Small dishes of fried bananas, pineapple slices, grated fresh coconut, peanuts, pistachios, cashews, cucumbers, gherkins, and various chutneys are also offered.

To Americanize it, use little sausages, sliced hard-boiled eggs, toasted almonds, raisins, kumquats, and fried onion rings. Once you get into the mood, the little extra dishes will be fun to dream up.

Rijsttafel is definitely a party dish (increase the ingredients according to the number of guests), perfect for dramatically different entertaining. It hasn't yet caught on in the United States, but with rice's current popularity, rijsttafel may soon be with us.

We have two dishes we favor for the rice table, a shrimp curry and a saté of chicken. We also make our own chutney, so we'll offer all here.

First on the agenda for a rice table is the rice. Cook plenty as it not only is the flavor conveyor, but the tastemaker.

# Rice for Rijsttafel

7½ cups water
3 cups long-grain rice
1½ tablespoons salt (optional)
4 tablespoons (½ stick) butter or margarine

In a large saucepan, over high heat, bring the water to a boil, stir in the rice, salt, and butter or margarine. Cover, lower the heat, and simmer for 25 minutes, or until the rice is tender and the water has been absorbed. Fluff up the rice with a metal fork and keep it warm in a very low oven.

*Serves 8*


# Curry of Shrimp for Rijsttafel

2½ pounds medium shrimp, shelled and deveined
6 tablespoons butter or margarine
5 large scallions (white part only), minced
1 bay leaf
1½ tablespoons curry powder, or to taste (see page 79)
3 tablespoons all-purpose flour
3 cups clam juice, warmed
½ cup half-and-half
½ tablespoon dried dill
Salt to taste

1. Bring a large pot of water to a boil. Add the shrimp and cook for 2 minutes, or until they just turn pink. Do not overcook. Immediately remove from the water.
2. In a large saucepan, over medium heat, melt the butter or margarine and cook the scallions for 3 minutes. Do not brown. Add the bay leaf and stir in the curry powder and flour, blending well. Simmer, stirring, for 3 minutes. Gradually add the clam juice, stir-

ring into a smooth, medium-thick sauce. Stir in the half-and-half and dried dill. Simmer, stirring, for 3 minutes. Remove and discard the bay leaf. Taste for seasoning before adding salt.

3. Add the shrimp, heat for 1 minute, and serve immediately.

*Serves 8*


# Saté of Chicken Breast for Rijsttafel

2½ pounds skinned and boned chicken breasts, cut into 1-inch
   cubes
¼ cup olive oil
3 tablespoons minced scallions
¼ cup fresh lemon juice
3 garlic cloves, minced
½ teaspoon ground ginger
½ teaspoon ground cumin
⅛ teaspoon cayenne
1 teaspoon salt (optional)
½ teaspoon freshly ground black pepper

1. In a large bowl, combine and mix well all ingredients. Marinate for 3 hours. Preheat the broiler.

2. Using skewers, spear 5 or 6 pieces (or more, depending upon the length of the skewer used) of chicken. Broil the satés 5 inches from the heat, turning several times to brown evenly. Do not overcook. A total cooking time of 7 minutes should do it.

*Serves 8*

# Fruit Chutney for Rijsttafel

5 tablespoons butter or margarine
1 tablespoon curry powder, or to taste (see page 79)
½ cup dark brown sugar
4 cups fresh fruit, such as apples, peaches, pineapple, pears, and
   pitted dark cherries (canned fruits can be used, but fresh are
   better), peeled and cut into chunks

1. In a saucepan, over medium heat, melt the butter or margarine. Add the curry powder and sugar and blend well. Preheat the oven to 350 degrees.
2. Arrange the fruit chunks in a deep baking dish. Pour the curry-sugar mixture over the fruit and bake, uncovered, for 45 minutes. Stir once, halfway through the cooking period. This can be jarred and frozen.

*Makes about 3 cups*


# Riso all'Onda

*This is what the Italians call "rippling rice," a risotto that bubbles just before it is served. Actually, this recipe, called* insaporito *(tasty), is a base for various risottos, but as we are anchovy fans we often serve it as is.*

3 tablespoons olive oil
2 medium onions, finely chopped
2 garlic cloves, minced
One 2-ounce can (or 2 cans, if you are an anchovy fan) flat
   anchovy fillets, drained
1 cup long-grain rice
2 cups chicken broth, heated
Salt and freshly ground black pepper to taste
3 tablespoons chopped broadleaf (Italian) parsley leaves

1. In a saucepan, over medium heat, heat the oil and cook the onions and garlic for 5 minutes, or until they are soft. Do not brown. Add the anchovies and cook for 1 minute.

2. Stir in the rice and cook for 1 minute, or until it is well coated with the oil. Pour in 1 cup of the broth and simmer, uncovered, for 10 minutes, or until the rice has absorbed the liquid. Add the remaining broth, and again cook until the rice expands and absorbs nearly all of the broth. The rice should be moist when served and al dente, with a small amount of liquid still bubbling when it is taken off the heat. Taste before seasoning, since the anchovies and broth may have supplied enough seasoning. Stir in the parsley and spoon into a hot serving dish.

*Note:* Sometimes we can't resist stirring in a cup of hot cooked shrimp and using the rippling rice as a light supper.

*Serves 4*

## Risotto in Cagnone

2½ cups water
1 cup long-grain rice
1 teaspoon salt (optional)
8 tablespoons (1 stick) butter or margarine
2 garlic cloves, crushed and peeled
1 tablespoon chopped fresh sage, or 1 teaspoon dried leaf sage, crumbled
½ cup grated Asiago or Parmesan cheese

1. In a pot, bring the water to a boil. Stir in the rice and salt. Lower the heat, cover, and simmer for 20 minutes, or until the rice is tender and the liquid has been absorbed.
2. In a saucepan, over medium heat, melt the butter or margarine. Add the garlic and sage and cook until the garlic is golden brown. Remove and discard the garlic. Pour half of the butter-sage sauce over the rice and mix in well with a metal fork, fluffing up the rice. Taste for seasoning, adding more salt if needed. Transfer to a hot serving dish. Pour the remaining sauce over the rice. Sprinkle on 2 tablespoons of the cheese and serve the remaining cheese at the table.

*Serves 4*

# Risotto alla Genovese

*Risotto bases are created in various ways. One we favor is this vegetable mixture, with main ingredients, such as Genoa salami in this recipe, added after the rice has cooked.*

2 tablespoons olive oil
5 tablespoons butter or margarine
1 small white onion, finely chopped
1 garlic clove, minced
1 small carrot, scraped and finely chopped
1 small celery stalk, scraped and finely chopped
1 cup long-grain rice
2½ cups chicken broth, heated
3 tablespoons tomato sauce (homemade or canned)
4 medium fresh mushrooms, thinly sliced
Four ½-inch slices Italian Genoa salami, skin removed, diced
¼ cup grated Parmesan cheese
Salt and freshly ground black pepper to taste

1. In a saucepan, over medium heat, heat the oil and 2 tablespoons of the butter or margarine. Add the onion, garlic, carrot, and celery and cook for 7 minutes, or until the vegetables are soft. Do not brown. Stir in the rice and cook, stirring, for 2 minutes. Pour in 1 cup of the broth and simmer, uncovered, for 10 minutes, stirring frequently with a wooden fork, until the liquid has been absorbed.

2. Add the tomato sauce, mushrooms, and the remaining broth. Cook, uncovered, stirring several times, for about 10 minutes, or until the rice is al dente and the liquid has been mostly absorbed. With a metal fork, stir in the salami and cheese, fluffing up the rice. Taste for seasoning before adding salt and pepper.

3. Top with the remaining butter or margarine (in small pieces). Remove from the heat and keep covered until the risotto is served.

*Serves 4*

# Baked Green Risotto

2 tablespoons butter or margarine
1 small onion, minced
1 garlic clove, minced
1 celery stalk, scraped and minced
2 whole eggs plus 1 egg yolk
1½ cups milk
½ cup finely chopped spinach leaves
½ cup finely chopped watercress leaves
1 cup finely chopped broadleaf (Italian) parsley leaves
3 cups al dente–cooked long-grain rice (cooked in chicken broth)
1 cup grated Gruyère or Fontina cheese
Salt and freshly ground black pepper to taste

1. Melt the butter or margarine in a saucepan, over medium heat. Add the onion, garlic, and celery and cook for 5 minutes, or until they are soft. Do not brown. Preheat the oven to 360 degrees.

2. Beat the eggs with the egg yolk in a large bowl. Add the milk, spinach, watercress, parsley, rice, cheese, salt, pepper, and the onion-garlic-celery mixture and blend well

3. Spoon into a buttered baking dish and bake for 35 minutes, or until puffed, golden, and set.

*Serves 6*

# Risotto Piemontese

*Risotti are all similar and yet they are all different. The rices are alike because they are cooked mostly in the same, or almost the same, manner, but ingredients vary according to the region from which they originate.*

*Italians insist that a risotto must be stirred almost constantly, adding hot broth as the rice absorbs it, then adding more, and so on until the rice is tender. The rice, they also insist, must be moist, never dry.*

*We've run numerous tests and find that all this isn't necessary; techniques in various countries differ, mainly because of the variety and quality of the rices. Anyway, this is a favorite risotto of northern Italy—cooked our way. We served it to an Italian friend from Milan, and he pronounced it perfect. But maybe he was hungry.*

3-inch length of beef or veal shank bone with marrow
3 tablespoons butter or margarine
1 medium onion, finely chopped
½ teaspoon salt (optional)
1½ cups long-grain rice
¾ cup dry red wine
2½ to 3 cups chicken broth
Pinch of powdered saffron (less than ¼ teaspoon)
Salt and freshly ground black pepper to taste
½ cup grated Parmesan cheese

1. Poach the shank in water until the marrow is barely cooked, pinkish, but can be easily pried out of the bone. Chop and reserve the marrow.

2. In a deep saucepan, over medium heat, melt the butter or margarine, and stir in the onion and salt. Cook, stirring, for 3 minutes. Do not brown. Stir in the rice, coating it well with the butter or margarine. Stir in the marrow, the wine, 2½ cups of the broth, and the saffron. Stir well with a wooden fork, bring to a boil, lower the heat, cover, and simmer for 17 minutes, or until the rice is tender, but still slightly al dente, and the liquid has been mostly absorbed. If the liquid is absorbed before the rice is tender, add a small amount of hot broth so that the rice will be slightly moist while the cooking is finished. Taste for seasoning, adding salt and pepper if needed.

3. With a metal fork, stir in the cheese, fluffing up the rice. Serve immediately.

*Serves 6*

# Chicken Risotto

5 fresh ripe plum tomatoes, peeled, seeded, and chopped
8 tablespoons (1 stick) butter or margarine
3 small shallots, finely chopped
½ chicken breast, skinned, boned, and cut into julienne
4 chicken livers, trimmed and each cut into 6 pieces
4 medium fresh mushrooms, chopped
Salt and freshly ground black pepper to taste
1½ cups long-grain rice
3½ to 4 cups chicken broth
¾ cup grated Asiago or Parmesan cheese
3 tablespoons chopped broadleaf (Italian) parsley leaves

1. In a saucepan, over medium heat, cook the tomatoes until most of the liquid has evaporated, about 15 minutes.

2. In a frying pan, over medium heat, melt 3 tablespoons of the butter or margarine. Add the shallots and cook until soft, about 2 minutes. Do not brown. Add the chicken breast strips and cook, stirring occasionally, for about 5 minutes, or until the pieces start to become firm. Add the chicken livers and mushrooms and cook until the livers are brown on the outside and pink inside. Add the tomatoes and cook for 5 minutes. Season with salt and pepper.

3. In a deep saucepan, melt 3 tablespoons of the butter or margarine. Add the rice and cook, stirring, for 1 or 2 minutes to coat it well. Add 3½ cups of the broth, bring to a boil, and stir with a wooden fork. Lower the heat, cover, and simmer for 15 minutes, or until most of the liquid has been absorbed and the rice is tender but slightly al dente. If the liquid is absorbed before the rice is cooked, add a small amount of hot broth. The rice should be slightly moist.

4. With a metal fork, stir in the remaining butter or margarine, 4 tablespoons of the cheese, half of the chicken-liver-tomato sauce, and half of the parsley. Cook for 5 minutes over low heat, fluffing up the rice with a metal fork. Transfer to a hot serving dish and spoon the remaining sauce on top. Sprinkle with the remaining parsley and pass the remaining cheese at the table.

*Serves 6*

# Rodos Rizi

*This was served to us with broiled fish on the Greek Island of Rhodes. It may seem odd to blend rice cooked in fish stock with cheese, but the Greeks believe that their feta cheese mates with everything. This combination proves their point.*

6 tablespoons butter or margarine
1½ cups long-grain rice
3½ cups Fish Stock (page 48)
1½ cups crumbled feta cheese
5 fresh basil leaves, chopped
Salt and freshly ground black pepper to taste

1. In a saucepan, over medium heat, melt 3 tablespoons of the butter or margarine. Stir in the rice and cook, stirring, for 2 minutes, or until the rice is well coated with butter or margarine. Stir in the stock and bring to a boil. Lower the heat, stir with a wooden fork, cover, and simmer for 20 minutes, or until the rice is tender and the liquid has been absorbed.

2. In another saucepan, melt the remaining butter or margarine. Add the cheese and stir just long enough to melt the cheese and blend well. With a metal fork, blend the butter-cheese mixture and basil with the rice, fluffing up the rice. Taste before adding salt and pepper.

*Serves 6*

# Arroz Rojo

4 tablespoons extra-virgin olive oil
1 large onion, finely chopped
1 celery stalk, scraped and finely chopped
½ cup finely chopped green bell pepper
1½ cups long-grain rice
⅛ teaspoon cayenne, or to taste
1 teaspoon sugar
3 medium ripe tomatoes, peeled, seeded, and chopped
¼ teaspoon dried thyme
2½ cups chicken broth
Salt to taste

1. In a deep frying pan, heat the oil over medium heat. Add the onion, celery, and green pepper and cook for 5 minutes, or until the onion is soft. Do not brown.

2. Stir in the rice and cook, stirring, for 2 minutes. Stir in the cayenne, sugar, tomatoes, thyme, and broth. Bring to a boil, lower the heat, stir with a wooden fork, cover, and simmer for 20 minutes, or until the rice is tender and the liquid has been absorbed. If the liquid has been absorbed before the rice is tender, add a small amount of hot broth (or water) and continue to cook. Taste for seasoning before adding salt.

3. Just before serving, use a metal fork to fluff up the rice.

*Serves 6*


# Deep-fried Rice Rolls

3 cups cooked short- or medium-grain rice
1 cup grated Swiss cheese
½ teaspoon ground mace
Salt and freshly ground black pepper to taste
1 egg, beaten (to be mixed with the rice)
1 egg (for dipping the rice rolls before frying)
Fine dry unseasoned bread crumbs for dredging
Vegetable oil for deep-frying

1. In a large bowl, combine and mix well the rice, cheese, mace, salt, pepper, and the beaten egg.

2. Form the rice mixture into rolls, 1 inch in diameter and 2 inches long.

3. Beat the remaining egg in a shallow bowl. Dredge the rice rolls in the bread crumbs, dip into the beaten egg, and dredge again in the bread crumbs. Place in the refrigerator for 3 hours to set, removing about 1 hour before cooking.

4. Heat the vegetable oil to 370 degrees, or until a 1-inch cube of bread dropped into it becomes golden in 40 to 50 seconds. Lower the rolls into the hot oil with a slotted spoon a few at a time and cook until golden. Drain on paper towels and serve immediately.

*Serves 4 to 6*

## Croquettes

Prepare as above but shape the rice mixture into oval patties instead of rolls.

# Tromso Scallion Rice

3 tablespoons butter or margarine
8 scallions, trimmed and chopped
1 cup long-grain rice
2½ cups beef broth
Salt and freshly ground black pepper to taste
1 teaspoon Worcestershire sauce
3 tablespoons chopped fresh parsley leaves

1. In a large saucepan, over medium heat, melt the butter or margarine. Add the scallions and cook for 3 minutes, stirring.

2. Add the rice to the saucepan and cook for 1 minute, stirring, until the rice is well coated with butter or margarine.

3. Pour in the broth and bring to a boil. Stir with a wooden fork, lower the heat, cover, and simmer for 20 minutes, or until the rice is tender and the liquid has been absorbed. Taste for seasoning, adding salt and pepper if needed.

4. Stir in the Worcestershire and fluff up the rice with a metal fork. Sprinkle with the parsley before serving.

*Serves 4*

# Soubise

*This purée of onions and rice is a famous French dish, found nowhere but in France. At least we have never encountered it in French restaurants in the United States. This method was taught us by our mentor, Antoine Gilly, one of the four greatest living French chefs. We like to serve it with a nice rare fillet of beef.*

6 tablespoons sweet butter or unsalted margarine
1 pound Bermuda onions, thinly sliced
1 cup long-grain rice
3 cups chicken broth
⅛ teaspoon ground nutmeg
Bouquet garni made of a sprig fresh parsley, 1 bay leaf, 1
    teaspoon of chopped fresh thyme (or ⅛ teaspoon dried), and a
    few celery leaves tied in cheesecloth
Salt and freshly ground black pepper to taste
½ cup half-and-half, beaten with 2 eggs

1. In a flameproof casserole with a lid, over medium-low heat, melt the butter or margarine and cook the onions for 15 minutes, or until they are soft. Do not brown. Preheat the oven to 350 degrees.

2. Stir in the rice and cook for 2 minutes, stirring. Then gradually stir in the broth. Add the nutmeg and the bouquet garni. Bring to a boil. Cover with aluminum foil and then the lid, and bake for 25 minutes, or until the rice is tender and the liquid has been absorbed. Raise the oven temperature to 450 degrees.

3. Remove the rice from the oven and discard the bouquet garni. Put the rice and onions in a fine sieve, pushing them through into a bowl. Or use your blender or food processor to purée them. Taste before adding salt and pepper, as the broth may have supplied enough seasoning.

4. Stir in the half-and-half–egg mixture.

5. Lightly butter a 1½-quart soufflé dish and pour in the mixture. Place in a pan of boiling water that comes halfway up the side of the dish. Bake, uncovered, for 20 minutes, or until the top is crusty and light brown and the *soubise* is set. Serve immediately.

*Serves 4 to 6*

## Sesame Rice

*Many of us haven't discovered the culinary value and unique flavor of sesame seeds. Native to Asia, and cultivated extensively in China and India, the seeds are the dried, hulled fruit of a tropical annual herb. Creamy white and oval-shaped, the flavor is delicate, somewhat like that of toasted almonds. The seeds are a natural rice plate mate. Here's a dish with an Asian touch. We like to serve this with a poached chicken with velouté sauce.*

3½ cups water
1½ teaspoons salt (optional)
1½ cups long-grain rice
2 medium onions, chopped
4 tablespoons sesame seeds
½ teaspoon ground cumin
5 tablespoons butter or margarine
1 tablespoon mustard seeds, preferably black

1. In a deep saucepan, bring the water to a boil. Stir in the salt, rice, and onions. Lower the heat, cover, and simmer for 20 minutes, or until the rice is tender and most of the liquid has been

absorbed. The rice should still be moist. Remove from the heat and reserve.

2. In another saucepan, over medium heat, shaking the pan, heat the sesame seeds until they are golden and stop popping and sputtering. With a metal fork, stir the sesame seeds and cumin into the rice.

3. Over medium heat, in the pan in which the sesame seeds were toasted, melt 2 tablespoons of the butter or margarine. Add the mustard seeds, and cook for a minute or two, or until they start to crackle. Stir the seeds, the butter or margarine they cooked in, and the remaining butter or margarine into the rice. Heat the rice, fluffing it up with a metal fork and serve.

*Serves 4 to 6*

# Rice Soufflé

2 tablespoons butter or margarine
3 scallions, trimmed and finely chopped
1 tablespoon all-purpose flour
¾ cup milk
1½ cups cooked short- or medium-grain rice
½ cup chopped fresh parsley leaves
½ cup grated Gruyère cheese
½ cup grated Parmesan cheese
3 egg yolks, beaten
3 egg whites, stiffly beaten
Salt and freshly ground black pepper to taste

1. Preheat the oven to 350 degrees.

2. In a saucepan, over medium heat, melt the butter or margarine. Add the scallions and cook for 2 minutes. Do not brown. Stir in the flour, blending well. Gradually add the milk, stirring into a smooth sauce.

3. Remove from the heat and stir in the rice, parsley, cheeses, and egg yolks. Fold in the egg whites and season with salt and pepper.

**4.** Pour into a buttered 1½-quart soufflé dish and bake for 30 minutes, or until set. A knife blade inserted just off center should come out clean.

*Serves 4*


## Rice Stuffings and Dressings

Rice is a stuffing's star, second to none in this role that enhances other food, be it just a festive plate mate; dressing up a serving of sliced turkey, chicken, or fish; or a major part of a holiday or special occasion meal, stuffing a bird or a leg of lamb. (We show rice in action in this regard on pages 103, 111, 133, 144, and 145.)

If used as a dressing, that is as an accompaniment, long-grain rice can be used and it should be cooked the full length of time. If, however, it is being used to stuff poultry or meats, short- or medium-grain rice should be used, because they hold together better than long grain.

Also, the stuffing rice should be cooked al dente, less than the normal time, since the rice will have further cooking. Two further points: Use less liquid in this shorter cooking—for example, rather than 2½ cups, use 2 cups, and cook for 15 minutes rather than 20 minutes—and if the liquid hasn't been absorbed in that length of time, drain the rice.

Rice starts right off better than bread as a spectacular stuffer. Run a simple test: Cook some rice, place it hot on a plate with a dab of butter or margarine, then taste it. Then cut some bread into cubes and repeat the process. Without the addition of a single other ingredient, the flavor of rice is superb. Bread needs all the help it can get. Rice responds with stuffing mixtures by magnifying and enhancing other flavors.

Besides, it's innovative and will delight many of your dinner guests. Rice, as we hope this book exemplifies, is full of surprises, as you will see on the following pages.

# Almond-Rice Dressing

*We like to serve this with* goujonettes *(slender strips) of sole sautéed in butter or margarine.*

3 tablespoons butter or margarine
2 medium onions, finely chopped
2 celery stalks, scraped and finely chopped
1 cup finely chopped celery leaves
1 cup long-grain rice
¾ teaspoon combined thyme and tarragon
2 cups boiling chicken broth
8 medium fresh mushrooms, sliced
Salt and freshly ground black pepper to taste
½ cup chopped toasted almonds

1. In a saucepan, over medium heat, melt the butter or margarine. Add the onions, celery, celery leaves, rice, and thyme and tarragon, blending well. Cook for 5 minutes, stirring. Preheat the oven to 350 degrees.

2. Transfer the rice mixture to a buttered shallow 2-quart casserole. Stir in the boiling broth. Cover and bake for 10 minutes. Remove from the oven and stir in the mushrooms. Return to the oven for 10 minutes, or until the rice is tender and the liquid has been absorbed. Taste for seasoning, adding salt and pepper if needed. The broth may have supplied enough.

3. Sprinkle with the almonds before serving as an accompaniment.

*Serves 6*

# Chestnut Stuffing

*We favor this simple stuffing, with surprisingly excellent flavor, for a small turkey that we stuff, truss, rub well with butter or margarine, and roast in foil. We roast an 8- to 12-pound bird for 3 to 4 hours, the first hour in a preheated 350-degree oven; the remaining time at 300 degrees. A meat thermometer in the thigh should register 180 degrees when the bird is done.*

2 tablespoons olive oil
3 medium onions, finely chopped
3 cups al dente–cooked short- or medium-grain rice
1 pound chestnuts, peeled, cooked, and chopped
1 teaspoon salt (optional)
½ teaspoon ground sage
½ cup chicken broth

1. In a deep saucepan, heat the oil over medium heat. Cook the onions for 5 minutes. With a metal fork stir in the rice, chestnuts, salt, sage, and chicken broth, tossing as you mix. Taste for seasoning, adding salt and pepper if needed.

2. Loosely stuff the bird. The rice will expand as the bird cooks. Any extra stuffing can be wrapped in foil and cooked with the bird.

*Makes approximately 5 cups*

# Brown Rice Stuffing

*We use this to stuff a capon, but you can stuff anything from a chicken to a goose with this combination.*

5 tablespoons butter or margarine
1 cup medium-grain brown rice
2 cups chicken broth
1 medium onion, chopped
3 tender (inside) celery stalks, scraped and chopped

1 cup chopped cooked chestnuts
½ teaspoon dried leaf sage, crumbled
½ teaspoon dried thyme
1 teaspoon salt (optional)
¼ teaspoon freshly ground black pepper
½ cup half-and-half

1. In a saucepan, over medium heat, melt 2 tablespoons of the butter or margarine. Stir in the rice and cook, stirring, for 1 minute. Pour in the broth, stir with a wooden fork, cover, lower the heat, and simmer for 35 minutes, or until the rice is al dente.

2. In a frying pan, over medium heat, melt the remaining 3 tablespoons of butter or margarine. Stir in the onion and celery and cook until they are just crisp-tender. Stir in the chestnuts, sage, thyme, salt, and pepper. Add the cooked rice and half-and-half and mix thoroughly. Taste for seasoning, adding salt and pepper if needed.

3. Loosely stuff the bird. The rice will expand as the bird cooks. Any extra stuffing can be wrapped in foil and cooked with the bird.

*Makes approximately 4½ cups*

# Chili-Rice Stuffing

*We find this gives Cornish game hens a dash of personality.*

4 tablespoons (½ stick) butter or margarine
2 onions, finely chopped
1 garlic clove, minced
1 cup long-grain rice
2 cups chicken broth
1½ cups chopped cooked ham
2 tablespoons chopped broadleaf (Italian) parsley leaves
2 teaspoons chili powder, or to taste
½ teaspoon ground cumin
1 egg, beaten
¼ cup melted butter or margarine
Salt and freshly ground black pepper to taste

1. In a saucepan, over medium heat, melt the butter or margarine. Add the onions, garlic, and rice and cook for 4 minutes, stirring. Pour in the chicken broth and bring to a boil. Stir with a wooden fork, cover, lower the heat, and simmer for 15 minutes. The rice should be al dente.

2. In a bowl, combine and blend well the rice mixture with the ham, parsley, chili powder, cumin, egg, and butter or margarine. Taste for seasoning before adding salt or pepper, as the broth and ham may have supplied enough.

3. Loosely stuff the birds; the rice will expand as the birds cook. Any extra stuffing can be wrapped in foil and cooked with the birds.

*Makes approximately 4½ cups, ample for 4 game hens*

## Italian Po Valley Rice Stuffing for Poultry

*We discovered this in northern Italy, the same area where Thomas Jefferson risked his life by stealing a handful of rice. Rice is used in this region instead of pasta and the innovations are all unique. This stuffing is a good example, giving poultry a new taste dimension.*

2 Italian sweet sausages, casings removed
3 tablespoons butter or margarine
2 medium onions, finely chopped
3 cups al dente–cooked short- or medium-grain rice (cooked in chicken broth)
¼ cup grated Asiago or Parmesan cheese
2 eggs, beaten
¼ teaspoon dried oregano
⅛ teaspoon dried basil
Salt and freshly ground black pepper to taste
Soft butter or margarine to rub on the outside of the bird

In a frying pan, over medium heat, cook the sausage meat for 10 minutes, breaking it up with a fork. Drain off any fat. Transfer the sausage to a large bowl. Add the butter or margarine to the frying pan and cook the onions until they are soft. Do not brown. Add the onions to the sausage along with all other ingredients except the soft butter or margarine. Mix well, but lightly, with a fork. Loosely spoon the stuffing into the cavity of the bird. Do not pack it in. Truss the bird, rub with soft butter or margarine and sprinkle with salt and pepper. Roast by any method you prefer.

*Makes enough to stuff a 5- to 6-pound bird*

# Oyster Stuffing

*We use this to stuff a large chicken, a capon, or a small turkey. For larger birds just increase the amount of rice.*

4 tablespoons (½ stick) butter or margarine
2 medium onions, chopped
3 celery stalks, scraped and chopped
Salt and freshly ground black pepper
½ teaspoon thyme combined with ½ teaspoon tarragon
3 cups al dente–cooked short- or medium-grain rice
2 tablespoons chopped broadleaf (Italian) parsley leaves
¼ cup grated Asiago or Parmesan cheese
2 eggs, beaten
1 pint fresh oysters with their liquid

1. In a deep saucepan, over medium heat, melt the butter or margarine. Add the onions and celery and cook for 4 minutes, or until they are crisp-tender. Remove from the heat and season with 1 teaspoon salt, ½ teaspoon pepper, and the combined thyme and tarragon.

2. In a large bowl, combine and blend well the onions and celery with the rice, parsley, cheese, and eggs. Taste for seasoning, adding salt and pepper if needed.

3. Carefully mix in the oysters with their liquid.

4. Loosely stuff the bird. The rice will expand as the bird cooks. Any extra stuffing can be wrapped in foil and cooked with the bird.

*Makes approximately 5 cups*

# Piquant Turnip Stuffing

*This is one we created for squab, our all-time favorite bird. This will handle six of those delicious, butter-tender baby pigeons. The turnips offer a delightfully different taste change.*

5 tablespoons butter or margarine
3 small turnips, peeled and finely chopped
1 cup finely chopped celery hearts with leaves
4 shallots, minced
1 teaspoon salt (optional)
⅛ teaspoon ground allspice
⅛ teaspoon ground nutmeg
3 cups al dente–cooked short- or medium-grain rice
Salt and freshly ground black pepper to taste

1. In a deep saucepan, over medium heat, melt the butter or margarine and cook the turnips, celery, and shallots for 5 minutes. Stir in the remaining ingredients, blending lightly with a metal fork. Cook for 5 minutes. Taste for seasoning, adding salt and pepper if needed.

2. Loosely stuff the squabs, game hens, or whatever birds you prefer (or can obtain). The rice will expand as the birds cook. Any extra stuffing can be wrapped in foil and cooked with the birds.

*Makes approximately 4 cups*

# Rice Stuffing with Pecans

*This will stuff a 15-pound turkey.*

4 tablespoons (½ stick) butter or margarine
2 medium onions, chopped
2 celery stalks, scraped and chopped
2 tablespoons broadleaf (Italian) parsley leaves
1 turkey liver, chopped
Salt and freshly ground black pepper to taste
1 teaspoon dried thyme
1 teaspoon dried leaf sage, crumbled
6 cups al dente–cooked long-grain rice
2 eggs, beaten
½ cup grated Asiago or Parmesan cheese
1 cup chopped pecans
¼ cup brandy

1. In a saucepan, over medium heat, melt the butter or margarine. Add the onions and celery and cook for 5 minutes. Add the parsley, liver, 1 teaspoon salt, ½ teaspoon pepper, thyme, and sage, blending well. Cook for 1 minute.

2. In a large bowl, combine and blend well with a metal fork the rice, eggs, cheese, pecans, and brandy. Blend in the onions, celery, parsley, and liver. Taste for seasoning, adding salt and pepper if needed.

3. Loosely stuff the bird. The rice will expand as it cooks. Any extra stuffing can be wrapped in foil and cooked with the bird.

*Makes approximately 7½ cups*

# Wild Rice as Garnish or Stuffing for Game

*Wild rice (which, as we've pointed out, is not rice at all) is very expensive, but it is also impressive when served as a garnish or stuffing for game, pheasant, quail, partridge, or duck. Game itself is expensive, not an everyday meal, so pairing it with wild rice is most appropriate. Here's a garnish with a French touch, in what is called a* mirepoix.

3 quarts water
1 tablespoon salt (optional)
2 cups wild rice
5 tablespoons butter or margarine
4 large scallions (white part only), minced
3 small carrots, scraped and minced
1 large celery stalk, scraped and minced
½ teaspoon dried marjoram
1 bay leaf
3 cups beef broth

1. Bring the water to a boil in a large pot. Stir in the salt and rice, lower the heat, and simmer for 10 minutes. Drain. Preheat the oven to 325 degrees.

2. In a flameproof casserole, over medium heat, melt the butter or margarine and cook the scallions, carrots, and celery for 5 minutes. Stir in the drained rice and simmer, stirring, until the rice has absorbed the butter or margarine.

3. Stir in the marjoram, bay leaf, and beef broth. Bring to a simmer. Cover and bake for 1 hour, or until the rice is tender and the liquid has been absorbed. If the rice is cooked before the liquid has been absorbed, quickly cook off the excess liquid on top of the stove, being careful not to burn the rice. If the liquid has cooked off before the rice is tender, add a small amount of hot broth or water and continue to cook. Be careful: The rice should be quite dry and the grains separate. Do not overcook or it will be mushy. Discard the bay leaf.

*Note:* If you are using this for stuffing, cook the rice in 2½ cups of beef broth instead of 3 and cook for 45 minutes instead of 1 hour. The rice should be slightly underdone.

*Serves 6 to 8*

# Rice Texarkana

2¼ cups water
1 teaspoon salt (optional)
1 tablespoon butter or margarine
1 cup long-grain rice
½ cup sour cream
2 teaspoons chili powder
1 cup grated Monterey Jack cheese

1. In a saucepan, over medium heat, combine the water, salt, butter or margarine, and rice and bring to a boil. Stir with a wooden fork, lower the heat, cover, and simmer for 20 minutes, or until the rice is tender, but still a little al dente, and the liquid has been absorbed. Preheat the oven to 350 degrees.

2. Combine the rice with the sour cream, chili powder, and half of the cheese. Blend with a metal fork and spoon into a buttered, shallow baking dish.

3. Sprinkle with the remaining cheese and bake for 20 minutes.

*Serves 4 to 6*

# Swiss Baked Rice with Cheese and Tomatoes

*We had this in a restaurant by the lake in Geneva and wheedled the recipe out of the chef.*

4 tablespoons (½ stick) butter or margarine
4 small white onions, minced
1 garlic clove, minced
2 cups long-grain rice
2 large ripe tomatoes, peeled, seeded, and chopped
1 teaspoon salt (optional)
¼ teaspoon dried thyme
1 small bay leaf
3½ cups chicken broth
Salt and freshly ground black pepper to taste
½ cup grated Swiss cheese
¼ cup grated Parmesan cheese

1. In a flameproof casserole, over medium heat, melt the butter or margarine. Add the onions and garlic and cook for 5 minutes, or until they are soft. Do not brown. Stir in the rice, blending it well with the onion, garlic, and butter or margarine. Stir in the tomatoes, salt, thyme, and bay leaf, blending well. Preheat the oven to 350 degrees.

2. Stir in the chicken broth and bring to a boil. Cover and bake for 25 minutes, or until the rice is tender and the liquid has been absorbed. If the liquid is absorbed before the rice is tender, add a small amount of hot broth and continue to cook. If the rice is tender but the liquid has not been absorbed, remove the cover and cook on top of the stove until the liquid evaporates. Watch carefully and do not burn the rice. Taste for seasoning, adding salt and pepper if needed.

3. Remove from the oven, discard the bay leaf, and, with a metal fork, stir in the cheeses. Return to the oven for 5 minutes, or until the cheeses have melted.

*Serves 4 to 6*

# Tomato Rice with Mornay Sauce

2 tablespoons olive oil
1 medium onion, finely chopped
One 1-pound can imported Italian plum tomatoes with their
    liquid, chopped
1½ cups chicken broth
1 teaspoon sugar
1 cup long-grain rice
Salt and freshly ground black pepper to taste
Mornay Sauce (see below)

1. In a saucepan, over medium heat, heat the olive oil. Add the onion and cook for 3 minutes, or until it is soft. Do not brown. Add the tomatoes with their liquid, the broth, and sugar. Simmer for 2 minutes.

2. Stir in the rice and bring to a boil. Lower the heat, stir with a wooden fork, cover, and simmer for 20 minutes, or until the rice is tender and the liquid has been absorbed. If the liquid is absorbed before the rice is tender, add a small amount of hot broth or water and continue to cook until the rice is cooked. Taste for seasoning, adding salt and pepper if needed. Preheat the broiler.

3. Transfer to a shallow casserole coated with butter or margarine. Spoon on the mornay sauce and place under the broiler until the top is golden. Remove and serve immediately.

*Serves 4 to 6*

## Mornay Sauce

1½ tablespoons butter or margarine
1½ tablespoons all-purpose flour
1 cup milk, heated
⅛ teaspoon cayenne
½ cup grated Gruyère or Cheddar cheese
¼ cup grated Asiago or Parmesan cheese
Salt to taste

1. In a saucepan, over medium heat, melt the butter or margarine. Add the flour and stir into a smooth paste. Gradually stir in the milk and cook, stirring constantly into a smooth sauce.

2. Stir in the cayenne and the cheeses and cook just long enough to melt the cheese, making a smooth sauce. Taste for seasoning, adding salt if needed.

*Makes approximately 1½ cups*

## Aromatic Stuffed Grape Vine Leaves

*These little morsels can be served hot or cold. The Greeks like to offer them cold as an appetizer.*

   40 or more vine leaves, fresh or preserved (Vine leaves are
      available in 1-pound jars containing 40 to 50 leaves.)
   4 tablespoons olive oil
   2 tablespoons butter or margarine
   1 large onion, finely chopped
   ½ cup long-grain rice
   1¼ cups water
   2 tablespoons pignoli or chopped walnuts
   2 tablespoons currants
   2 teaspoons ground allspice
   ¼ teaspoon ground cinnamon
   1 teaspoon chopped fresh mint leaves
   Salt and freshly ground black pepper to taste
   1 cup chicken broth
   Juice of 1 lemon
   1 cup plain yogurt
   Lemon wedges

1. If fresh leaves are used, bring a large pot of water to a boil. Drop the leaves in, a few at a time, and blanch them for 5 minutes. Carefully remove with a slotted spoon or skimmer and plunge into cold water. Remove and drain on paper towels. If preserved leaves

are used, rinse well but carefully in cold water and drain. Cut off the stems.

2. In a saucepan, over medium heat, heat 3 tablespoons of the oil and 1 of the butter or margarine and cook the onion for 3 minutes, or until it is soft. Do not brown. Add the rice and cook, stirring, for 2 minutes. Add the water and bring to a boil. Cover, lower the heat, and simmer for 15 minutes, or until the rice is al dente and the liquid has been absorbed. Transfer to a mixing bowl.

3. Heat the remaining oil and butter or margarine in a frying pan and cook the pignoli until they are golden. Do not brown. Remove with a slotted spoon and add to the rice bowl. Add the currants to the frying pan and cook for 1 minute, or until they are slightly plumped. Transfer to the rice bowl. Add the allspice, cinnamon, mint, salt, and pepper to the bowl, and mix well with a metal fork.

4. Line the bottom of a flameproof casserole with 6 leaves. Arrange the remaining leaves, a few at a time, on a flat surface, rough side down. Place a heaping teaspoonful (or more, depending on the size of the leaf) on the stem side of the leaf. Fold the sides of the leaf over the filling, then roll, fairly tightly, from the stem end to the tip of the leaf, without breaking the leaf. Do not roll too tightly because the rice may expand.

5. Arrange the stuffed leaves, seam side down, side by side in snug layers in the leaf-lined casserole.

6. Pour on the broth and lemon juice. Lay a plate on top of the leaves, cover the pot with aluminum foil, and then with its cover. Bring to a boil, lower the heat, and simmer for 45 minutes. Remove the cover and let the rolls cool. Lift them out with a slotted spoon onto a serving dish and serve with the yogurt and/or lemon wedges.

*Makes enough to stuff approximately 34 leaves*

# Rice Timbales

*In the section on Rice Molds (page 14), we've pointed out how interesting and decorative offerings of rice can dress up a meal. Here's one, made slightly spicy with watercress, that we like to serve with a piece of fish or a scaloppine of chicken or veal.*

6 medium fresh mushrooms
2½ cups beef broth
2 tablespoons butter or margarine
1 medium onion, finely chopped
1 cup short- or medium-grain rice
Salt and freshly ground black pepper to taste
½ cup finely chopped watercress
2 tablespoons melted butter or margarine

1. In a saucepan, combine the mushrooms and beef broth. Bring to a boil, lower the heat, and simmer for 5 minutes. With a slotted spoon remove the mushrooms, cool, and finely chop them. Reserve the broth.

2. In another saucepan, over medium heat, melt the 2 tablespoons of butter or margarine. Stir in the onion and rice and pour in the broth in which the mushrooms cooked. Bring to a boil, stir with a wooden fork, cover, lower the heat, and simmer for 20 minutes, or until the rice is tender and the liquid has been absorbed. Taste for seasoning, adding salt and pepper if needed. The broth may have supplied enough.

3. Combine and blend well the rice, mushrooms, watercress, and melted butter or margarine. Butter four 5-ounce timbale molds and fill with the rice mixture, pressing the rice into the molds. You'll be tempted to unmold these on a large platter, centered with the entrée. Don't do it. The molds can break up when served. Unmold them on the individual plates.

*Serves 4*

# Rice Waffles

*These are excellent served with creamed chicken, tuna, or other sauced foods.*

2 cups sifted all-purpose flour (sifted before measuring)
1 tablespoon baking powder
½ teaspoon salt (optional)
3 egg yolks, beaten
1¾ cup milk
4 tablespoons (½ stick) butter or margarine, melted
¾ cup cooked short- or medium-grain rice
3 egg whites, beaten stiffly

1. Sift the flour, baking powder, and salt into a large bowl. Combine the egg yolks, milk, melted butter or margarine, and rice in another bowl. Add the liquid ingredients to the dry and mix thoroughly. Fold in the egg whites.

2. Pour a little batter into a hot, greased waffle iron and cook according to the manufacturer's directions, usually about 4 minutes.

*Serves 4 to 6*

# 9

# Rice Salads

There was a time when salads, especially potato salads, were considered suitable only for picnic fare. Today, salads have become so popular and so exotic that they're running away with many menus. Some cookbooks have made salads so complicated that a number of the recipes may take over an hour to prepare. That is nonsense. One of the virtues salads always had (and should have) is their simplicity.

In this regard, rice has always ruled supreme throughout the world. Rice salads are also light, easily digested, attractive to the eye, and, as some devotees claim, seductive. They come cold or hot with a "dress up" or presentation advantage that few other foods have. We doubt that any other salad could so successfully combine all of these assets as do Dilled Shrimp and Rice Salad, Tomato-Stuffed Eggplant Rice Salad, or a Rice-Crabmeat Salad.

For all rice salads, be sure to use parboiled or converted rice. Rice grains for salads should be firm, fluffy, and separate, never sticky or gummy. Parboiled or converted rice ensures perfect salad rice every time.

# Rice and Beet Salad

3 cups cooked long-grain rice, cooled
2 cups cubed cooked beets
One 7-ounce can tuna, drained and broken into bite-size pieces
2 scallions (white part only), minced
1 cup cubed heart of fennel
12 black Greek olives, pitted and halved
5 tablespoons olive oil
1 tablespoon red or white wine vinegar
½ cup mayonnaise
Salt and freshly ground black pepper to taste
Boston lettuce leaves
1 hard-boiled egg, sliced
6 anchovy fillets
6 cooked asparagus spears

1. In a large bowl, combine the rice, beets, tuna, scallions, fennel, and olives. In a smaller bowl, combine the olive oil, wine vinegar, mayonnaise, salt, and pepper, then add to the rice bowl. Toss with two metal forks. Taste for seasoning, adding salt and pepper if needed.

2. Line a salad bowl with the lettuce leaves. Spoon in the salad. Garnish with the egg slices in the center, like the hub of a wheel, and the asparagus and anchovy fillets like the spokes.

*Serves 6*

# Rice-Crabmeat Salad

1½ cups cooked long-grain rice, cooled
1 pound fresh cooked crabmeat, or two 7½-ounce cans, picked
    over to remove any cartilage or shell
One 4-ounce can water chestnuts, drained and sliced
2 small tender (inside) celery stalks, scraped and chopped
2 whole scallions, trimmed and thinly sliced
¼ cup mayonnaise
¼ cup sour cream
3 tablespoons fresh lemon juice
1 teaspoon salt (optional)
¼ teaspoon cayenne
Six ¾-inch slices ripe, firm large tomatoes (use just the center
    portion of the tomato), seeds scooped out
6 lettuce leaves
3 tablespoons chopped fresh dill
2 hard-boiled eggs, yolks and whites sieved separately

1. In a large bowl, combine the rice, crabmeat, water chestnuts, celery, and scallions.

2. Combine the mayonnaise, sour cream, lemon juice, salt, and cayenne and blend well. Fold two-thirds of the dressing into the salad, mixing well but gently. Taste and add more dressing if desired.

3. Lay a slice of tomato on a lettuce leaf on individual plates or on one large, flat serving dish. Spoon on the salad, dividing it equally. Sprinkle on the dill, the sieved egg white, and then the sieved egg yolk. Serve any remaining salad dressing at the table.

*Serves 6*

# Rice and Ham Salad

3 cups cooked long-grain rice, cooled
2 cups cubed cooked ham
2 hard-boiled eggs, coarsely chopped
½ cup black Greek olives, halved
4 tender (inside) celery stalks, scraped and cut into small dice
3 scallions (white part only), thinly sliced
¾ cup mayonnaise, blended with 3 tablespoons lemon juice, 2
    tablespoons honey, and salt and pepper to taste
6 large Boston lettuce leaves
3 ripe tomatoes, peeled and each cut into 6 wedges

1. In a large bowl, combine and mix well with a metal fork the rice, ham, eggs, olives, celery, and scallions.
2. Spoon half of the mayonnaise onto the rice mixture and mix with a metal fork. Taste and add more mayonnaise, salt, and pepper if needed.
3. Spoon the salad onto the lettuce leaves on one large serving dish or individual plates. Garnish with the tomato wedges.

*Serves 6*

# Mussel and Rice Salad

30 mussels, scrubbed and beards removed
2 shallots, chopped
Leaves from 2 celery stalks
½ bay leaf
4 tablespoons (½ stick) butter or margarine
½ cup water
1½ cups dry white wine
3 tablespoons white wine vinegar
¾ cup olive oil
½ teaspoon each fresh tarragon, fresh chives, fresh basil, and
    fresh thyme, or use one-third that amount of dried herbs

Salt and freshly ground black pepper to taste
¾ cup water
¾ cup long-grain rice
Salt to taste
3 tablespoons chopped broadleaf (Italian) parsley leaves

1. In a large saucepan, combine the mussels, shallots, celery leaves, bay leaf, butter or margarine, water, and wine. Bring to a boil over high heat. Cover, and cook for 2 minutes, stir and cook for another 2 minutes, or until the mussels open; discard any that do not. Drain the mussels, saving the liquid in which they cooked. Reduce the liquid to ¾ cup over high heat. Strain through a double thickness of cheesecloth.

2. Combine the wine vinegar, olive oil, tarragon, chives, basil, thyme, salt, and pepper, and blend well

3. Shell the mussels and set them aside in a bowl. Mix with ⅛ cup of the salad dressing. Set aside.

4. In a saucepan, heat to a boil ¾ cup of water with the ¾ cup of reduced mussel broth. Add the rice and bring to a boil. Lower the heat, stir with a wooden fork, cover, and cook for 15 minutes, or until the rice is tender and the liquid has been absorbed. Taste for seasoning, adding salt if needed. Cool.

5. Mix the rice with one-third of the salad dressing. Taste and add more dressing if desired.

6. Arrange the mussels in the center of a serving bowl. Surround them with the rice. Sprinkle the rice with parsley. Pass the remaining dressing at the table.

*Serves 4*

# Cold Chicken Salad

3 cups cooked long-grain rice, cooled
3 cups cubed cooked chicken breast
1 large firm ripe tomato, peeled, seeded, and diced
1 cup scraped and diced celery heart
½ cup diced pimiento
2 whole scallions, trimmed and diced
1 cup mayonnaise, blended with 2 tablespoons lemon juice and ¼
   teaspoon ground cumin
Salt and freshly ground black pepper to taste
6 to 8 Boston lettuce leaves

1. In a large bowl, combine and blend well the rice and chicken, using two metal forks. Add the tomato, celery, pimiento, scallions, and two-thirds of the mayonnaise, mixing well but carefully. Season with salt and pepper. Taste, adding more mayonnaise if desired.

2. Spoon onto the lettuce leaves on individual plates and serve, passing any remaining mayonnaise at the table.

*Serves 6 to 8*

# Hot Rice Salad

4 cups cooked, warm long-grain rice
3 tender (inside) celery stalks, scraped and chopped
8 to 10 large black Greek olives, pitted and halved
1 dill pickle, chopped
¼ cup hot chicken broth
2 tablespoons dry white wine
½ cup vinaigrette (see String Beans Vinaigrette, page 267)
Salt and freshly ground black pepper to taste
Boston or Bibb lettuce leaves
1 teaspoon chopped fresh chives
1 tablespoon chopped fresh parsley

1. The rice should be warm and all the other ingredients at room temperature. Combine the rice, celery, olives, pickle, broth, wine, and half of the vinaigrette. Blend with a metal fork, fluffing as you mix. Taste and add more dressing, if desired, and salt and pepper.

2. Spoon the salad into a lettuce-lined salad bowl. Sprinkle with the chives and parsley. Serve while still tepid. Pass any remaining vinaigrette at the table.

*Serves 4 to 6*

# Rice Rex

*This superb summer salad could be the king of the rice salads, combining cold meat, seafood, and vegetables. Actually it is also a unique cold "casserole."*

3 cups al dente–cooked long-grain rice, cooled
1 cup vinaigrette (see String Beans Vinaigrette, page 267)
1 cup chopped scallions (including some of the green)
2 tender (inside) celery hearts, scraped and chopped
2 small cucumbers, peeled, halved lengthwise, seeds scooped out, and sliced
1 cup thinly sliced radishes
3 or 4 baby carrots, scraped and blanched in boiling water; then cooled and thinly sliced
One 4-ounce jar pimientos, drained and julienned
2 tablespoons rinsed and drained capers
One 7½-ounce can red salmon, drained and flaked
12 medium cooked shrimp, halved lengthwise
1 cup diced pickled lamb's tongue (optional)
Salt and freshly ground black pepper to taste
Boston lettuce leaves

1. Put the rice in a large bowl. It is important that the rice be cooked al dente, with the grains separate and firm.

2. Pour on the vinaigrette a tablespoonful at a time, tossing well with a metal fork as each spoonful is added.

3. Add all remaining ingredients, except the lettuce, blending and tossing well with one or two forks. The ingredients should not be stirred together or mashed. Taste for seasoning, adding salt and pepper if needed. Serve on lettuce leaves.

*Serves 6 to 8*


# Ricotta-Rice-Vegetable Salad

3 cups cooked long-grain brown rice, cooled
1 cup ricotta, set in a sieve over a bowl to drain
1 cup broccoli florets, cooked tender-crisp
½ cup julienned carrots, cooked tender-crisp
2 whole scallions, trimmed and cut into ¼-inch lengths
6 tablespoons olive oil
3 tablespoons fresh lemon juice
Salt and freshly ground black pepper to taste
Bibb or Boston lettuce leaves
⅓ cup drained small capers

Combine the rice with all the ingredients except the lettuce and capers, and mix with a metal fork, fluffing up the rice as you mix. Taste for seasoning, adding whatever your taste demands. Spoon into a bowl lined with the lettuce leaves and sprinkle with the capers.

*Serves 4 to 6*

# Rice-Stuffed Pimientos

1 cup cooked long-grain rice, cooled
½ cup finely diced Genoa salami
½ cup finely diced Swiss cheese
½ cup finely diced radishes
2 scallions (white part only), minced
½ cup mayonnaise
2 tablespoons olive oil
2 tablespoons white vinegar
1 tablespoon chopped fresh tarragon, or 1 teaspoon dried
Salt and freshly ground black pepper to taste
4 to 6 large whole canned pimientos
½ pound String Beans Vinaigrette (see below)
4 to 6 Boston lettuce leaves

1. In a bowl, combine and mix well the rice, salami, cheese, radishes, and scallions.

2. In another bowl, combine the mayonnaise, olive oil, vinegar, tarragon, salt, and pepper and blend well. Add this salad dressing to the rice mixture and blend well with a fork. Taste for seasoning, adding more vinegar, salt, pepper, or whatever your taste demands.

3. Divide and fill the pimientos, handling the pimientos gently, since they are very fragile.

4. Set each stuffed pimiento on a lettuce leaf and arrange the string beans around it.

*Serves 4 to 6, depending on the size of the pimientos*


## String Beans Vinaigrette

½ pound young, tender string beans, trimmed
3 tablespoons olive oil
1 tablespoon wine vinegar
Salt and freshly ground black pepper to taste
1 shallot, minced
3 tablespoons chopped fresh parsley leaves

1. Cook the beans in boiling salted water for 5 minutes, or until they are tender but still slightly crisp. Plunge in cold water to cool and drain well. Cut into 1-inch lengths.

2. In a bowl, combine the remaining ingredients and blend well. Pour this salad dressing over the beans and toss to coat.

# Dilled Shrimp and Rice Salad

1 pound medium shrimp, shelled and deveined
½ cup olive oil
3 tablespoons fresh lemon juice
⅛ teaspoon cayenne, or to taste
Salt and freshly ground black pepper to taste
½ garlic clove, minced
2 tablespoons chopped fresh dill, or 2 teaspoons dried
1½ cups cooked long-grain rice, cooled
Bibb or Boston lettuce leaves
1 tablespoon chopped fresh dill, or 1 teaspoon dried, or 1
   tablespoon chopped fresh parsley leaves

1. Cook the shrimp in boiling salted water for 3 minutes, or just until they turn pink and become firm. Do not overcook as they will toughen. Immediately drain and cool. Cut into halves lengthwise.

2. Combine the olive oil, lemon juice, cayenne, salt, garlic, and the 2 tablespoons of dill and blend well.

3. In a large bowl, combine the shrimp, two-thirds of the salad dressing, and the rice. Mix with a metal fork, lifting as you mix. Taste and add more lemon juice, pepper, or salt to taste.

4. Line a salad bowl with the lettuce leaves and spoon the salad into it. Or serve on individual salad plates on a lettuce leaf. Garnish the top with the 1 tablespoon of dill or parsley. Serve the remaining salad dressing at the table.

*Serves 4 to 6*

# Stella Insalata

1½ cups cooked long-grain rice, cooled
¼ cup quartered pimiento-stuffed olives
¼ cup scraped and chopped celery
¼ cup scraped and shredded carrots
⅛ cup small Provolone cubes
1 teaspoon chopped chives
½ cup olive oil
2 tablespoons red wine vinegar
⅛ teaspoon dried oregano
Salt and freshly ground black pepper to taste
4 large ripe firm tomatoes
4 rolled anchovies
1 tablespoon chopped broadleaf (Italian) parsley leaves

1. In a bowl combine and blend with a metal fork the rice, olives, celery, carrots, cheese, and chives.

2. In a measuring cup, combine and blend well the oil, vinegar, oregano, salt, and pepper. Pour half of the dressing over the rice mixture and toss with a fork. Taste for seasoning. Add more salad dressing to taste. Chill for 30 minutes.

3. Set the tomatoes stem side down. Cut each tomato nearly through forming 6 wedges held together by the stem end. Carefully open each tomato to form a star. Spoon one-quarter of the rice mixture into each tomato. Top each with a rolled anchovy. Sprinkle on the parsley and pass any remaining salad dressing at the table.

*Serves 4*

# Singapore Rice Salad

6 tablespoons peanut oil or light vegetable oil
3 eggs, lightly beaten, seasoned with salt and black pepper
1 cup tiny fresh peas or frozen peas, defrosted
1 cup fresh corn kernels or frozen corn, defrosted
¼ pound small firm fresh mushrooms, quartered
½ cup currants
½ cup rich chicken broth
4 cups cooked long-grain rice, cooled
2 crisp lettuce leaves (the heart of romaine is good), shredded
½ of a medium cucumber, peeled, seeded, and cut into bean-sized
   pieces
3 tablespoons soy sauce
2 tablespoons sesame oil
½ teaspoon salt (optional)
1 teaspoon sugar
2 tablespoons dry sherry
3 whole scallions, trimmed and finely chopped

1. In a wok or frying pan over medium heat, heat 3 tablespoons of the oil. Pour in the eggs and cook much like an omelet, until the eggs have set. Remove and cut into ½-by-1-inch strips. Set aside.

2. Heat the remaining oil in the wok or frying pan. Stir in the peas and corn and cook for 2 minutes. Add the mushrooms and currants and cook for 1 minute, or until the currants are somewhat plump. Add the chicken broth and bring to a boil.

3. Spoon the vegetable mixture, including its liquid, over the rice. Mix with a fork. Add the egg, lettuce, and cucumber and mix well. Combine the soy sauce, sesame oil, salt, sugar, and dry sherry and blend well. Pour the mixture over the salad and mix thoroughly. Sprinkle the scallions on top. Serve hot or cold.

*Serves 6 to 8*

# Rizi Tabbouleh

4 cups cooked long-grain rice, cooled
½ cup finely chopped fresh mint leaves
1 large red onion, coarsely chopped
¼ cup olive oil
3 tablespoons fresh lemon juice
Salt and freshly ground black pepper to taste
Blanched grape vine leaves (see Note below) to line the salad
  bowl (optional)
1 large ripe firm tomato, peeled and cut into 4 or 6 wedges

1. In a bowl, combine and blend well all the ingredients, except the vine leaves and tomato. Taste, adding more oil, lemon juice, and so on if needed.

2. Line a glass salad bowl with the grape leaves, rough side against the glass. Spoon the rice salad into the bowl and garnish with the tomato wedges.

*Note:* To blanch vine leaves, wash the leaves and drop them into boiling water. Blanch for 3 minutes. Lift out with a large fork and plunge into cold water. Drain well on paper towels.

*Serves 4 to 6*

# Tomatoes Stuffed with Eggplant-Rice Salad

6 large ripe firm tomatoes
1 eggplant (about 1 pound), peeled and cut into cubes slightly
    smaller than ½ inch
Salt
3 tablespoons olive oil
1 garlic clove, minced
½ cup chopped tender celery
1½ cups cooked long-grain rice, cooled
¼ cup chopped black Greek olives
¼ cup chopped pimiento-stuffed green olives
6 anchovy fillets, chopped
1 tablespoon drained capers
2 tablespoons cider vinegar
½ cup olive oil
2 scallions (white part only), minced
1 hard-boiled egg yolk, sieved
Freshly ground black pepper to taste

1. Peel the tomatoes, dipping them in hot water if necessary. Cut a slice from the stem end and scoop out the inside, leaving a firm shell. Invert on a plate to drain.

2. Sprinkle the eggplant with salt; set it in a strainer over a bowl and allow to stand for 30 minutes to drain. Rinse and pat dry.

3. In a frying pan, over medium heat, heat the 3 tablespoons of olive oil. Add the eggplant, garlic, and celery and cook for 5 minutes, or until they are tender, but still slightly crisp. Cool.

4. Combine the eggplant mixture, rice, olives, anchovies, and capers in a bowl and blend well with a metal fork. Combine the vinegar, ½ cup olive oil, scallions, sieved egg yolk, and black pepper and blend well. Pour over the salad and mix thoroughly. Taste for seasoning and add more of whatever your taste demands.

5. Divide the mixture equally and mound it in the tomatoes. Serve on lettuce leaves.

*Serves 6*

# Baked German Rice Salad

3 cups al dente–cooked long-grain rice
4 knockwurst, cut into ¼-inch slices
2 celery stalks, scraped and diced
1 small onion, finely chopped
½ cup mayonnaise
1 teaspoon prepared mustard
Salt and freshly ground black pepper to taste
½ cup half-and-half
2 hard-boiled eggs, sliced
3 tablespoons chopped fresh parsley leaves

1. Preheat the oven to 350 degrees.

2. Combine the rice, knockwurst, celery, and onion in a large bowl.

3. Combine and blend into a salad dressing the mayonnaise, mustard, salt, pepper, and half-and-half.

4. Stir the salad dressing into the rice bowl.

5. Spoon into a buttered shallow baking dish. Cover and bake for 30 minutes. Garnish with the egg slices, each topped with a dab of mayonnaise and then sprinkled with parsley.

*Serves 6*

# Valencia Salad

½ pound shrimp, peeled and deveined
3 cups al dente–cooked long-grain rice, cooled
One 6½-ounce can minced clams, drained
1½ cups diced cooked chicken
1 cup sliced celery heart (Scrape the celery before slicing it.)
1 cup cut-up small cooked string beans
1 medium red onion, thinly sliced and separated into rings
1 tablespoon chopped fresh mint leaves
1 cup mayonnaise
3 tablespoons dry white wine
3 tablespoons rinsed and drained capers
Salt and freshly ground black pepper to taste
2 medium ripe firm tomatoes, peeled and each cut into 6 wedges

1. Cook the shrimp in boiling salted water, just until they turn pink. Do not overcook. Drain and cut lengthwise into halves.

2. In a large glass bowl, combine the shrimp, rice, clams, chicken, celery, string beans, onion, and mint.

3. Combine the mayonnaise, wine, capers, salt, and pepper and blend well. Spoon over the salad and mix well but carefully with a metal fork. Taste for seasoning. Chill.

4. Garnish with the tomato wedges.

*Serves 6*

# Wild Rice Salad with Aïoli Sauce

3 cups cooked wild rice
½ pound small white fresh mushrooms, sliced
3 tablespoons olive oil
2 tablespoons fresh lemon juice
2 hard-boiled eggs, coarsely chopped
1 small green bell pepper, chopped
2 cups cooked bay scallops or shrimp (If you are using the
    scallops, slice them, but cut the shrimp in half lengthwise.)
1 cup Aïoli Sauce (see below)

1. In a large bowl, combine all the ingredients except the Aïoli Sauce.

2. Spoon in half of the Aïoli Sauce and mix well but carefully with a metal fork, fluffing.

3. Taste and add more sauce if desired. Serve the remaining sauce at the table.

*Serves 4 to 6*

## Aïoli Sauce

1 cup mayonnaise
3 garlic cloves, minced
½ teaspoon dry mustard
½ teaspoon paprika
1 tablespoon fresh lemon juice

Combine and blend all the ingredients well.

# Summer Rice Salad

4 cups cooked long-grain rice, cooled
4 scallions (white part only), thinly sliced
½ cup finely chopped sweet pickles
1 small pimiento, cut into short strips
4 hard-boiled eggs, chopped
1 cup mayonnaise, blended with 1 teaspoon Dijon mustard
Salt and freshly ground black pepper to taste
2 bunches watercress
1 ripe firm avocado, cut into 6 wedges
2 ripe firm tomatoes, peeled and each cut into 6 wedges

1. In a large bowl, combine and blend well but gently with a metal fork the rice, scallions, pickles, pimiento, eggs, and two-thirds of the mayonnaise. Add salt and pepper. Taste and add more mayonnaise if desired.

2. Serve on a bed of watercress, garnished with the avocado and tomato wedges.

*Serves 6*

# 10
# Rice Desserts

Antoine Gilly, one of the greatest of the French chefs, once observed, "It probably isn't fair, but one of the strongest and very often the most favorable impressions of a dinner is the last course. Maybe we have short taste memories.

"I still remember," he went on, "serving the Maharaja of Bharatpur one of my own favorites, smoked salmon wrapped around caviar, pheasant under feather, and several other offerings, including barquettes of crayfish. It was, admittedly, a rather full meal, so, for dessert, I served another favorite of mine, something light, cool, and refreshing—a goblet of orange sherbet topped with light rum. *That* got the applause."

Rice surprises many of us when it appears as a dessert. We once forgot all that went before (at a remarkable dinner of smoked trout followed by quail) when Strawberry Rice Custard Pie was served. As rice often does, it stole the show.

In cooking the following desserts, we've run tests with various rices and found that short- or medium-grain rice worked best. We also checked many markets and found that medium grain is available just about everywhere.

# Almond-Date Cream

2 whole eggs plus 1 egg yolk
1½ cups milk
1½ cups cooked short- or medium-grain rice
¼ cup firmly packed light brown sugar
⅛ teaspoon salt (optional)
3 tablespoons butter or margarine
½ cup chopped pitted dates
½ teaspoon vanilla extract
⅛ cup chopped blanched and toasted almonds
¼ teaspoon cream of tartar
4 tablespoons granulated sugar
½ teaspoon almond extract

1. Separate the whole eggs. In a bowl, beat the 3 egg yolks slightly; stir in the milk, rice, brown sugar, salt, butter or margarine, and dates. Transfer to a deep saucepan and cook over medium-low heat, stirring constantly, until thickened. Do not overcook. Stir in the vanilla. Preheat the oven to 350 degrees.

2. Butter a shallow baking dish. Sprinkle the almonds on the bottom. Then spoon in the custard.

3. Beat the egg whites until frothy. Beat in the cream of tartar. When stiff, add the granulated sugar, a small amount at a time, and continue beating after each addition. Beat until the mixture holds its shape. Beat in the almond extract.

4. Spread the meringue over the rice custard. Bake for 20 minutes, or until the top is golden brown. Serve warm or cold.

*Serves 4*

# Algarve Rice Pudding

*We call this excellent dessert the "Algarve" pudding, for it was in that southern province, Portugal's Riviera, that we found it.*

1 cup short- or medium-grain rice
2½ cups water
Peel of 1 lemon, cut into strips
2 cups of half-and-half
2 egg yolks
¼ cup sugar
1 teaspoon ground mace

1. In a saucepan, combine the rice, water, and lemon peel. Bring to a boil, stir well with a wooden fork, lower the heat, cover, and simmer for 15 minutes, or until the rice is tender. Drain off any liquid that remains. Discard the lemon peel.

2. In a bowl, combine and beat well the half-and-half, egg yolks, and sugar. Stir this mixture into the rice and simmer over low heat, until the rice is very soft, of pudding consistency, and the custard is creamy. Serve warm in bowls, sprinkled with the mace.

*Serves 4*

# Apricot Twist

3 cups cooked short- or medium-grain rice
2½ cups milk
⅔ cup sugar
1 tablespoon butter or margarine
3 egg yolks beaten with ½ cup milk
1 teaspoon vanilla extract
3 egg whites beaten with ¼ teaspoon cream of tartar and ⅛
    teaspoon salt until stiff but not dry
¾ cup well-drained and chopped cooked dried apricots
2 teaspoons brandy

1. Combine the rice, milk, ⅓ cup of the sugar, and the butter or margarine in a saucepan. Cook over low heat until thick and creamy, about 20 minutes, stirring occasionally.

2. Stir the egg yolk mixture into the rice mixture and cook for 2 or 3 minutes. Stir in the vanilla. Turn into a buttered 1½-quart baking dish. Preheat the oven to 350 degrees.

3. A tablespoonful at a time, beat the remaining ⅓ cup of sugar into the egg whites.

4. Fold the apricots and brandy into the egg whites. Spread over the pudding in little twists or swirls, completely covering it. Bake for 10 minutes, or until golden brown. Serve immediately.

*Serves 6 to 8*


## Apple-Walnut Crisp

2 cups cooked short- or medium-grain rice
2 cups thinly sliced tart apples
1 tablespoon fresh lemon juice
1 cup firmly packed light brown sugar
½ teaspoon ground cinnamon
¼ teaspoon salt (optional)
¾ cup all-purpose flour
6 tablespoons butter or margarine
½ cup chopped walnuts
1 cup heavy cream, whipped

1. In a bowl, combine and mix well, but carefully, the rice, apples, lemon juice, ½ cup of the brown sugar, cinnamon, and salt. Transfer to a shallow baking dish coated with butter or margarine. Preheat the oven to 350 degrees.

2. Mix the flour and remaining sugar together. With a pastry cutter, cut in the butter or margarine until the mixture is crumbly. Stir in the nuts. Evenly spoon over the rice and bake for 30 minutes, or until the top is crispy and golden brown. Serve warm or cool, topped with the whipped cream.

*Serves 6*

# Apple-Rum Pudding

1 cup cooked short- or medium-grain rice
2 cups light cream or half-and-half
⅓ cup sugar
½ teaspoon salt (optional)
1 envelope (1 tablespoon) unflavored gelatin
¼ cup water
2 tablespoons light rum
1 cup sour cream
Apple-Rum Topping (see below)

1. Combine the rice, cream or half-and-half, sugar, and salt in a saucepan. Bring to a boil, stir with a wooden fork, lower the heat, and cook, stirring occasionally, until creamy, about 20 minutes.

2. Soften the gelatin in the water. Heat the mixture over hot water until it is clear and liquid. Add to the rice mixture and stir to blend well. Cool until thickened but not set.

3. Fold in the rum and sour cream. Spoon into individual 1-cup molds. Chill until firm. Unmold and serve with the hot Apple-Rum Topping spooned on top.

*Serves 6*

## Apple-Rum Topping

½ cup firmly packed light brown sugar
2 teaspoons cornstarch
¼ teaspoon salt (optional)
½ teaspoon ground cinnamon
½ cup water
2 cups coarsely chopped tart apples
3 tablespoons butter or margarine
2 tablespoons light rum

Combine and blend well the sugar, cornstarch, salt, cinnamon, and water in a saucepan. Add the apples. Bring to a boil, lower the heat, and simmer, stirring occasionally, for 15 to 20 minutes, or until the apples are tender. Remove from the heat and stir in the butter or margarine and rum.

# Apple-Ricot Soufflé

3½ cups light cream or half-and-half
1¼ cups short- or medium-grain rice
2 eggs, separated
6 tablespoons superfine sugar
6 tablespoons apricot jam
4 tablespoons applesauce
¼ teaspoon cream of tartar
½ teaspoon almond extract
1 tablespoon light rum (optional)

1. In a saucepan, over medium heat, bring the cream or half-and-half to a boil. Stir in the rice, turn the heat to the lowest setting, cover, and simmer, stirring frequently, for 30 minutes, or until the rice is very tender and most of the liquid has been absorbed. Remove from the heat.

2. Beat the egg yolks with 3 tablespoons of the sugar and stir into the rice. Preheat the oven to 350 degrees.

3. Butter a 2-quart soufflé dish and spread a layer of rice over the bottom. Spread a thin layer of jam over the rice. Repeat until all the rice is used, ending with a layer of jam. The number of layers depends on the size of the dish. Spread the applesauce over the last layer of jam.

4. Beat the egg whites until they are frothy. Add the cream of tartar and beat until stiff enough to form peaks. Add the remaining sugar in small amounts, beating after each addition. Beat in the almond extract. Spread over the applesauce and bake for 20 minutes, or until golden. Just before serving, spoon the rum over the top and ignite it. A few minutes' time to stand will allow the rum to burn off.

*Serves 4 to 6*

# Dolce Budino Velluto con Salsa di Fragole

1½ cups ricotta
2 cups milk
3 cups cooked short- or medium-grain rice
½ cup sugar
½ teaspoon salt (optional)
1 tablespoon grated lemon rind
2 eggs, beaten in a bowl
1 teaspoon vanilla extract
1 quart fresh strawberries, hulled, rinsed, and sliced
½ cup red currant jelly
Pinch of salt

1. Mash or process the cheese in a blender or food processor until it is smooth. Transfer to a deep saucepan; stir in the milk, rice, sugar, salt, and lemon rind, blending well. Cook over low heat, stirring frequently, until thick and creamy, about 20 minutes.

2. Stir a small amount of the hot mixture into the eggs; return all to the saucepan. Cook, stirring constantly, until the eggs have set, about 1 minute. Stir in the vanilla. Cool.

3. Meanwhile, to make the sauce, mash 1 cup of the strawberries. Combine with the jelly and pinch of salt in a saucepan. Heat to boiling. Stir in the remaining berries and cook for about 1 minute. Chill.

4. Spoon the pudding into serving dishes and cover with the strawberry sauce.

*Serves 6 to 8*

# Danish Rice Cream

*While staying at an elegant small hotel near the railway station in Copenhagen, we attended cooking classes offered free by the Danish government.*

*Four pink-cheeked, robust women in aprons worked on a platform, the wall behind them mirrored so spectators could observe the hands of the skilled cooks at work. One woman explained the actions in Danish, another in English, while the other two cooked. We learned how to cook Danish chickens in nothing but "the world's best butter" and lemon, with a currant jelly-cheese-mustard sauce, and the following rice dish. The dessert is varied with different nuts and sometimes tart wild "cloudberries."*

1 quart milk
4 tablespoons superfine sugar
¾ cup short- or medium-grain rice
1 large egg yolk, beaten
½ cup chopped walnuts
1 teaspoon vanilla extract
1 cup heavy cream, whipped
One 1-pound can pitted Bing (black) cherries with their liquid
1 tablespoon Crème de Cassis (black currant liqueur)
1 tablespoon cornstarch, dissolved in 1 tablespoon cold water

1. Pour the milk into a deep saucepan, stir in the sugar, and bring to a boil. Stir in the rice, lower the heat, and simmer, uncovered, for 20 minutes, or until thick and creamy. Stir frequently.

2. Remove the rice from the heat and stir in the egg yolk, walnuts, and vanilla. Pour the rice mixture into a chilled mixing bowl and let sit at room temperature until it cools. Fold in the whipped cream. Cover and refrigerate.

3. Pour the cherries and their liquid into a saucepan with the Crème de Cassis. Simmer, stirring, for 5 minutes. Add the cornstarch mixture and cook, stirring, for 30 seconds, or until thickened and clear.

4. Transfer the rice to a fairly shallow serving dish, smooth the top, and evenly spoon on the cherry mixture. Refrigerate for 2 hours before serving.

*Serves 4 to 6*

# President Grant's Rice Pudding

1 tablespoon butter or margarine, softened
3 cups hot cooked short- or medium-grain rice
2 cups light cream or half-and-half
2 cups milk
½ cup sugar
1 tablespoon grated lemon rind
1 teaspoon vanilla extract
⅛ teaspoon salt (optional)
4 egg yolks, beaten in a large bowl
4 egg whites, beaten until stiff but not dry
Lemon Sauce (see below)

1. Preheat the oven to 350 degrees.

2. Stir the butter or margarine into the rice. Add the rice, cream, milk, sugar, lemon rind, vanilla, and salt to the bowl with the beaten egg yolks and blend well. Fold in the beaten egg whites.

3. Turn into a buttered shallow 2½-quart baking dish. Set in a pan of hot water. Bake for 1 hour, or until a knife blade inserted just off center comes out clean. Serve warm with Lemon Sauce.

*Serves 8*

## Lemon Sauce

½ cup sugar
1 tablespoon cornstarch
⅛ teaspoon salt (optional)
1 cup boiling water
1 tablespoon butter or margarine
1 tablespoon grated lemon rind
1 tablespoon fresh lemon juice

1. Combine and blend well the sugar, cornstarch, and salt in a saucepan. Gradually stir the hot water into the sugar-cornstarch mixture.

2. Cook over medium-low heat, stirring constantly, until it thickens, about 5 minutes. Blend in the butter or margarine, lemon rind, and lemon juice.

# Cherries Jubilee Pudding

1 recipe for rice pudding, as prepared for Raspberry Parfait
(page 302). Do not use the fruit for that recipe but do use the
almonds if desired.
Cherries Jubilee Sauce (see below)

1. Prepare pudding and cool.
2. Serve in individual dessert dishes, spooning Cherries Jubilee
Sauce over each serving.

*Serves 6*


## Cherries Jubilee Sauce

One 1-pound can pitted Bing (black) cherries
1 tablespoon sugar
1 tablespoon cornstarch, blended with 1 tablespoon cold water
¼ cup Kirschwasser, heated

1. Drain cherries, reserving the syrup. In a saucepan, combine
and blend well the sugar and cornstarch mixture. Gradually stir in
the reserved cherry syrup. Cook over low heat, stirring constantly,
until the sauce starts to thicken, about 2 minutes. Add the cherries
and heat through.
2. Pour the Kirschwasser over the cherries and ignite it (stand
back as it will flare).
3. Spoon the sauce over the pudding. This will extinguish the
flames.

# Cream Mold

¼ cup short- or medium-grain rice
½ cup water
½ teaspoon salt (optional)
2 cups milk
1 tablespoon butter or margarine
1½ envelopes (1½ tablespoons) unflavored gelatin
6 tablespoons sugar
2 teaspoons grated lemon rind
1 teaspoon vanilla extract
1 cup heavy cream, whipped

1. Combine the rice, ¼ cup of the water, and the salt. Heat to boiling, stir with a wooden fork, lower the heat, cover, and cook for 5 minutes. Add the milk and butter or margarine, and return to a boil. Lower the heat, cover, and simmer until the rice is tender, about 20 minutes, stirring occasionally.

2. Soften the gelatin in the remaining water; stir over hot water until it is dissolved, clear, and liquid. Stir into the rice mixture. Stir in the sugar, lemon rind, and vanilla. Remove from the heat and cool until it just starts to set. Fold in the whipped cream.

3. Pour into a 1-quart mold. Cover and chill until the mixture sets.

4. Unmold and serve with a raspberry, strawberry, peach, or other fruit sauce.

*Serves 4 to 6*

# Flan de Arroz

4 cups (2 pints) light cream or half-and-half
⅛ cup short- or medium-grain rice
Thin strips of zest from 1 large lemon
9 tablespoons sugar
6 egg yolks

1. Heat the cream or half-and-half in the top of a double boiler. Stir in the rice and lemon zest. Bring the water in the bottom of the double boiler to a boil, lower the heat, and cook the rice over the simmering water for 25 minutes, or until it is very tender. Stir frequently.

2. Spoon 6 tablespoons of the sugar into a heavy saucepan or frying pan and cook over medium heat for 3 minutes (or until the sugar starts to melt), shaking the pan to keep the sugar from burning. Turn the heat to low and cook, stirring until the sugar is syrupy and dark brown, being careful that it doesn't burn. Spoon the syrup into a 2-quart Pyrex bowl, spinning the bowl around until the sugar syrup evenly coats the sides and bottom. Preheat the oven to 300 degrees.

3. In a bowl, beat the egg yolks with the remaining sugar until they are lemony in color. Remove and discard the lemon zest in the cream-rice mixture. Gradually blend the cream-rice mixture with the beaten egg yolks. Carefully pour into the bowl coated with the sugar syrup. Set the bowl in a pan of very hot water. The water should come halfway up the sides of the bowl. Bake for 35 minutes, or until the flan is set. A knife blade inserted just off center will come out clean. Do not overbake. Cool and refrigerate until ready to serve. Just before serving, run a knife blade around the side of the bowl and turn the flan out onto a serving dish with a slightly raised rim.

*Serves 6*

# A Georgia Peach

1 cup cooked short- or medium-grain rice
3 eggs, beaten
¼ teaspoon salt (optional)
⅓ cup sugar
1 teaspoon vanilla extract
1 teaspoon grated lemon rind
2½ cups milk
1½ cups sliced fresh peaches, sweetened to taste, or drained
    canned or frozen sliced peaches
1 teaspoon fresh lemon juice
1 tablespoon brandy
⅔ cup shredded coconut

1. Preheat the oven to 350 degrees.

2. Combine and blend well all the ingredients, except the peaches, lemon juice, brandy, and coconut. Turn into a 1-quart baking dish coated with butter or margarine. Set the dish in a pan of hot water and bake for 45 minutes, or until a knife blade inserted just off center emerges clean. Halfway through the cooking time, use a spoon to stir from the bottom, bringing the rice to the surface.

3. Combine and mix well the peaches, lemon juice, brandy, and coconut. Chill until serving time. Arrange on top of the custard just before serving.

*Serves 4*

# Rice-Coconut Custard

½ cup sugar
¼ teaspoon salt (optional)
3 eggs, beaten in a mixing bowl
2 cups milk
1 cup cooked short- or medium-grain rice
¼ cup raisins
1 teaspoon vanilla extract
½ cup shredded coconut
¼ teaspoon ground nutmeg
1 tablespoon butter or margarine
¼ cup shredded coconut, toasted until golden

1. Preheat the oven to 350 degrees.
2. Add the sugar and salt to the beaten eggs and blend well. Stir in the milk. Stir in the rice, raisins, vanilla, and the ½ cup of coconut. Pour into a buttered 1½-quart baking dish. Set it in a pan of hot water.
3. Bake for 30 minutes. Stir from the bottom to the top, bringing the rice to the surface as much as possible.
4. Sprinkle with nutmeg and dot with butter or margarine. Bake for 30 minutes longer, or until the custard has set.
5. Sprinkle with the toasted coconut just before serving.

*Serves 6*

# Pineapple Pudding

3 cups cooked short- or medium-grain rice
1 quart milk
⅔ cup sugar
½ teaspoon salt (optional)
One 3-ounce package cream cheese, softened
2 eggs, beaten in a bowl
1 teaspoon vanilla extract
Pineapple Sauce (see below)

1. Combine and blend well the rice, 3½ cups of the milk, sugar, and salt in a deep saucepan. Cook over low heat, stirring occasionally, until thick and creamy, about 20 minutes.

2. Add the remaining milk and the cheese to the beaten eggs and beat to blend. Stir into the rice mixture in the saucepan. Cook, stirring constantly, for 2 minutes, or until the eggs have set.

3. Stir in the vanilla. Spoon into serving dishes.

4. Serve warm or chilled with Pineapple Sauce.

*Serves 6*

## Pineapple Sauce

One 20-ounce can pineapple chunks
1 tablespoon cornstarch, dissolved in 1 tablespoon cold water
1 tablespoon butter or margarine
¼ cup firmly packed light brown sugar
⅛ teaspoon salt (optional)
½ teaspoon vanilla extract

1. Combine and blend well the pineapple with its juice and the cornstarch mixture in a saucepan.

2. Add the butter or margarine, brown sugar, and salt and cook over medium-low heat, stirring, until clear and thickened. Stir in the vanilla.

# Rice Pudding Glacé

3 cups cooked short- or medium-grain rice
3 cups milk
½ cup sugar
¼ teaspoon salt (optional)
2 teaspoons vanilla extract
2 teaspoons grated lemon rind
1 cup sour cream
2 cups mixed fruit, fresh, canned, or frozen, drained

1. In a deep saucepan, combine and blend well the rice, milk, 5 tablespoons of the sugar, and the salt. Cook over low heat, stirring occasionally, until thick and creamy, about 20 minutes. Add 1 teaspoon of the vanilla and 1 teaspoon of the lemon rind and blend. Turn into a buttered shallow 1½-quart baking dish. Preheat the broiler.

2. Combine and blend well the sour cream, remaining sugar, vanilla, and lemon rind. Spread over the pudding. Place under a broiler for about 5 minutes to form a glaze. Watch carefully to prevent burning. Serve hot or cold, topped with the mixed fruit.

*Serves 6*

# Orange Rice Ring

3 cups half-and-half
⅔ cup superfine sugar
1½ cups short- or medium-grain rice
1 teaspoon grated lemon rind
2 teaspoons grated orange rind
½ cup freshly squeezed orange juice
1 cup heavy cream, whipped
1½ cups Mandarin orange slices, marinated in Grand Marnier
    barely to cover

1. Bring the half-and-half to a boil in a deep saucepan. Stir in the sugar and then the rice. Turn the heat to the lowest possible setting, permitting the liquid to barely bubble. Cover and cook for 40 minutes, or until the liquid has been absorbed and the rice is tender, stirring occasionally. If the liquid is absorbed before the rice is tender, add a small amount of hot half-and-half or milk, and continue cooking. Remove from the heat and cool.

2. Stir in the lemon and orange rinds and orange juice, blending thoroughly. Fold in the whipped cream.

3. Spoon into a lightly oiled 9-inch ring mold. Refrigerate overnight. Unmold onto a cold serving dish and fill the center with the well-drained marinated orange slices.

*Serves 4 to 6*

# Pudding with Hazelnuts

3½ cups milk
1 cup heavy cream
1½ cups short- or medium-grain rice
¾ cup sugar
½ cup boiling water
¾ cup hazelnuts, toasted, skinned, and ground

1. In a saucepan, bring the milk and 2 tablespoons of cream to a boil. Stir in the rice, turn the heat to the lowest setting, cover, and cook for 25 minutes, or until the rice is tender and the liquid has been absorbed. Stir occasionally. Cool.

2. In a saucepan, over medium-low heat, melt the sugar, stirring so it doesn't burn, until it is syrupy and brown. Standing back, since the combining of hot sugar with water can cause spattering, slowly stir the water into the syrup and blend. Simmer for 5 minutes. Stir carefully into the cooled rice.

3. With a metal fork, add the ground hazelnuts to the rice, mixing well, lifting the rice as you mix.

4. Whip the remaining heavy cream with sweetening to taste, then fold in the rice. Serve cold in dessert glasses.

*Serves 4 to 6*

# Creamy Raisin Rice

½ cup short- or medium-grain rice
½ cup water
½ teaspoon salt (optional)
2¾ cups milk
½ cup raisins
Dark rum to cover the raisins, warmed
3 tablespoons butter or margarine
2 eggs, beaten in a bowl
⅛ cup sugar
½ teaspoon vanilla extract

1. In a deep saucepan, combine the rice, water, and salt. Bring to a boil, lower the heat, cover, and cook for about 5 minutes. Stir in 2¼ cups of the milk. Cover and cook over lowest heat for 1 hour, stirring occasionally.

2. Meanwhile, cover the raisins with the rum; let stand for 15 minutes. Drain in a sieve and set aside.

3. Stir the butter or margarine into the hot pudding.

4. Combine and blend well the eggs, sugar, and remaining milk. Add to the pudding mixture, stirring constantly. Cook for 2 to 3 minutes, or until the mixture thickens and the eggs have set. Remove from the heat and stir in the raisins and vanilla.

5. Spoon into serving dishes. Serve warm or cold.

*Serves 4 to 6*


# Old-fashioned American Rice Pudding

*This is an American classic, born in the South, and the favorite of several U.S. presidents.*

3 cups cooked short- or medium-grain rice, thoroughly drained
3 eggs, beaten
1 cup milk
1 cup half-and-half
½ cup light brown sugar (without lumps)
1 teaspoon vanilla extract
2 teaspoons fresh orange juice
⅛ teaspoon ground mace
½ cup golden raisins

1. Preheat the oven to 325 degrees.

2. In a bowl, combine all the ingredients and blend lightly with a metal fork. Spoon into a buttered 8-inch-square by 2-inch-deep baking dish and bake for 15 minutes. Stir and bake for 25 minutes longer, or until set. The pudding can be served either warm or cold.

*Serves 6 to 8*

# Strawberry-Rice Custard Pie

*The Rice Custard*

 2 egg yolks, beaten in a large bowl
 ½ cup cooked short- or medium-grain rice
 ½ cup sugar
 1 teaspoon grated lemon rind
 ½ teaspoon vanilla extract
 Pinch of salt (optional)
 1½ cups milk
 2 egg whites, stiffly beaten
 9-inch partially baked pastry shell

*The Strawberries*

 1 quart ripe strawberries, washed, hulled, and thoroughly
   drained
 1 cup sugar, mixed with 3 tablespoons cornstarch
 Whipped cream

1. To prepare the custard, preheat the oven to 325 degrees. Blend the egg yolks with the rice, sugar, lemon rind, vanilla, salt, and milk. Fold in the egg whites. Pour the mixture into the pastry shell and bake for 40 minutes, or until set. Remove and cool.

2. For the strawberry topping, select and set aside the most perfect, uniform berries. (They should amount to at least half of the berries.)

3. Mash the remaining berries and push them through a strainer (or process in a food processor) into a 2-cup measure. If you do not have 1½ cups, add water to yield that amount. Pour into a saucepan. Gradually stir in the sugar and cornstarch. Cook over medium heat, stirring, until the mixture simmers and thickens. Simmer for 1 minute, stirring. Cool.

4. Arrange the reserved whole berries attractively on top of the rice custard. Pour the sauce over and chill thoroughly. Decorate with whipped cream if desired.

*Serves 6*

# Top-of-the-Stove Rice Pudding

½ cup short- or medium-grain rice
4 tablespoons (½ stick) butter or margarine
1 cup water
½ teaspoon salt (optional)
1 quart milk
½ cup sugar
2 eggs, beaten
½ cup half-and-half
1 teaspoon vanilla extract
½ cup raisins, plumped in port wine and well drained
Ground cinnamon

1. In a saucepan, combine the rice, butter or margarine, water, and salt. Bring to a boil, lower the heat, cover, and simmer until all the water has been absorbed.

2. Pour in the milk and bring to a boil. Turn the heat to the lowest setting and simmer, stirring often, for 25 minutes, or until the rice is very tender.

3. Beat the sugar and eggs together. Stir into the cooked rice, stirring constantly until the mixture is set. Remove from the heat and blend in the half-and-half, vanilla, and raisins.

4. Spoon into a serving bowl and cool. Refrigerate until serving time. Sprinkle the top lightly with cinnamon before serving.

*Serves 6*

# Rice Tart

*We found this one in Parma, that region in Italy that is also famous for remarkable ham, the spicy* culatello, *and superb cheese,* parmigiano-reggiano.

5 cups milk
1 cup granulated sugar
1½ cups short- or medium-grain rice
3 egg yolks
½ cup chopped blanched and toasted almonds
Grated zest of 1 orange
½ teaspoon almond extract
3 egg whites, stiffly beaten
Confectioner's sugar
Amaretto (optional)

1. In a saucepan, bring the milk to a boil. Lower the heat and stir in ½ cup of the granulated sugar and then the rice. Simmer, covered, over the lowest heat for 15 minutes. Stir occasionally. Remove from the heat and cool. Preheat the oven to 325 degrees.

2. In a large bowl beat the egg yolks with the remaining granulated sugar. Blend in the rice and milk, almonds, orange zest, and almond extract. Fold in the egg whites.

3. Pour into a buttered 12-inch-square cake pan with high sides and bake for 50 minutes, or until set.

4. Before serving, sprinkle on the confectioner's sugar. Or sprinkle lightly with Amaretto and then the sugar.

*Serves 6 to 8*

# Raspberry-Rice Mold

3 cups cooked short- or medium-grain rice
3 cups milk
⅓ cup sugar
1 tablespoon butter or margarine
¼ teaspoon salt (optional)
2 eggs, beaten
½ cup golden raisins
½ cup drained crushed pineapple
1 teaspoon vanilla extract
⅔ cup raspberry jelly, melted
½ cup chopped pecans

1. In a deep saucepan, combine and blend well the rice, 2½ cups of the milk, sugar, butter or margarine, and salt. Cook over low heat until thick and creamy, 20 to 25 minutes, stirring occasionally.

2. Combine and blend well the eggs and the remaining milk. Stir into the rice mixture. Stir in the raisins. Cook, stirring constantly, for about 2 minutes, or until the eggs have set. Stir in the pineapple and vanilla. Spoon into individual molds or one large mold. Refrigerate for one full hour. Unmold and spoon on the melted raspberry jelly. Sprinkle with the pecans, and serve.

*Serves 6 to 8*

# Strawberry Rice Crème Brûlée

3 cups cooked short- or medium-grain rice
3 cups milk
⅓ cup granulated sugar
¼ teaspoon salt (optional)
Two 3-ounce packages cream cheese, softened
1½ teaspoons vanilla extract
1 cup heavy cream, whipped
1 pint strawberries, hulled, rinsed, sliced, and sweetened to taste, or one 16-ounce package frozen, sweetened whole strawberries, thawed, drained, and cut into halves
½ cup light brown sugar

1. In a deep saucepan, combine the rice, milk, granulated sugar, and salt. Cook over low heat until thick and creamy, about 20 minutes, stirring occasionally. Remove from the heat. Add the cream cheese, in small pieces, and the vanilla, stirring until the cheese has melted. Chill.

2. Fold in the whipped cream and chill thoroughly.

3. Arrange the strawberries on the bottom of a shallow baking dish. Spoon the pudding over the berries. Sprinkle evenly with the brown sugar, smoothing the top. Place under the broiler until the sugar melts, forming a glaze. Watch carefully so the sugar does not burn. Serve as soon as the glaze cools and hardens.

*Serves 6 to 8*

# Raspberry Parfait

1½ cups cooked short- or medium-grain rice
1½ cups milk
3 tablespoons sugar
¼ teaspoon salt (optional)
1 teaspoon vanilla extract
¼ cup toasted sliced almonds
1 cup heavy cream, whipped
One 10-ounce package frozen raspberries (or blueberries), thawed

1. Combine and blend well the rice, milk, sugar, and salt in a saucepan. Cook over low heat until thick and creamy, about 20 minutes, stirring occasionally. Remove from the heat and stir in the vanilla. Cool.

2. Fold in the almonds and two-thirds of the whipped cream.

3. In parfait glasses, alternate layers of the rice mixture and the fruit, ending with fruit and a dab of the remaining whipped cream. Chill until ready to serve.

*Serves 6*

# Index